MUSIC TELEVISION®

SELECTIONS FROM

Easy Guitar with Tab

100 greatest pop songs

P9-DFV-687

There are some things you'll never forget: Your first kiss. Your first love. Your first heartbreak. And you will never ever forget the songs that were playing while all that was going on. Pop music is the soundtrack to our lives—the songs that are burned into our memories. To honor the best of them, MTV and Rolling Stone have compiled the 100 most creative, important, and timeless pop songs of the last four decades, from Beatlemania to boy band-mania, and all the hits in between. We're sure you'll have as much fun playing them as you did listening to them.

ISBN 0-634-05377-9

HAL•LEONARD® CORPORATION

7777 W. BLUEMOUND RD. P.O. BOX 13819 MILWAUKEE, WI 53213

MAY 0 8 2008

Visit Hal Leonard Online at
www.halleonard.com

100 greatest pop songs

RANK	SONG	ARTIST	YEAR
1.	Yesterday	*The Beatles*	1965
2.	(I Can't Get No) Satisfaction†	*The Rolling Stones*	1965
3.	Smells Like Teen Spirit	*Nirvana*	1991
4.	Like a Virgin	*Madonna*	1984
5.	Billie Jean	*Michael Jackson*	1983
6.	I Want to Hold Your Hand	*The Beatles*	1964
7.	Respect	*Aretha Franklin*	1967
8.	One	*U2*	1992
9.	I Want You Back	*The Jackson 5*	1969
10.	I Want It That Way	*Backstreet Boys*	1999
11.	Hotel California	*Eagles*	1977
12.	Where Did Our Love Go	*The Supremes*	1964
13.	Sweet Child o' Mine	*Guns N' Roses*	1988
14.	Brown Sugar†	*The Rolling Stones*	1971
15.	Imagine	*John Lennon with The Plastic Ono Band*	1971
16.	Nothing Compares 2 U†	*Sinead O'Connor*	1990
17.	Superstition	*Stevie Wonder*	1972
18.	Losing My Religion	*R.E.M.*	1991
19.	Vogue	*Madonna*	1990
20.	Like a Rolling Stone	*Bob Dylan*	1965
21.	Brown Eyed Girl	*Van Morrison*	1967
22.	Beat It	*Michael Jackson*	1983
23.	Oh, Pretty Woman	*Roy Orbison*	1964
24.	What's Going On	*Marvin Gaye*	1971
25.	…Baby One More Time	*Britney Spears*	1998
26.	Go Your Own Way	*Fleetwood Mac*	1977
27.	When Doves Cry†	*Prince*	1984
28.	In My Life	*The Beatles*	1965
29.	Bohemian Rhapsody	*Queen*	1975
30.	Your Song	*Elton John*	1970
31.	Smooth	*Santana featuring Rob Thomas*	1999
32.	(Sittin' On) The Dock of the Bay	*Otis Redding*	1968
33.	My Generation	*The Who*	1965
34.	You Oughta Know	*Alanis Morissette*	1995
35.	Born to Run†	*Bruce Springsteen*	1975
36.	Waterfalls	*TLC*	1995
37.	O.P.P.	*Naughty By Nature*	1991
38.	Changes	*David Bowie*	1972
39.	Iris	*Goo Goo Dolls*	1998
40.	I Will Always Love You	*Whitney Houston*	1992
41.	Proud Mary	*Creedence Clearwater Revival*	1969
42.	Every Breath You Take	*The Police*	1983
43.	Miss You	*The Rolling Stones*	1978
44.	Dancing Queen	*ABBA*	1976
45.	Tears in Heaven	*Eric Clapton*	1992
46.	The Tracks of My Tears	*The Miracles*	1965

Ranking

RANK	SONG	ARTIST	YEAR
47.	Jump	Van Halen	1984
48.	Jeremy†	Pearl Jam	1992
49.	Tangled Up in Blue	Bob Dylan	1975
50.	Little Red Corvette†	Prince	1983
51.	Just My Imagination (Running Away with Me)	The Temptations	1971
52.	Maybe I'm Amazed	Paul McCartney	1970
53.	Faith	George Michael	1987
54.	Under the Bridge	Red Hot Chili Peppers	1992
55.	Bye Bye Bye	*NSYNC	2000
56.	I Will Survive	Gloria Gaynor	1979
57.	Our Lips Are Sealed	Go-Go's	1981
58.	One Headlight	The Wallflowers	1997
59.	You Are the Sunshine of My Life	Stevie Wonder	1973
60.	Just the Way You Are	Billy Joel	1977
61.	The One I Love	R.E.M.	1987
62.	Papa Don't Preach	Madonna	1986
63.	MMM Bop	Hanson	1997
64.	Bennie and the Jets	Elton John	1974
65.	Just What I Needed	The Cars	1978
66.	Time After Time	Cyndi Lauper	1984
67.	My Name Is	Eminem	1999
68.	Only Happy When It Rains	Garbage	1996
69.	Just Can't Get Enough	Depeche Mode	1981
70.	Good Vibrations	The Beach Boys	1966
71.	I Wanna Be Sedated	The Ramones	1979
72.	Free Fallin'	Tom Petty	1989
73.	Do You Really Want to Hurt Me	Culture Club	1982
74.	Tiny Dancer	Elton John	1972
75.	Hot Fun in the Summertime	Sly & The Family Stone	1969
76.	Creep	Radiohead	1993
77.	Let's Stay Together	Al Green	1971
78.	Longview	Green Day	1994
79.	Nasty	Janet Jackson	1986
80.	I Need Love	LL Cool J	1987
81.	Don't Speak	No Doubt	1996
82.	Rock with You	Michael Jackson	1979
83.	I Want to Know What Love Is	Foreigner	1984
84.	Wonderwall	Oasis	1995
85.	Surrender	Cheap Trick	1978
86.	Don't You Want Me	The Human League	1982
87.	Brass in Pocket	The Pretenders	1980
88.	Gone till November	Wyclef Jean	1998
89.	Careless Whisper	Wham! featuring George Michael	1984
90.	The Boy Is Mine	Brandy & Monica	1998
91.	No Diggity	Blackstreet	1996
92.	You Shook Me All Night Long	AC/DC	1980
93.	Stayin' Alive	Bee Gees	1977
94.	All the Small Things	blink-182	1999
95.	Good Times	Chic	1979
96.	Photograph	Def Leppard	1983
97.	Love Shack	The B-52's	1989
98.	She Drives Me Crazy	Fine Young Cannibals	1989
99.	Just a Friend	Biz Markie	1989
100.	Tainted Love	Soft Cell	1982

†Omitted from this publication because of licensing restrictions.

contents

STRUM AND PICK PATTERNS

This chart contains the suggested strum and pick patterns that are referred to by number at the beginning of each song in this book. The symbols ⊓ and ∨ in the strum patterns refer to down and up strokes, respectively. The letters in the pick patterns indicate which right-hand fingers plays which strings.

p = thumb
i = index finger
m = middle finger
a = ring finger

For example; Pick Pattern 2
is played: thumb - index - middle - ring

Strum Patterns   ## Pick Patterns

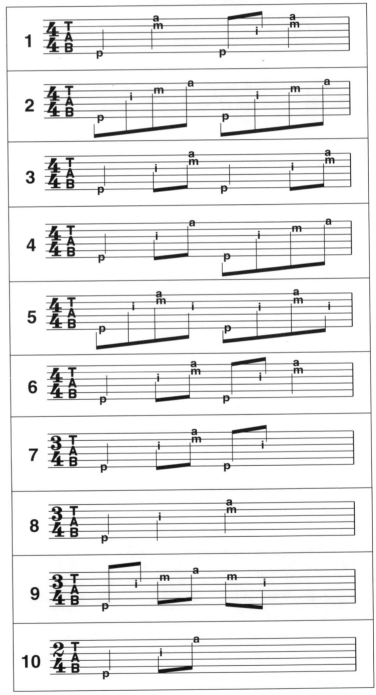

You can use the 3/4 Strum or Pick Patterns in songs written in compound meter (6/8, 9/8, 12/8, etc.).
For example, you can accompany a song in 6/8 by playing the 3/4 pattern twice in each measure.
The 4/4 Strum and Pick Patterns can be used for songs written in cut time (¢) by doubling the note time values in the patterns. Each pattern would therefore last two measures in cut time.

...Baby One More Time

Words and Music by Max Martin

*Capo III

Strum Pattern: 1, 2
Pick Pattern: 3, 4

Intro
Moderately

N.C.

Oh, ba - by, ba - by.

*Optional: To match recording, place capo at 3rd fret.

Oh, ba - by, ba - by.

Verse

Am

1. Oh, ba - by, ba - by, how
2. *See additional lyrics*

E7/G#   E7   C   Dm   E Am

was I sup - posed __ to know __ that some - thing was - n't right here?

E7/G#   E7   C

Oh, ba - by, ba - by, I should - n't have let __ you go. __ And

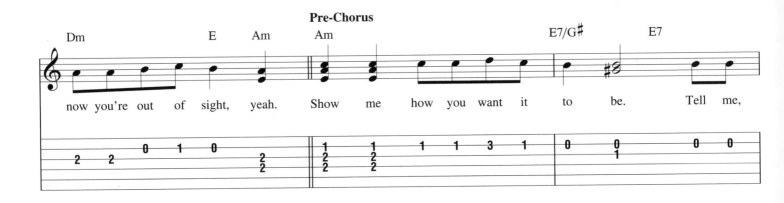

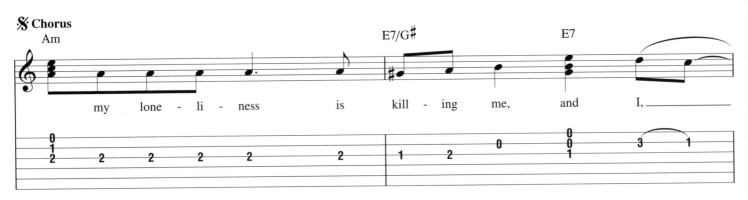

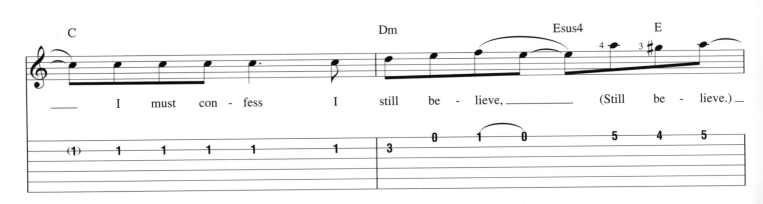

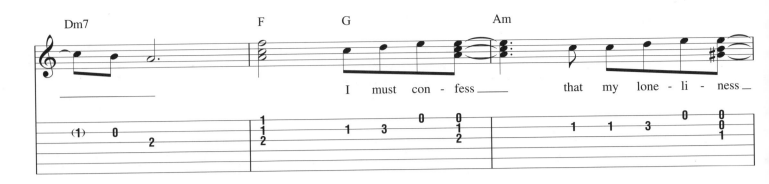

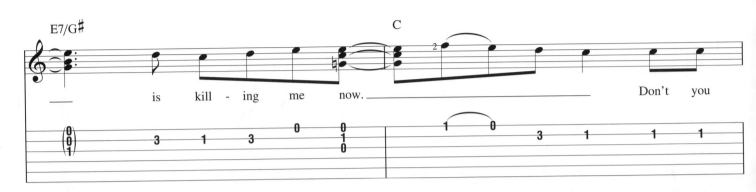

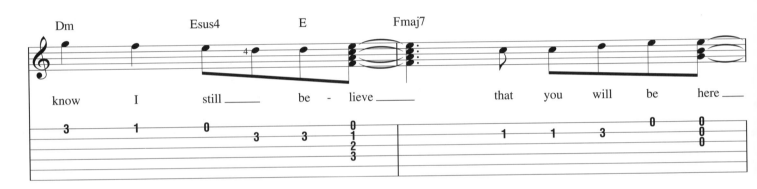

D.S. al Coda

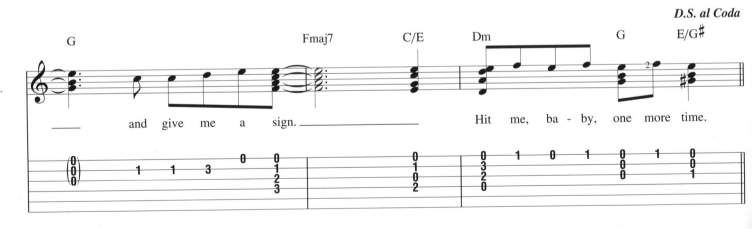

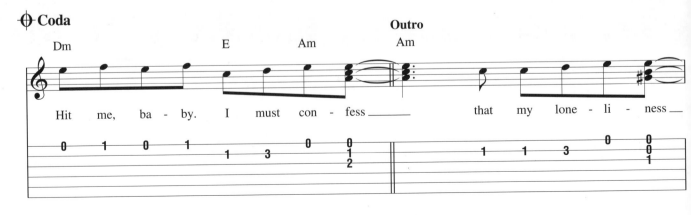

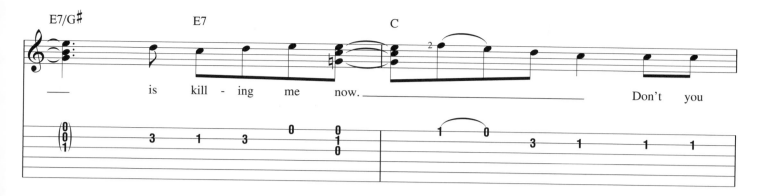

is kill - ing me now. _____ Don't you

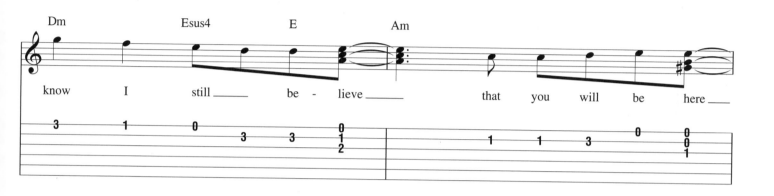

know I still _____ be - lieve _____ that you will be here _____

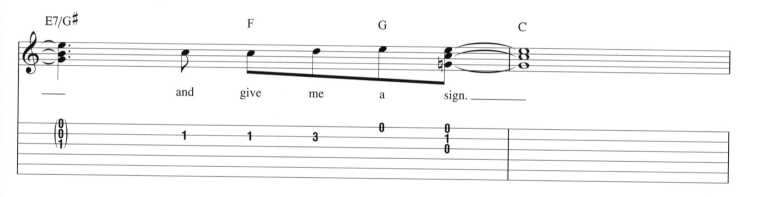

_____ and give me a sign. _____

Hit me, ba - by, one more time.

Additional Lyrics

2. Oh, baby, baby, the reason I breathe is you.
   Boy, you've got me blinded.
   Oh, pretty baby, there's nothing that I wouldn't do.
   It's not the way I planned it.

All the Small Things

Words and Music by Tom De Longe and Mark Hoppus

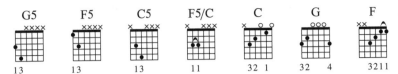

Strum Pattern: 1

Intro

Bright Rock

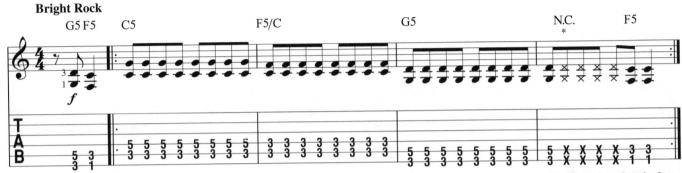

*Muffled strings: Lay the fret hand across the strings without depressing and strike them w/ the pick hand.

Verse

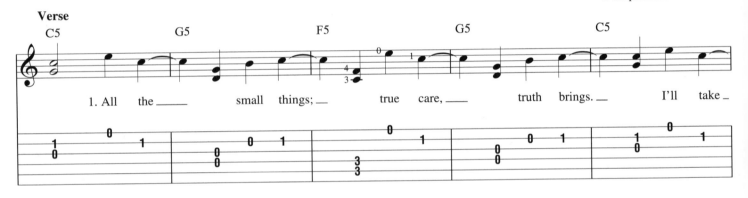

1. All the ____ small things; ____ true care, ____ truth brings. ____ I'll take ____

____ one lift. ____ Your ride, ____ best trip. ____ 2. Al - ways ____ I know, ____

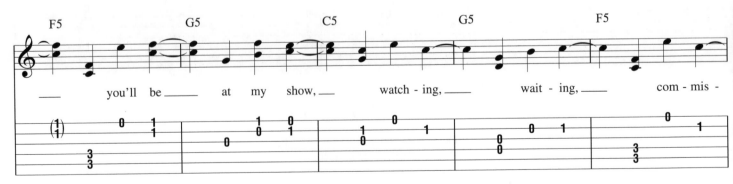

____ you'll be ____ at my show, ____ watch - ing, ____ wait - ing, ____ com - mis -

Pre-Chorus

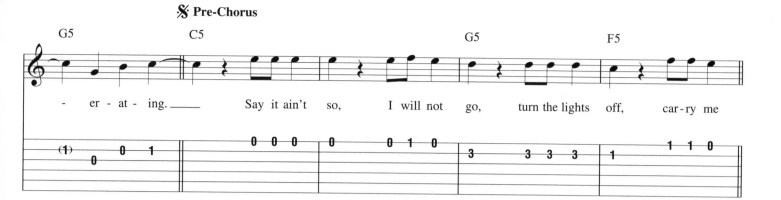

er-at-ing. ____ Say it ain't so, I will not go, turn the lights off, car-ry me

Chorus

home. Na, na, na, na, na, ___ na, na, na, na. Na, na, na, na, na, na, ___ na, na, na, na.

To Coda

Na, na, na, na, na, na, ___ na, na, na, na. Na, na, na, na, na, na, ___ na, na, na, na.

Interlude

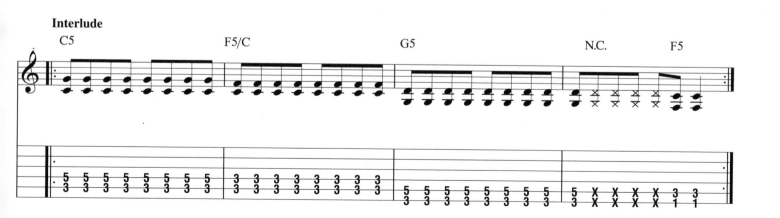

Verse

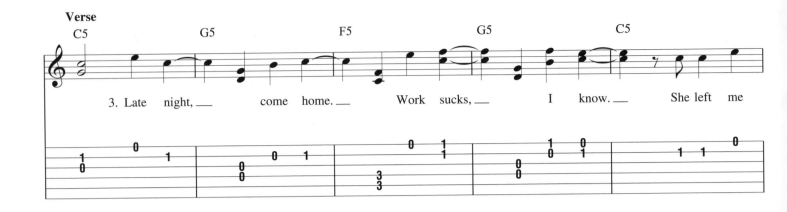

3. Late night, __ come home. __ Work sucks, __ I know. __ She left me

D.S. al Coda   Coda

Interlude

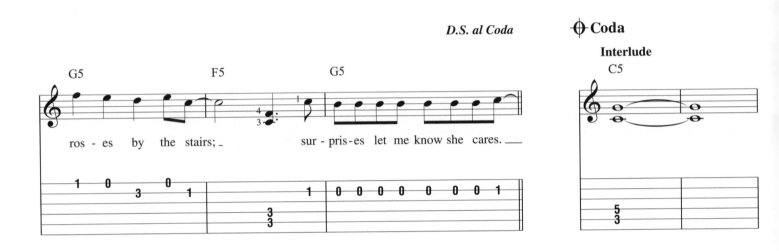

ros - es by the stairs; __ sur - pris-es let me know she cares. __

Outro

Play 3 times

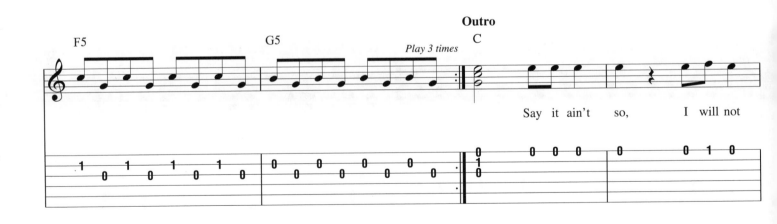

Say it ain't so, __ I will not

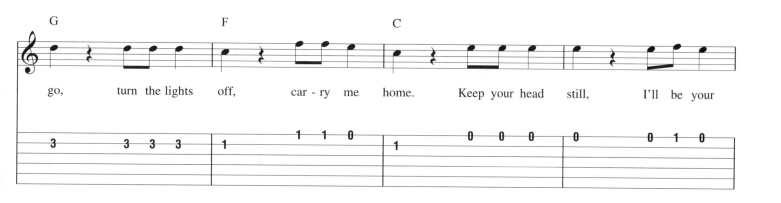

go, turn the lights off, car - ry me home. Keep your head still, I'll be your

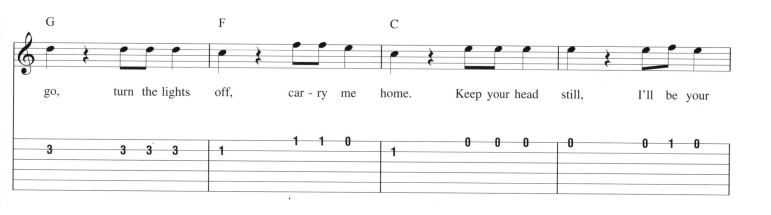

thrill, the night will go on, my lit - tle wind - mill. Say it ain't so, I will not

go, turn the lights off, car - ry me home. Keep your head still, I'll be your

thrill, the night will go on, the night will go on, my lit - tle wind - mill.

Beat It

Written and Composed by Michael Jackson

Strum Pattern: 1, 2
Pick Pattern: 2, 4

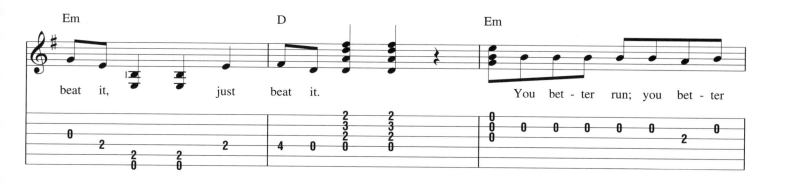

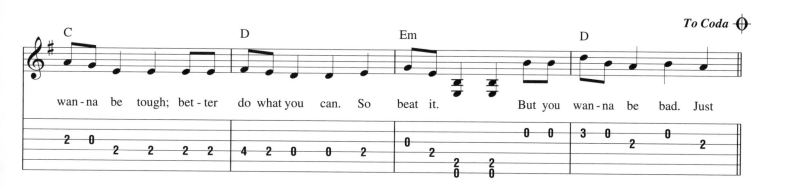

Chorus

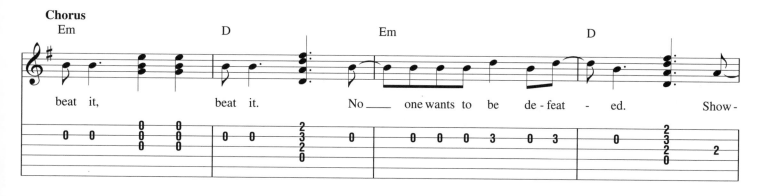

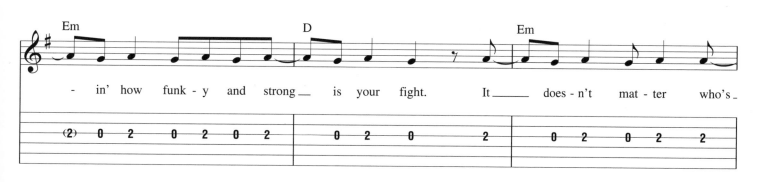

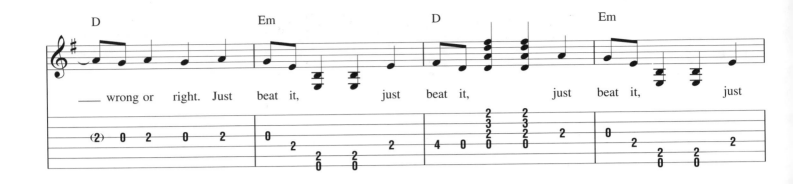

_____ wrong or right. Just beat it, just beat it, just beat it, just

$\oplus$ **Coda**

D.S. al Coda · **Outro-Chorus**

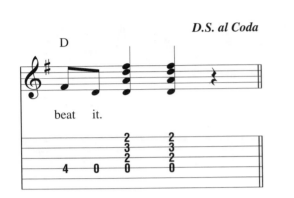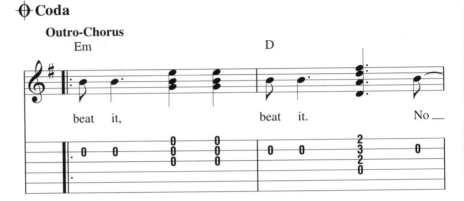

beat it. · beat it, beat it. No __

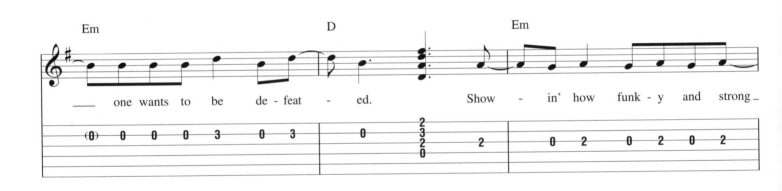

_____ one wants to be de-feat-ed. Show-in' how funk-y and strong__

Repeat and fade

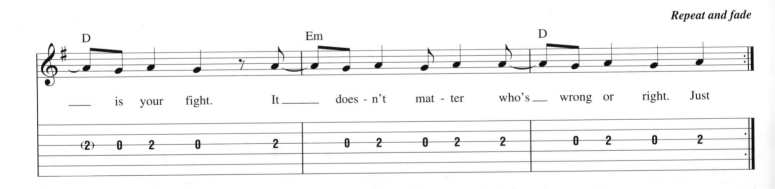

_____ is your fight. It_____ does-n't mat-ter who's__ wrong or right. Just

Additional Lyrics

2. They're out to get. Better leave while you can.
   Don't wanna be a bad boy; you wanna be a man.
   You wanna stay alive, better do what you can.
   So beat it, just beat it.
   You have to show them that you're not really scared.
   You're playin' with your life. This ain't no truth or dare.
   They'll kick you, then they beat you, then they'll tell you it's fair.
   So beat it. But you wanna be bad.

Brown Eyed Girl

Words and Music by Van Morrison

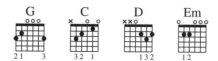

Strum Pattern: 6
Pick Pattern: 3

Intro
Bright Rock

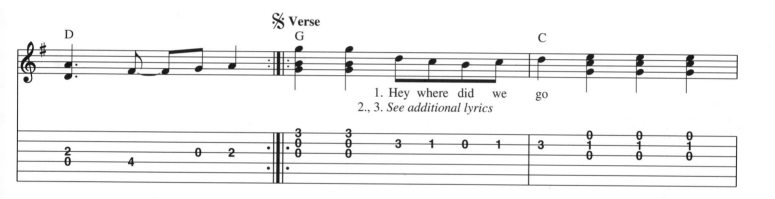

1. Hey where did we go
2., 3. *See additional lyrics*

days when the rains ___ came, down in the hol-

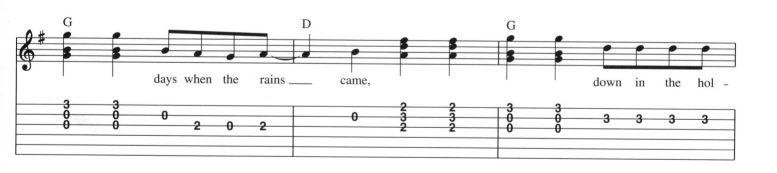

low, play-in' a new ___ game. Laugh-ing and a'

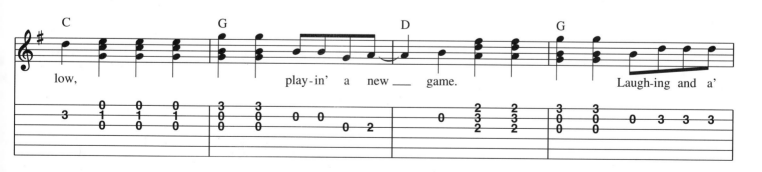

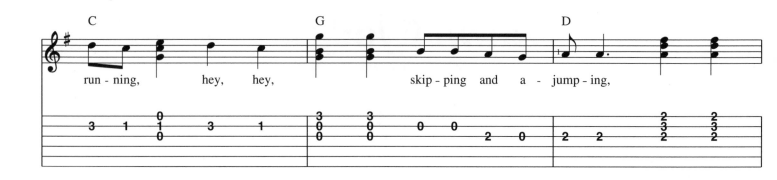

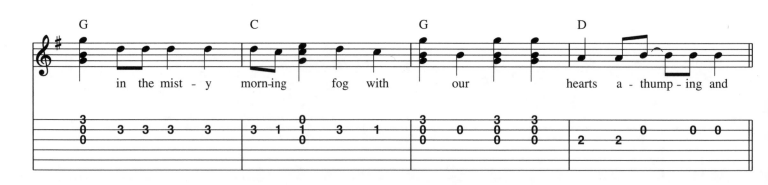

Pre-Chorus

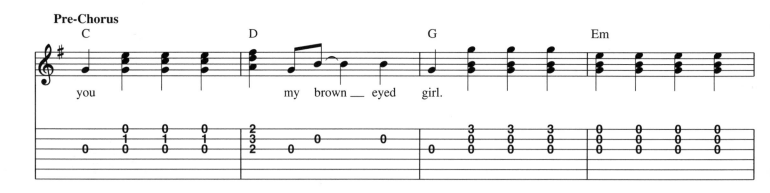

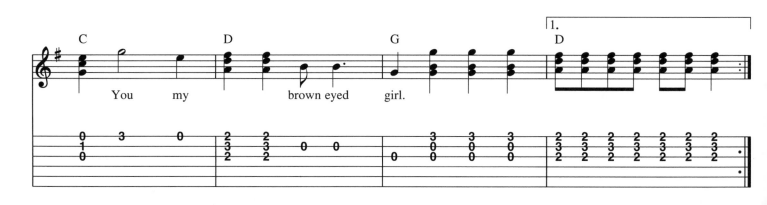

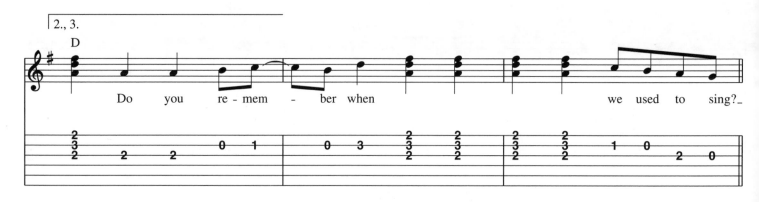

Chorus

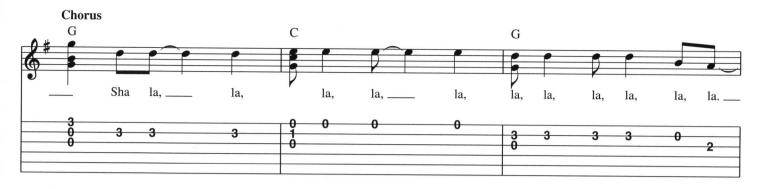

Sha la, la, la, la, la, la, la, la, la, la, la.

Sha la, la, la, la, la,

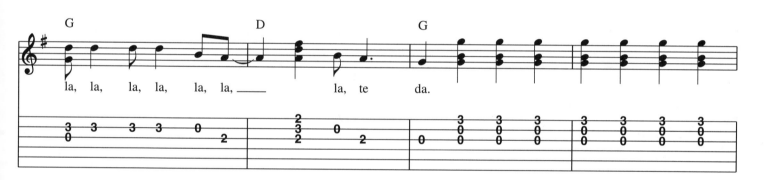

la, la, la, la, la, la, la, te da.

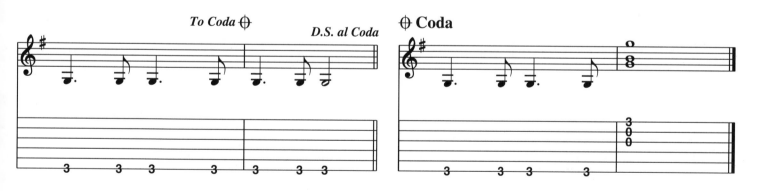

To Coda ⊕

D.S. al Coda

⊕ **Coda**

Additional Lyrics

2. Whatever happened
   To Tuesday and so slow,
   Going down the old mine
   With a transistor radio?
   Standing in the sunlight laughing,
   Hiding behind a rainbow's wall,
   Slipping and a-sliding
   All along the waterfall with you,
   My brown eyed girl.
   You, my brown eyed girl.

3. So hard to find my way
   Now that I'm all on my own.
   I saw you just the other day
   My, how you have grown.
   Cast my memory back there Lord,
   Sometimes I'm overcome thinkin' 'bout it.
   Laughing and a-running, hey, hey,
   Behind the stadium with you,
   My brown eyed girl.
   You, my brown eyed girl.

Bennie and the Jets

Words and Music by Elton John and Bernie Taupin

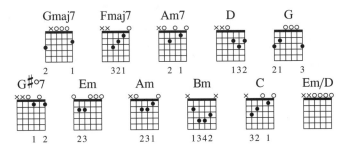

Strum Pattern: 4
Pick Pattern: 2

Intro
Moderately

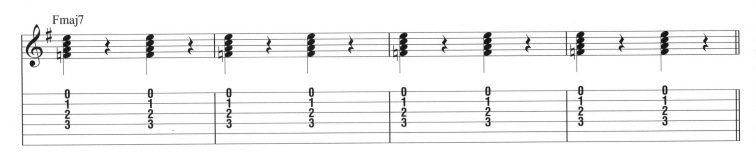

Verse

1. Hey, kids, shake it loose to-geth-er; the spot-light's hit-ting some-thing that's been
2. *See additional lyrics*
3. *Instrumental*

known to change the weath-er. We'll kill the fat-ted calf to-night, so stick a-

Chorus

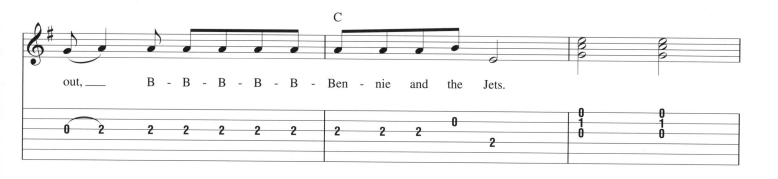

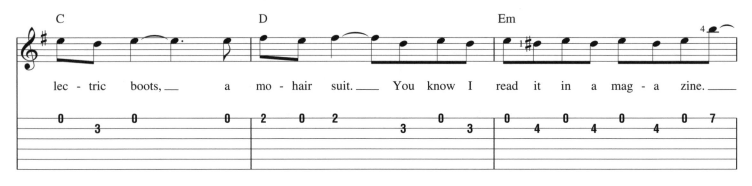

lec - tric boots, ___ a mo - hair suit. ___ You know I read it in a mag - a zine. ___

To Coda ⊕

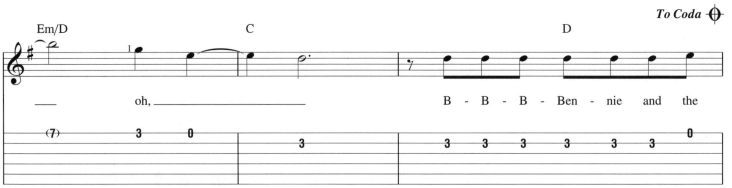

___ oh, ___ B - B - B - Ben - nie and the

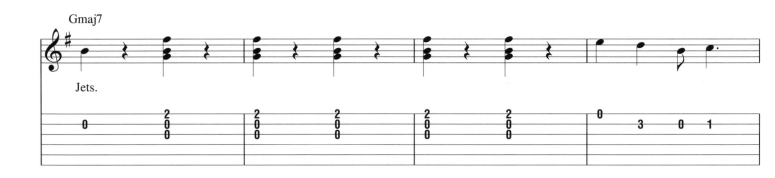

Jets.

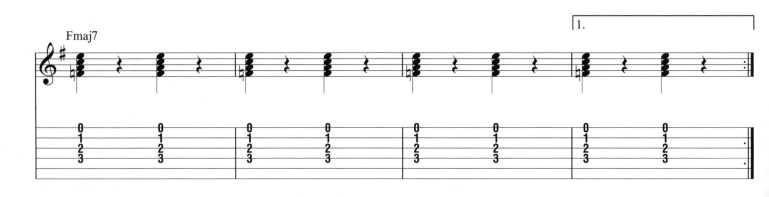

D.S. al Coda

⊕ **Coda**

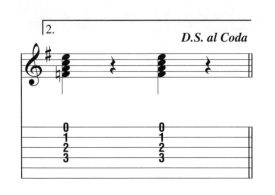

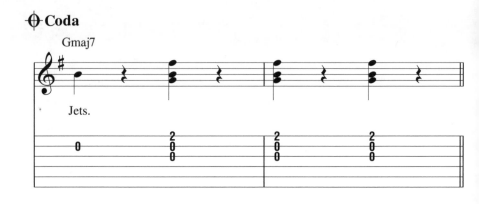

Jets.

Outro

Ben - nie. Ben - nie. Ben - nie, Ben - nie,

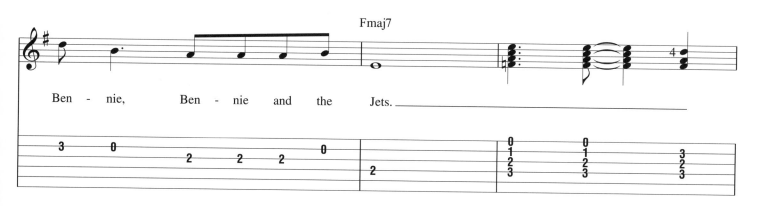

Ben - nie, Ben - nie and the Jets. _____

Repeat and fade

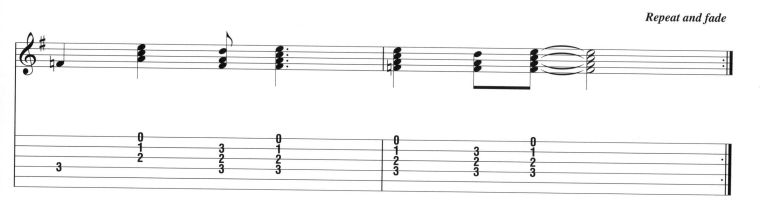

Additional Lyrics

2. Hey, kids, plug into the faithless,
   Maybe they're blinded, but Bennie makes them ageless.
   We shall survive; let us take ourselves along
   Where we fight our parents out in the streets
   To find who's right and who's wrong.

Billie Jean

Written and Composed by Michael Jackson

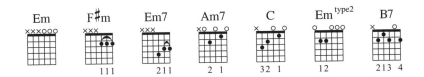

*Capo II

Strum Pattern: 1, 2
Pick Pattern: 2, 4

Intro
Moderately

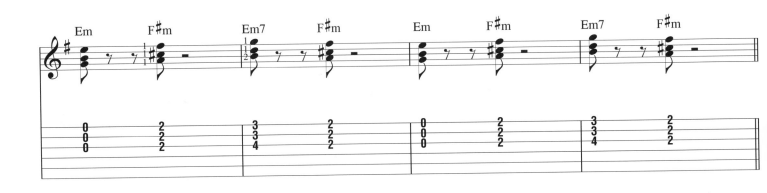

*Optional: To match recording, place capo at 2nd fret.

Verse

1. She was more like a beau - ty queen from a mov - ie scene. I said don't mind, but what do __
2. *See additional lyrics*

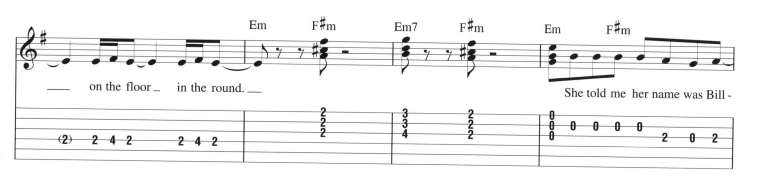

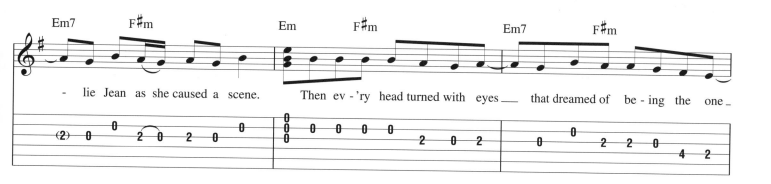

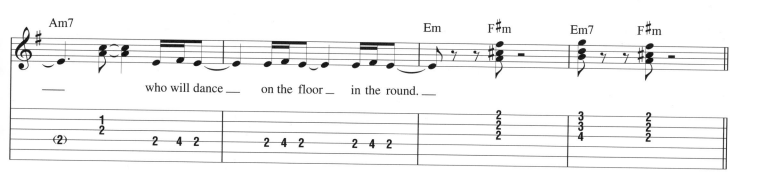

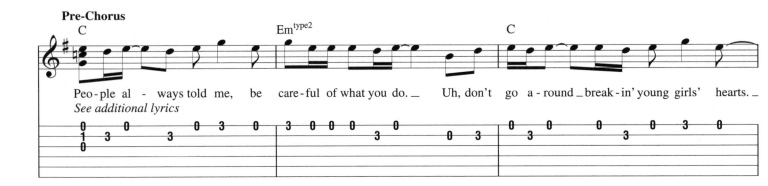

Peo-ple al - ways told me, be care-ful of what you do. __ Uh, don't go a - round __ break-in' young girls' hearts. __

See additional lyrics

__ And Moth-er al - ways told me, be care-ful of who you love. __ And be

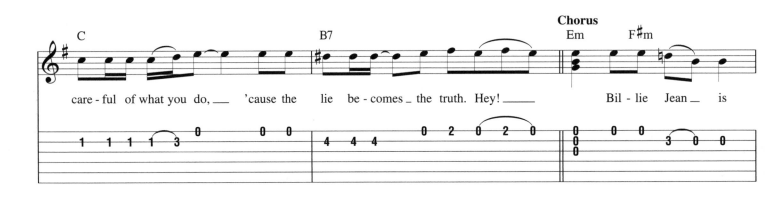

care - ful of what you do, __ 'cause the lie be - comes __ the truth. Hey! __ Bil - lie Jean __ is

Chorus

not my lov - er. She's just a girl __ who claims that I __ am the one,

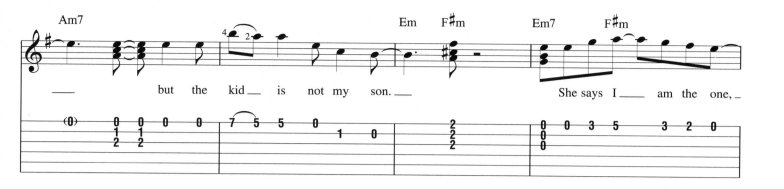

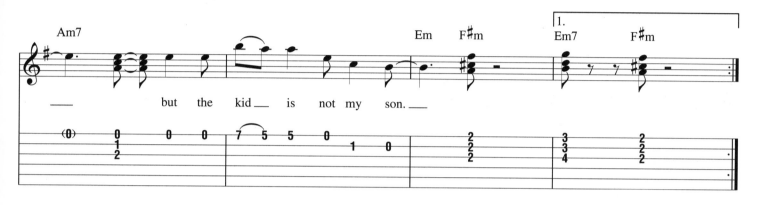

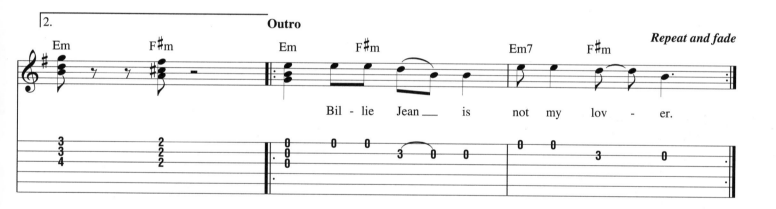

Additional Lyrics

2. For forty days and for forty nights,
Law was on her side.
But who can stand when she's in demand,
Her schemes and plans,
'Cause we danced on the floor in the round?
So take my strong advice:
Just remember to always think twice.
She told me my baby, we danced till three,
And then she looked at me, then showed a photo.
My baby cried. His eyes were like mine,
'Cause we dance on the floor in the round.

Pre-Chorus People always told me, be careful of what you do.
Uh, don't go around breakin' young girls' hearts.
But you came and stood right by me,
Just a smell of sweet perfume.
This happened much too soon.
She called me to her room. Hey!

Bohemian Rhapsody

Words and Music by Freddie Mercury

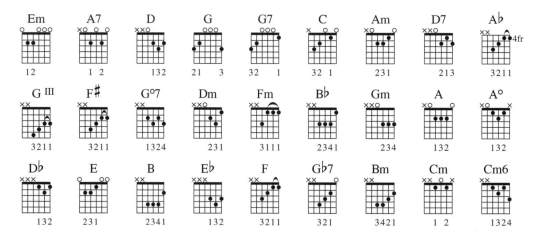

Strum Pattern: 3, 4
Pick Pattern: 2, 3

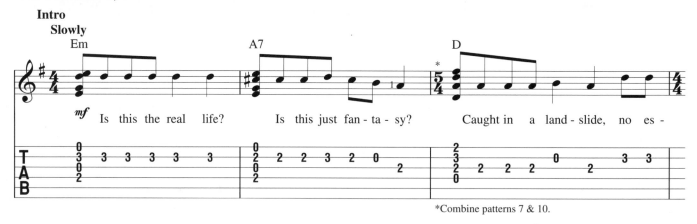

*Combine patterns 7 & 10.

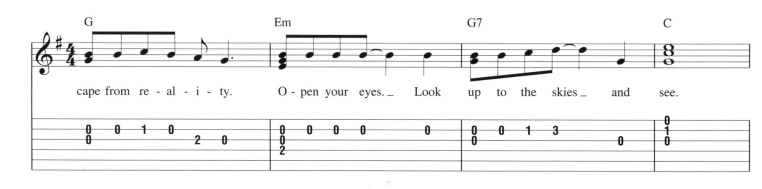

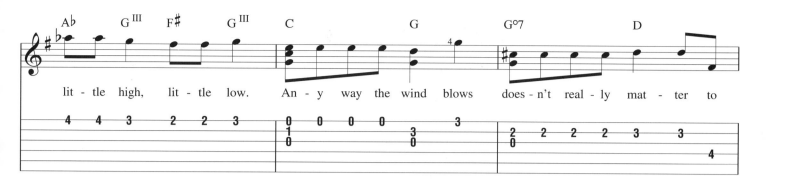

lit – tle high, lit – tle low. An – y way the wind blows does – n't real – ly mat – ter to

me, to ___ me. ____

Verse

1. Ma – ma, just
2. *See additional lyrics*

killed a man. Put a gun a – gainst his head, pulled my trig – ger, now he's dead.

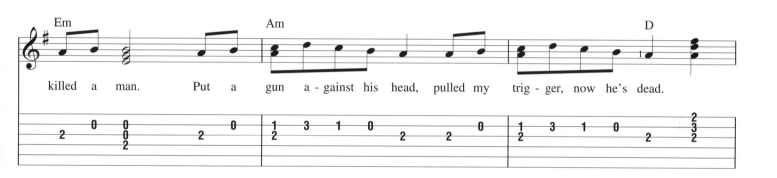

Ma – ma, life had just be – gun, but now I've gone and thrown it all a – way. ___

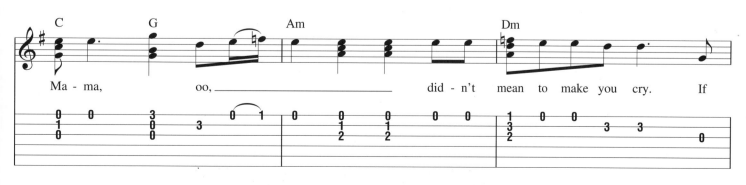

Ma – ma, oo, _____ did – n't mean to make you cry. If

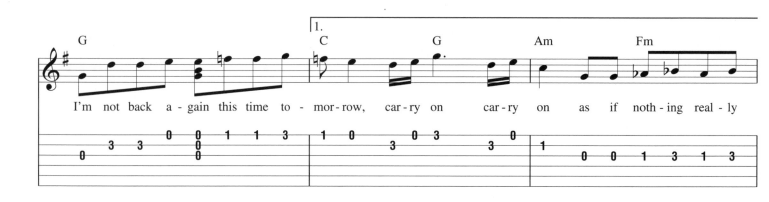

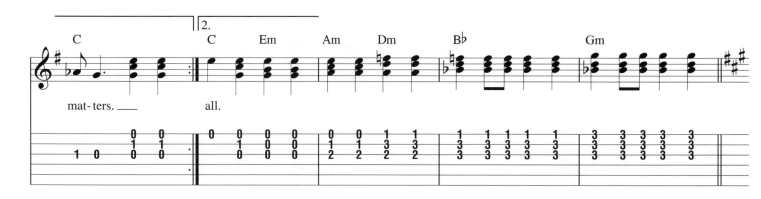

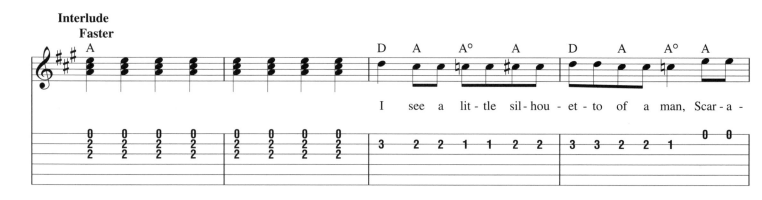

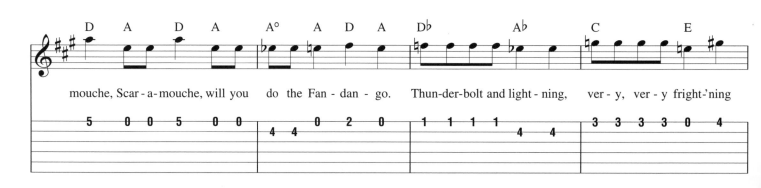

ro Mag - ni - fi - co. _____ I'm just a poor boy and no - bod - y loves me.

*Use Pattern 10

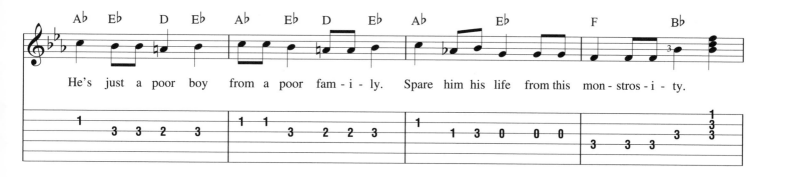

He's just a poor boy from a poor fam - i - ly. Spare him his life from this mon - stros - i - ty.

Eas - y come, eas - y go, will you let me go? Bis - mil - lah! No, we

will not let you go. Let him go! _____ Bis - mil - lah! We will not let you go. Let him go! _

_ Bis - mil - lah! We will not let you go. Let me go. Will not let you go. Let me go.

Will not let you go. Let me go. Ah. _____ No, no, no, no, no, no, no. Oh ma-ma

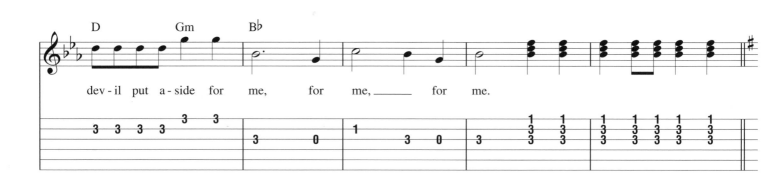

mi - a, ma-ma mi - a. Ma-ma mi - a, let me go. Be - el - ze-bub has a

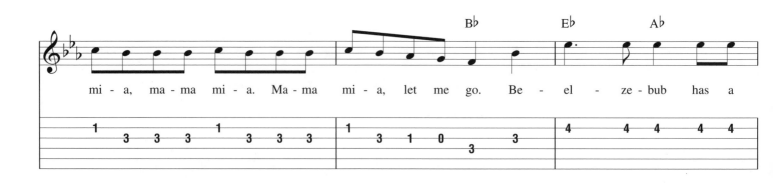

dev - il put a-side for me, for me, _____ for me.

Chorus

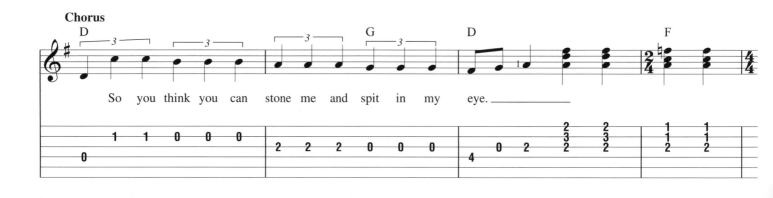

So you think you can stone me and spit in my eye. _____

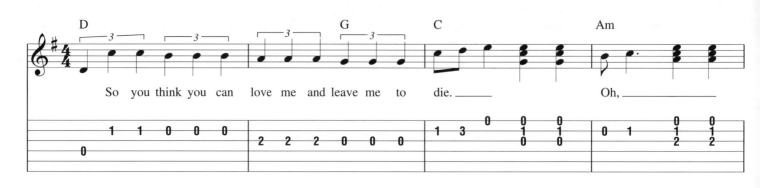

So you think you can love me and leave me to die. _____ Oh, _____

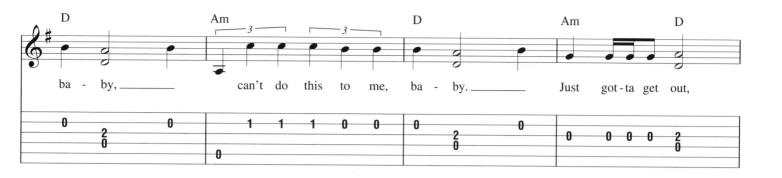

ba - by, _____ can't do this to me, ba - by. _____ Just got-ta get out,

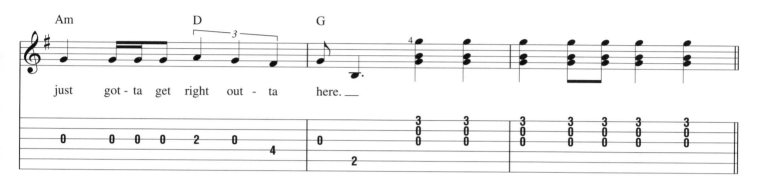

just got - ta get right out - ta here. __

Outro
Slowly

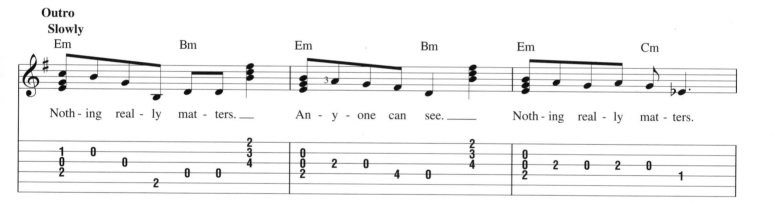

Noth - ing real - ly mat - ters. __ An - y - one can see. _____ Noth - ing real - ly mat - ters.

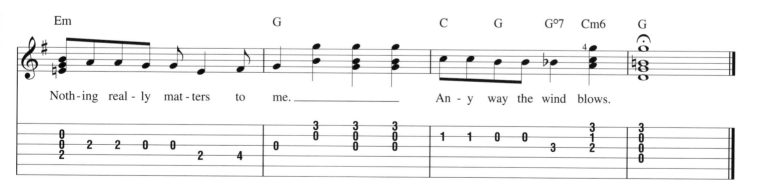

Noth - ing real - ly mat - ters to me. _____ An - y way the wind blows.

Additional Lyrics

2. Too late, my time has come.
Sends shivers down my spine, body's aching all the time.
Goodbye ev'ry body, I've got to go.
Gotta leave you all behind and face the truth.
Mama, oo, I don't want to die.
I sometimes wish I'd never been born at all.

The Boy Is Mine

Words and Music by LaShawn Daniels, Japhe Tejeda, Rodney Jerkins, Fred Jerkins and Brandy Norwood

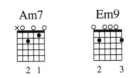

Strum Pattern: 2
Pick Pattern: 5

Intro
Moderately fast

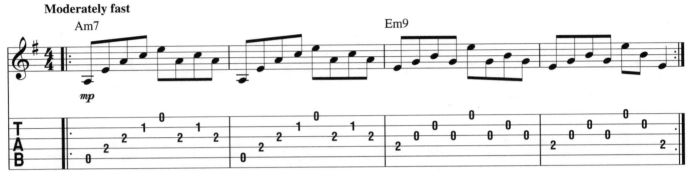

Spoken: Brandy: Excuse me, can I please talk to you for a minute?   *Monica: Uh huh, sure.*   You know,

you look kind of familiar.   Brandy: Yeah, you do too. But, um, I just wanted to know, do you know

somebody named... You know his name. Monica: Oh, yeah,   definitely.   I know his name.

Brandy: Well, I just want to let you know that he's mine. Monica: Heh, no no. He's mine.

Chorus

You need to give it up; I've had a-bout e-nough. It's not hard to

see; the boy is mine. I'm sor-ry that you seem to be con-

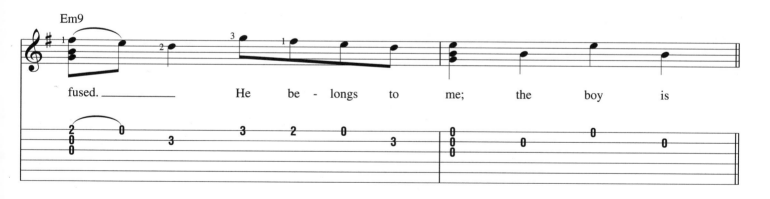

fused. ___ He be-longs to me; the boy is

Verse

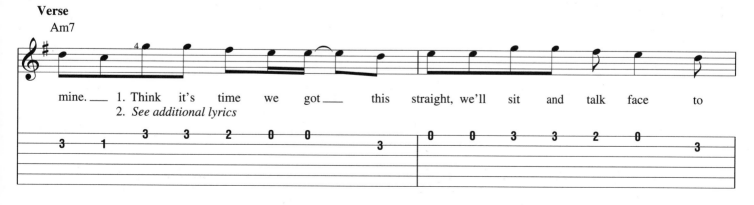

mine. ___ 1. Think it's time we got ___ this straight, we'll sit and talk face to
2. *See additional lyrics*

face. There is no way you could mis - take him for your man. Are you in -

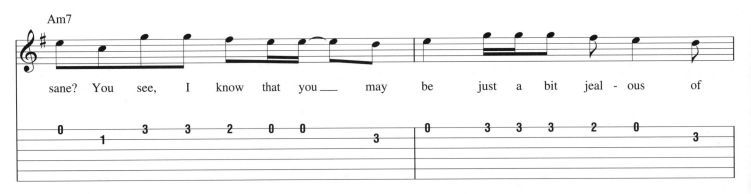

sane? You see, I know that you may be just a bit jeal - ous of

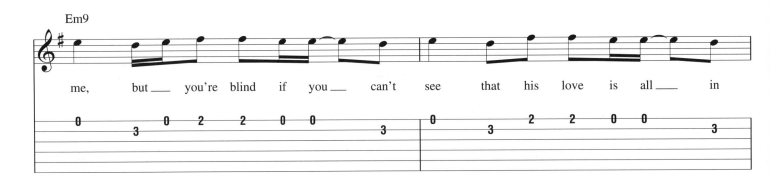

me, but you're blind if you can't see that his love is all in

me. See, I tried to hes - i - tate; I did - n't want to say what he told

me, he said with - out me he could - n't make it through the day. Ain't that a

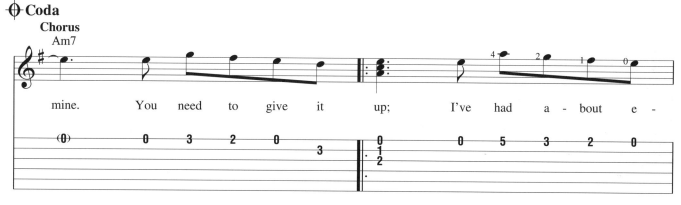

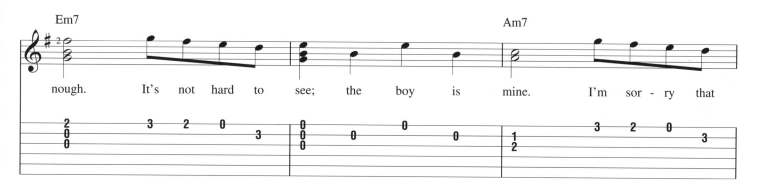

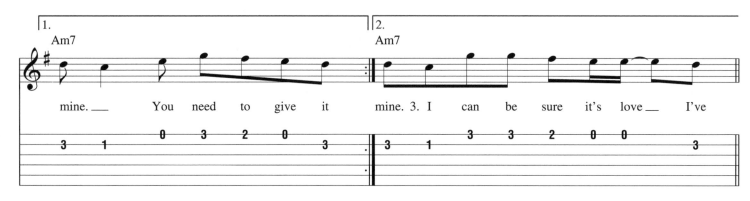

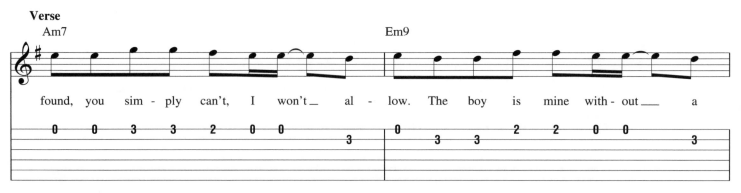

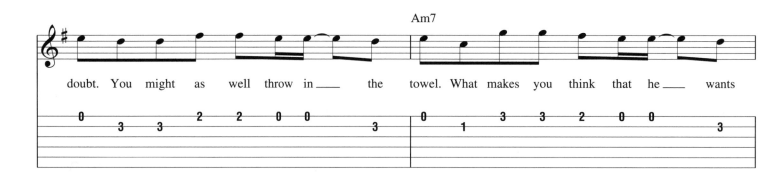

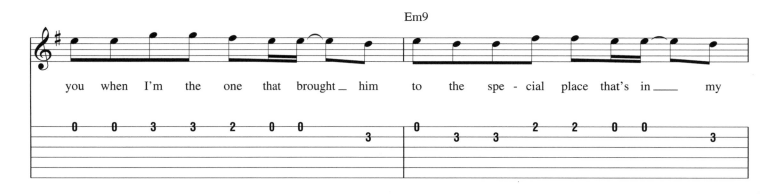

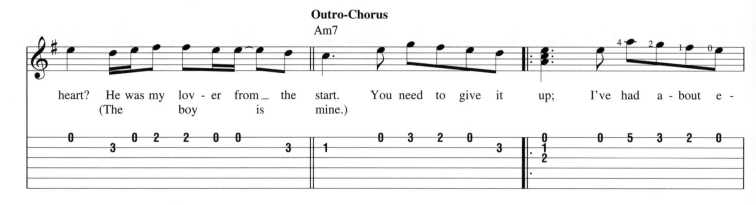

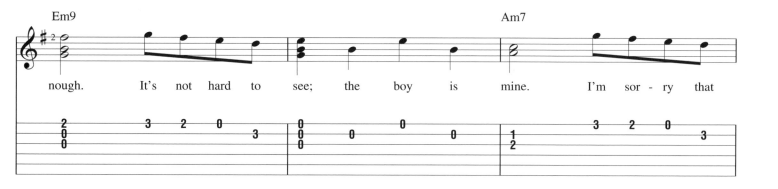

nough. It's not hard to see; the boy is mine. I'm sor - ry that

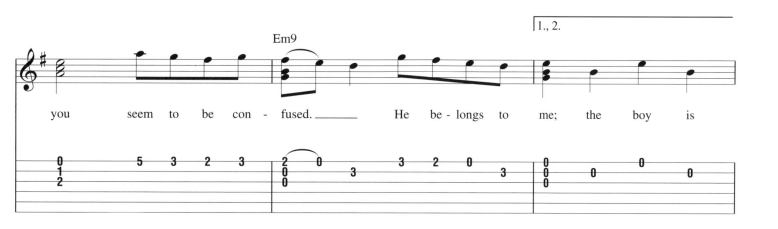

you seem to be con - fused. _____ He be - longs to me; the boy is

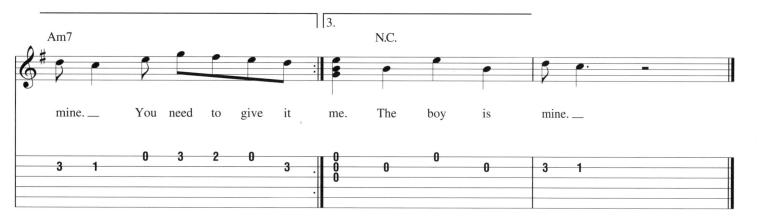

mine. __ You need to give it me. The boy is mine. __

Additional Lyrics

2. Must you do the things you do?
   You keep on acting like a fool.
   You need to know it's me, not you,
   And if you didn't know it, girl, it's true.
   I think that you should realize
   And try to understand why
   He is a part of my life.
   I know it's killing you inside.
   You can say what you wanna say,
   What we have you can't take.
   From the truth you can't escape.
   I can tell the real from the fake.
   When will you get the picture?
   You're the past and I'm future.
   Get away, it's my time to shine.
   If you didn't know, the boy is mine.

Brass in Pocket

Words and Music by Chrissie Hynde and James Honeyman-Scott

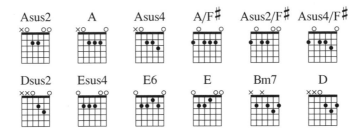

Strum Pattern: 1, 6
Pick Pattern: 2

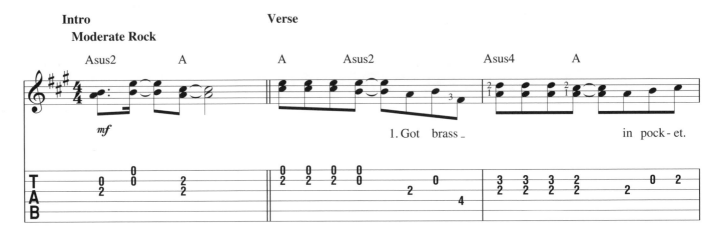

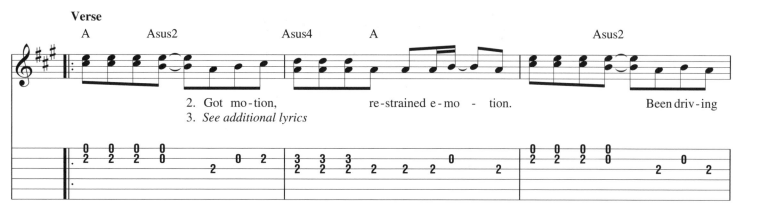

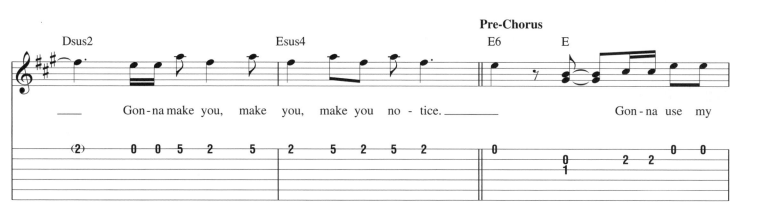

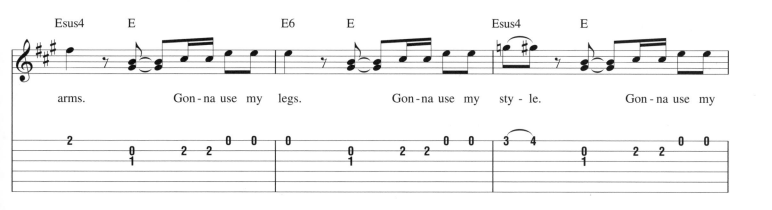

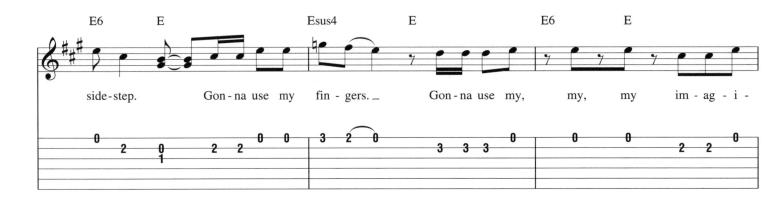

side-step. Gon-na use my fin-gers.___ Gon-na use my, my, my im-ag-i-

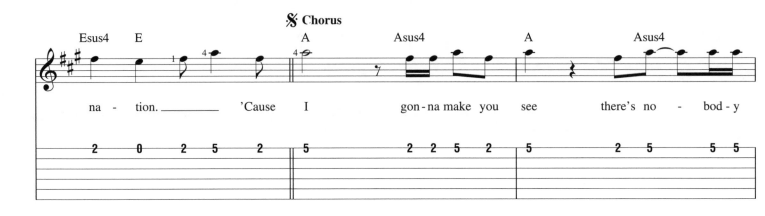

𝄋 Chorus

na - tion._____ 'Cause I gon-na make you see there's no - bod-y

else here, no one like me.___ I'm spe - cial. (Spe - cial.) So___

1.

To Coda ⊕

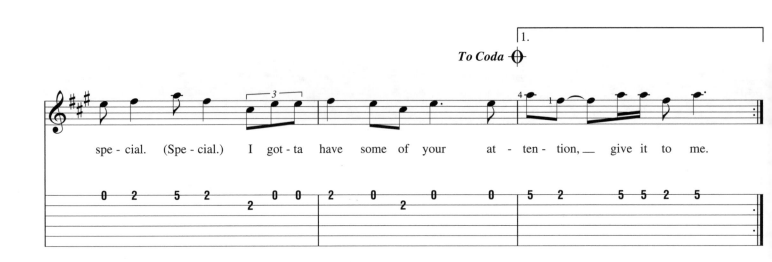

spe - cial. (Spe - cial.) I got - ta have some of your at - ten - tion,___ give it to me.

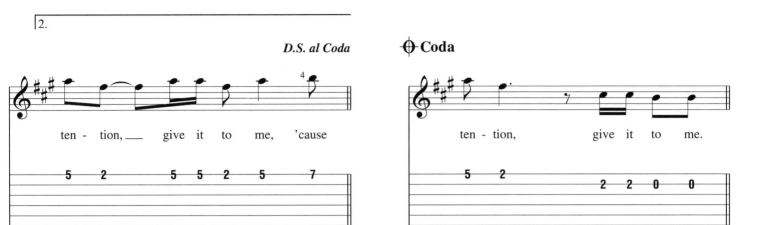

ten - tion, ___ give it to me, 'cause

D.S. al Coda

⊕ Coda

ten - tion, give it to me.

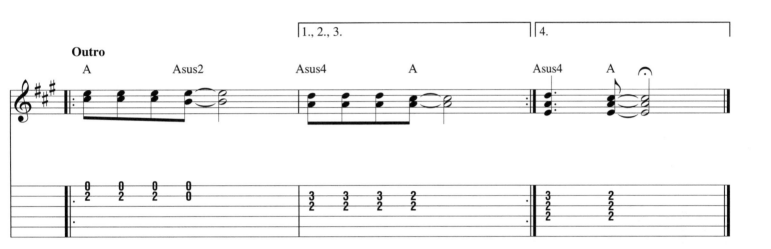

Outro

Additional Lyrics

3. Got rhythm, I can't miss a beat.
   I got new skank so reet,
   Got something I'm winking at you.
   Gonna make you, make you, make you notice.

Bye Bye Bye

Words and Music by Kristian Lundin, Jake Carlsson and Andreas Carlsson

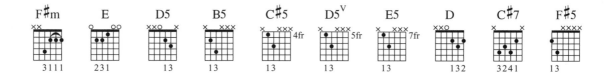

*Capo II

Strum Pattern: 2, 3
Pick Pattern: 3, 4

Intro
Moderately slow

*Optional: To match recording, place capo at 2nd fret.

Verse

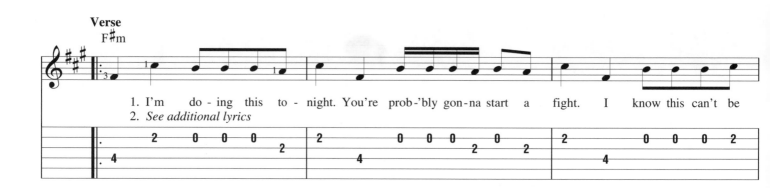

1. I'm do-ing this to-night. You're prob-'bly gon-na start a fight. I know this can't be
2. *See additional lyrics*

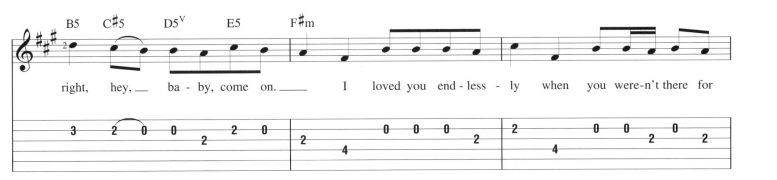

B5 C#5 D5ᵛ E5 F#m

right, hey, __ ba - by, come on. __ I loved you end - less - ly when you were-n't there for

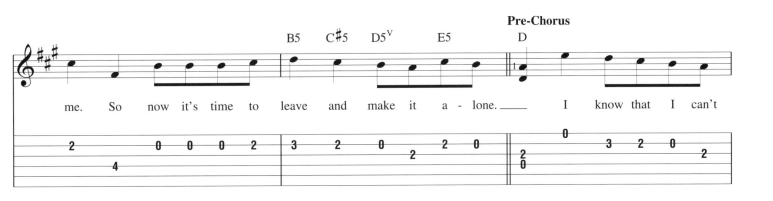

B5 C#5 D5ᵛ E5 **Pre-Chorus** D

me. So now it's time to leave and make it a - lone. __ I know that I can't

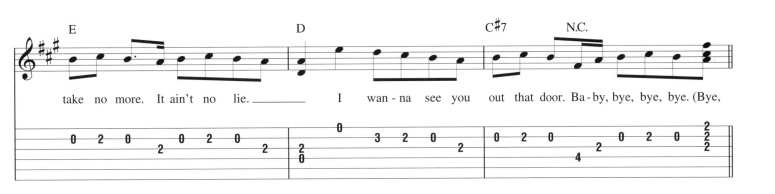

E D C#7 N.C.

take no more. It ain't no lie. __ I wan - na see you out that door. Ba - by, bye, bye, bye. (Bye,

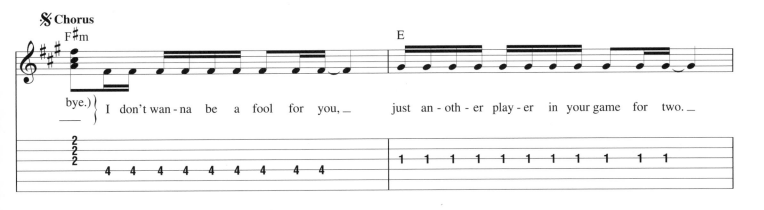

𝄋 **Chorus** F#m E

bye.) __ I don't wan - na be a fool for you, __ just an - oth - er play - er in your game for two. __

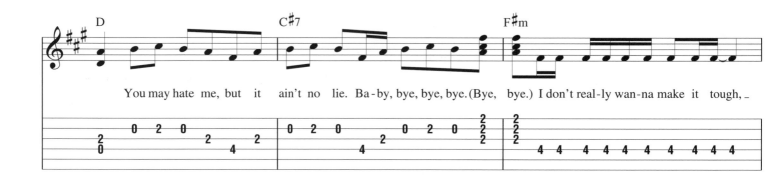

You may hate me, but it ain't no lie. Ba-by, bye, bye, bye. (Bye, bye.) I don't real-ly wan-na make it tough, __

To Coda

I just wan-na tell you that I've had e - nough. __ It might sound cra - zy, but it

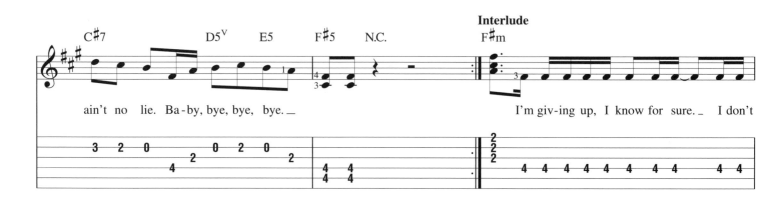

Interlude

ain't no lie. Ba-by, bye, bye, bye. __ I'm giv-ing up, I know for sure. __ I don't

wan-na be the rea-son for your love no more. __ (Bye, bye.) I'm check-ing out, I'm sign-ing off. __ I don't

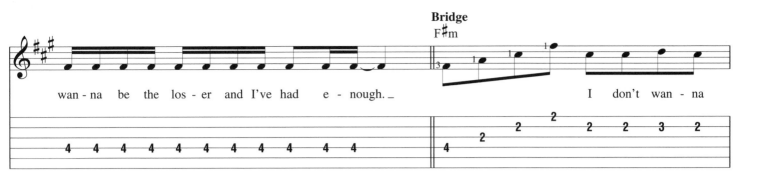

wan - na be the los - er and I've had e - nough. _ I don't wan - na

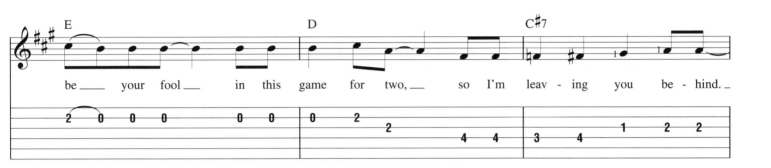

be _ your fool _ in this game for two, _ so I'm leav - ing you be - hind. _

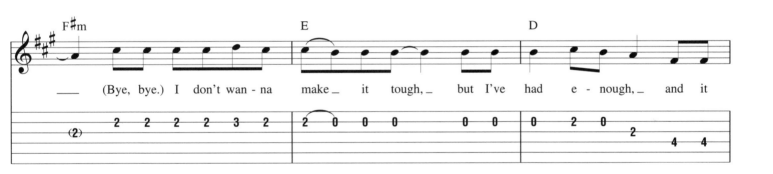

_ (Bye, bye.) I don't wan - na make _ it tough, _ but I've had e - nough, _ and it

Coda

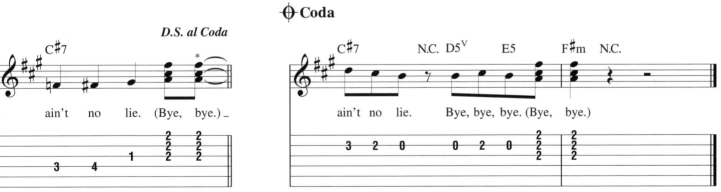

ain't no lie. (Bye, bye.) _

ain't no lie. Bye, bye, bye. (Bye, bye.)

*Tie into beat one on D.S.

Additional Lyrics

2. Just hit me with truth.
   Now, girl, you're more than welcome to.
   So give me one good reason, baby, come on.
   I live for you and me
   And now I really come to see
   That life would be much better once you're gone.

Careless Whisper

Words and Music by George Michael and Andrew Ridgeley

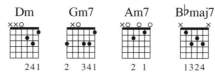

Strum Pattern: 2
Pick Pattern: 5

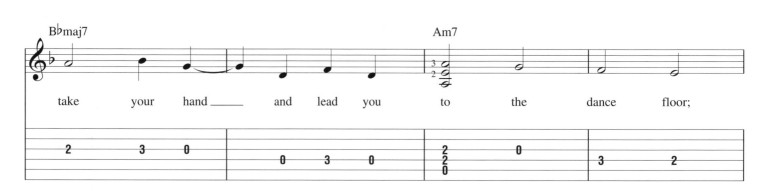

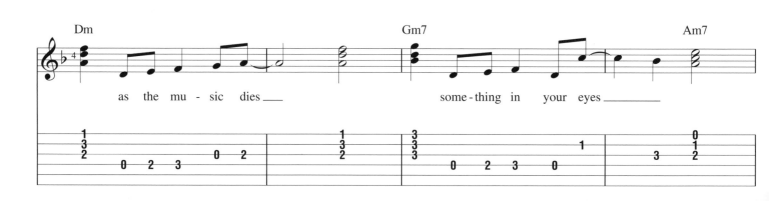

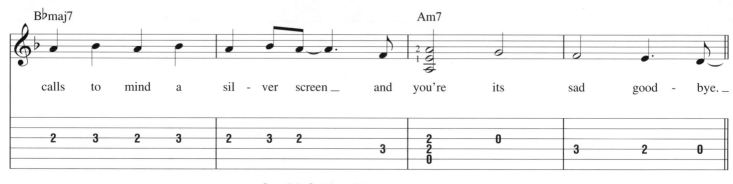

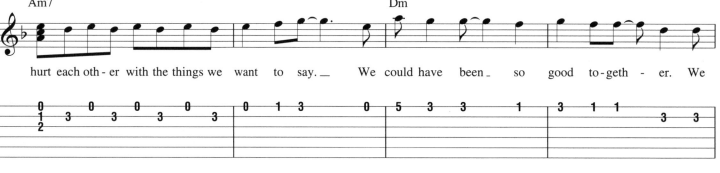

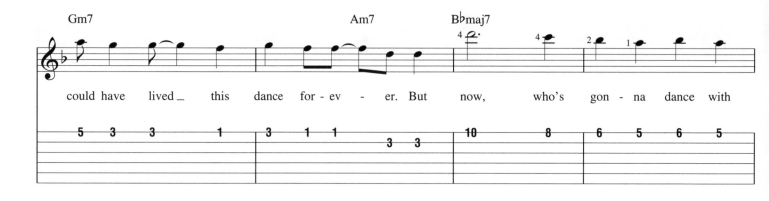

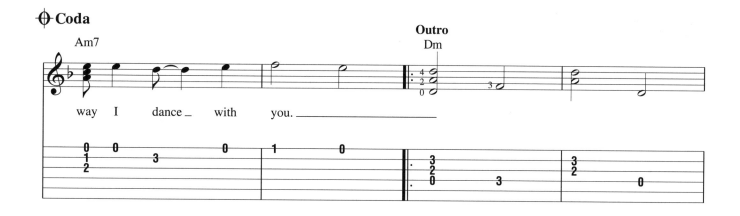

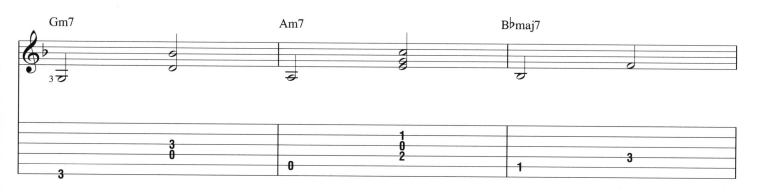

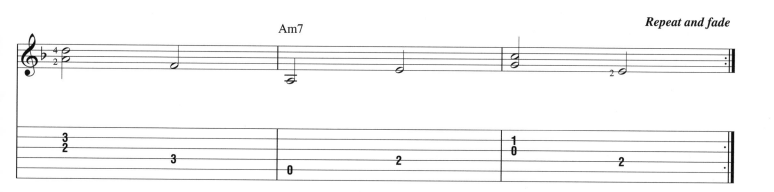

Additional Lyrics

2. Time can never mend the careless whisper of a good friend.
To the heart and mind ignorance is kind.
There's no comfort in the truth, pain is all you'll find.

Changes

Words and Music by David Bowie

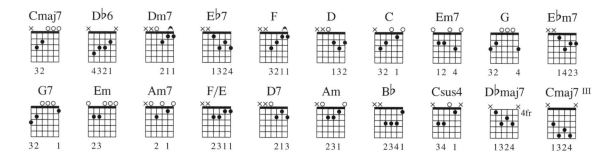

*Strum Pattern: 1, 5
*Pick Pattern: 2

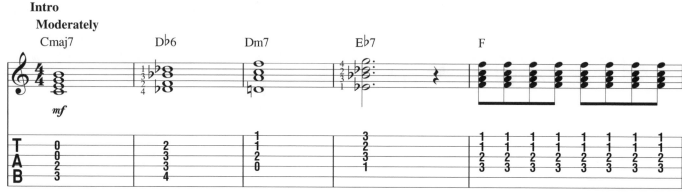

*Use Pattern 10 for $\frac{2}{4}$ meas.
 and Pattern 8 for $\frac{3}{4}$ meas.

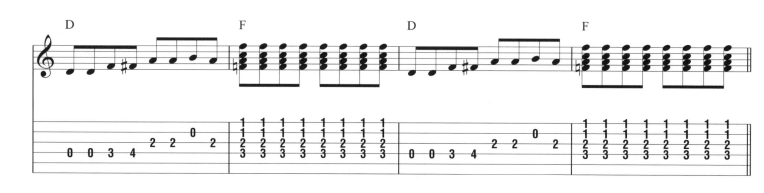

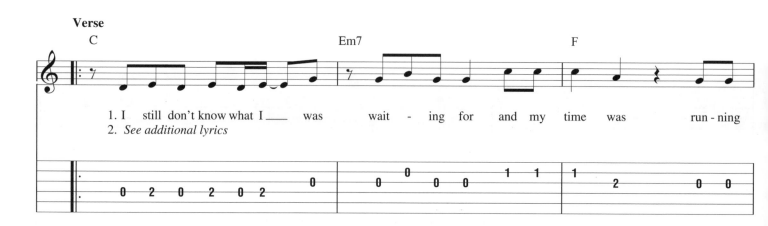

1. I still don't know what I ___ was wait - ing for and my time was run - ning
2. *See additional lyrics*

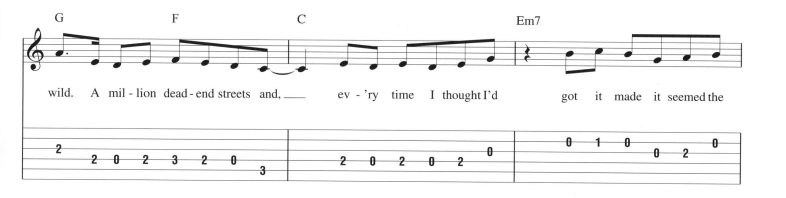

wild. A mil - lion dead - end streets and, ___ ev - 'ry time I thought I'd got it made it seemed the

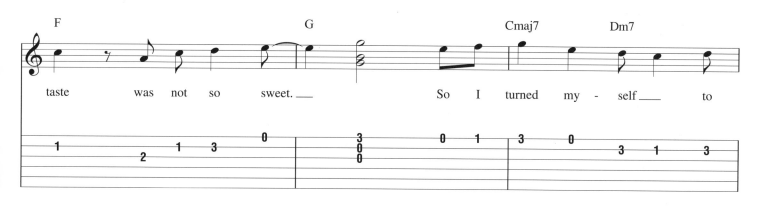

taste was not so sweet. ___ So I turned my - self ___ to

face me ___ but I've nev - er caught a glimpse how the

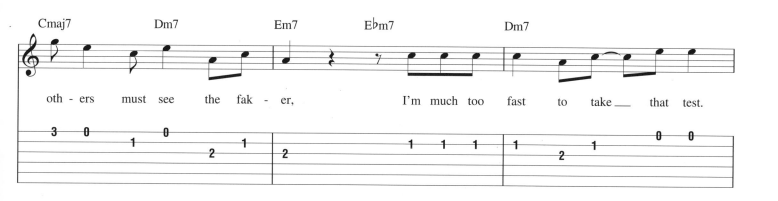

oth - ers must see the fak - er, I'm much too fast to take ___ that test.

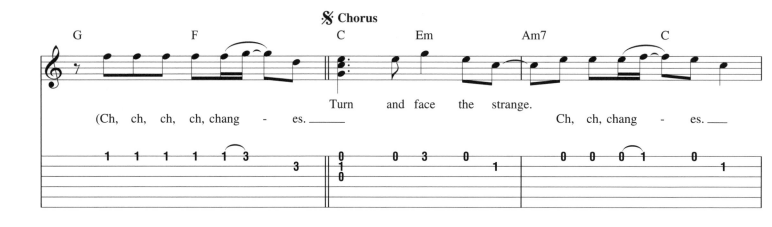

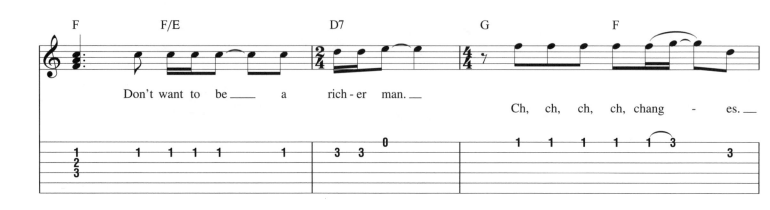

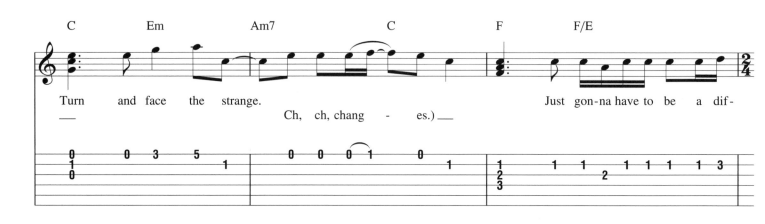

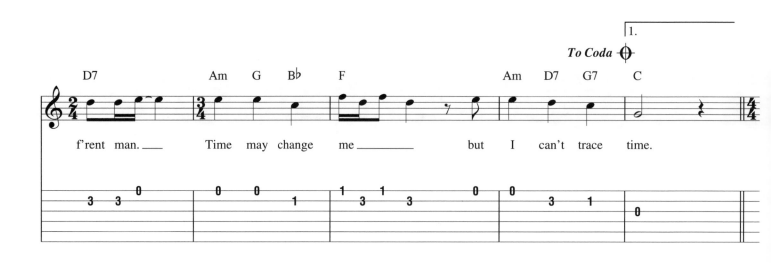

Interlude

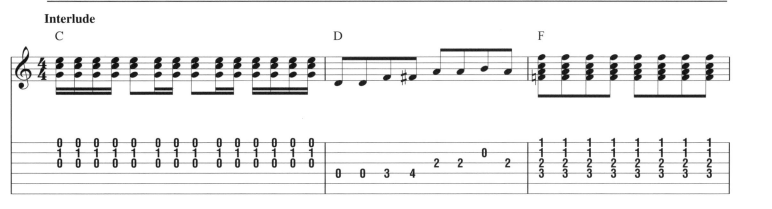

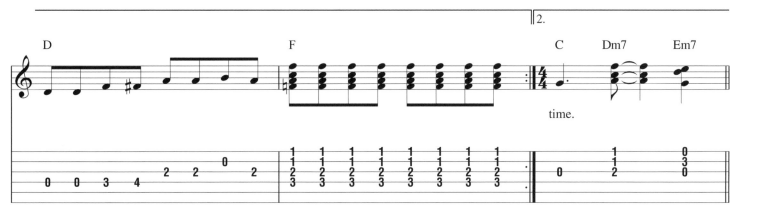

time.

Bridge

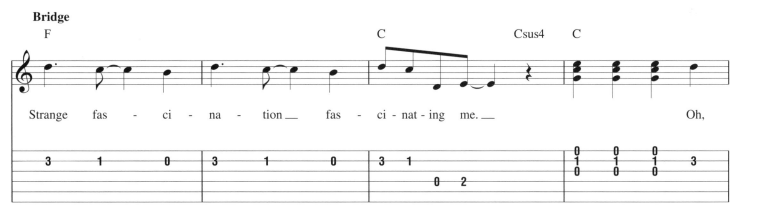

Strange fas - ci - na - tion __ fas - ci - nat - ing me. __ Oh,

D.S. al Coda

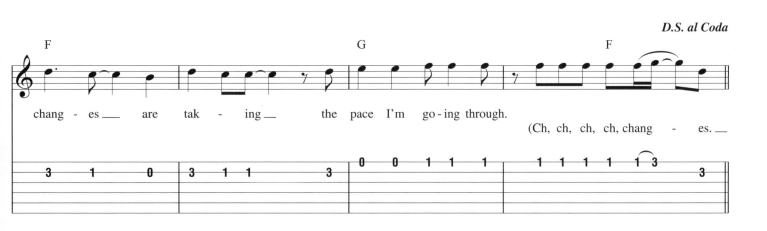

chang - es __ are tak - ing __ the pace I'm go - ing through.

(Ch, ch, ch, ch, chang - es. __

⊕ Coda

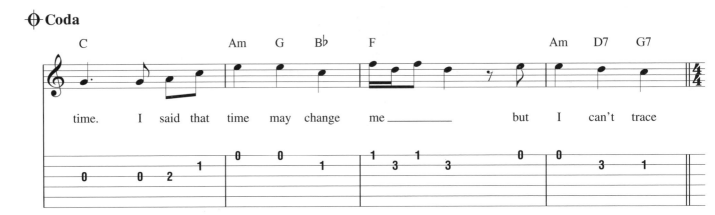

time.   I   said   that   time   may   change   me _____   but   I   can't   trace

Outro

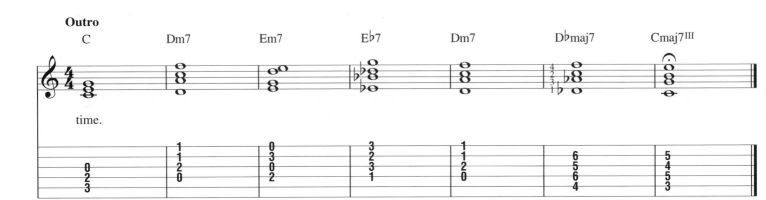

time.

Additional Lyrics

2. I watch the ripples change their size
   But never leave the stream of warm impermanence,
   And so the days flow through my eyes
   But still the days seem the same.
   And these children that you spit on,
   As they try to change their worlds,
   Are immune to your consultations,
   They're quite aware what they're going through.

Chorus 2. Turn and face the strange. (Ch, ch, changes.)
   Don't tell them to grow up and out of it.
   (Ch, ch, ch, ch, changes.)
   Turn and face the strange. (Ch, ch, changes.)
   Where's your shame, you've left us up to our necks in it.
   Time may change me but I can't trace time.

Chorus 3. Turn and face the strange. (Ch, ch, changes.)
   Oh, look out you rock 'n rollers.
   (Ch, ch, ch, ch, changes.)
   Turn and face the strange. (Ch, ch, changes.)
   Pretty soon now you're gonna get older.
   Time may change me but I can't trace time.
   I said that time may change me but I can't trace time.

Creep

Words and Music by Albert Hammond, Mike Hazlewood, Thomas Yorke, Richard Greenwood, Philip Selway, Colin Greenwood and Edward O'Brian

Strum Pattern: 5
Pick Pattern: 2

*Optional fingerings: Barre
3rd finger across 4th fret.

1. When you were here __ be-fore,

**As before: 5th fret

3. *See additional lyrics*

could-n't look you in the eye. ____

You're just like an an - gel, your skin makes me cry. __

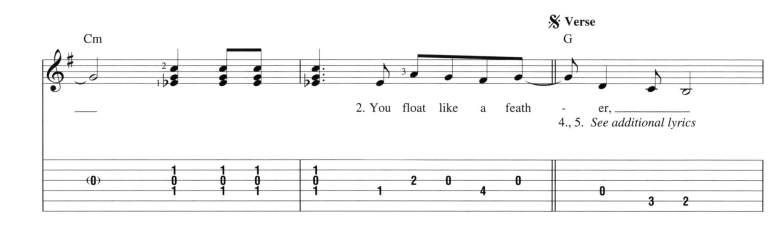

2. You float like a feath - er, _____

4., 5. *See additional lyrics*

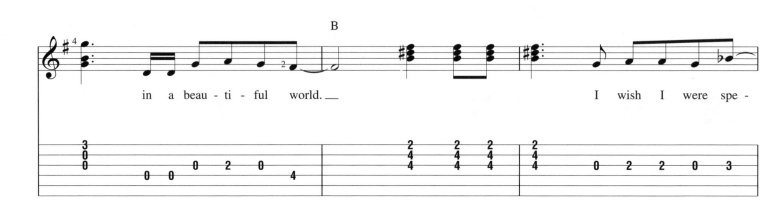

in a beau - ti - ful world. __   I wish I were spe -

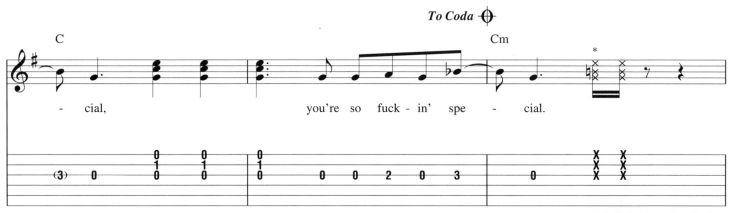

To Coda ⊕

- cial,   you're so fuck - in' spe - cial.

*Muffled strings: Lay the fret
hand across the strings with-
out depressing and strike them
w/ the pick hand.

Chorus

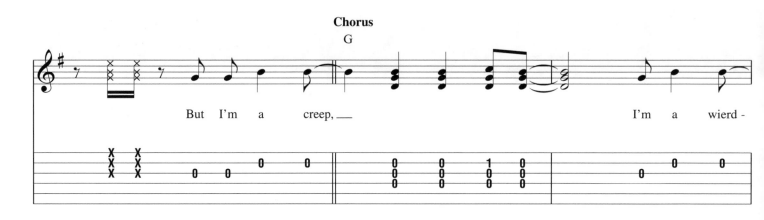

But I'm a creep, ___   I'm a wierd -

What the hell ___ am I do - ing here? ___

1.

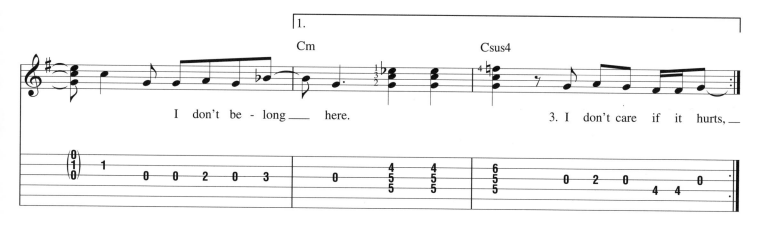

I don't be - long ___ here.   3. I don't care if it hurts, ___

2.

Bridge

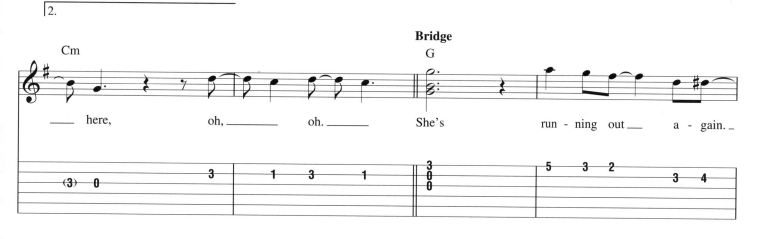

___ here,   oh, ___ oh. ___ She's   run - ning out ___ a - gain. _

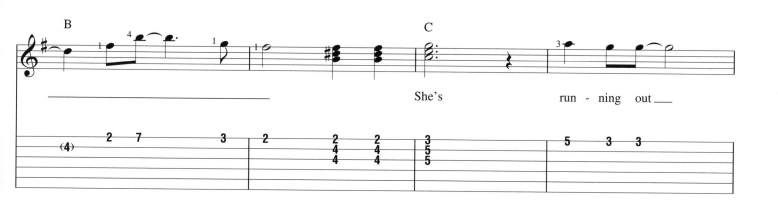

She's   run - ning out ___

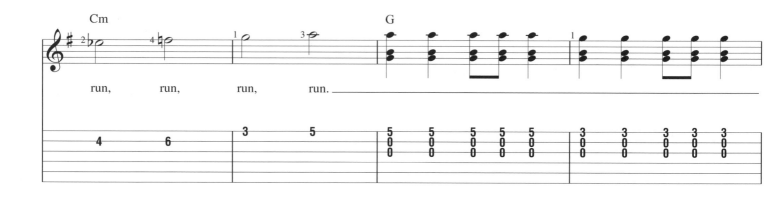

run,   run,   run,   run.

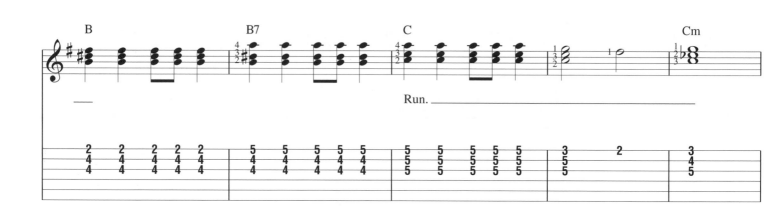

Run.

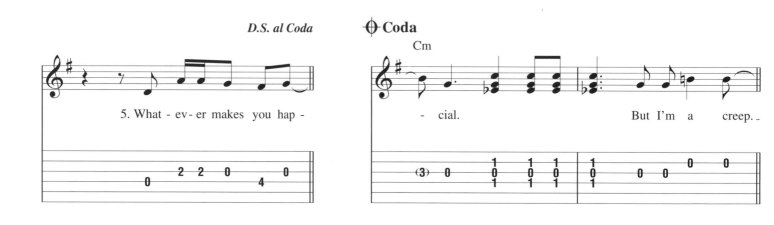

D.S. al Coda   Coda

5. What - ev - er makes you hap -   - cial.   But I'm a   creep.

Outro-Chorus

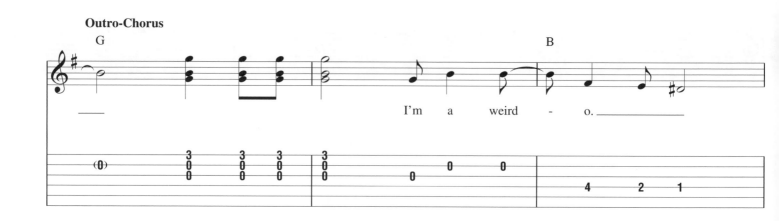

I'm a weird - o.

What the hell _ am I do - ing here? _ I don't be - long _

_ here. I don't be - long _____ here.

Additional Lyrics

3. I don't care if it hurts,
   I want to have control.
   I want a perfect body,
   I want a perfect soul.

4. I want you to notice
   When I'm not around.
   You're so fuckin' special,
   I wish I were special.

5. Whatever makes you happy,
   Whatever you want.
   You're so fuckin' special,
   I wish I were special.

Dancing Queen

Words and Music by Benny Andersson, Bjorn Ulvaeus and Stig Anderson

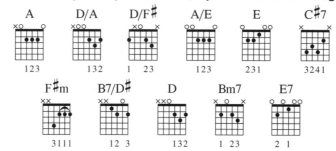

Strum Pattern: 3, 4
Pick Pattern: 4, 5

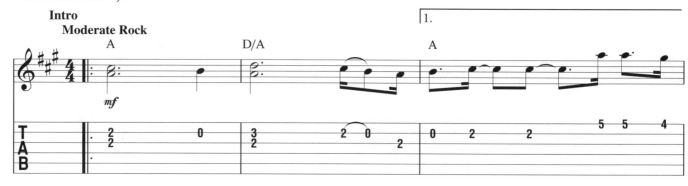

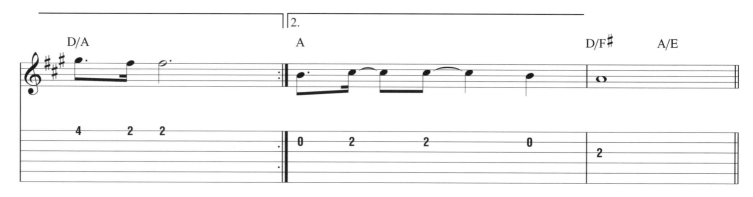

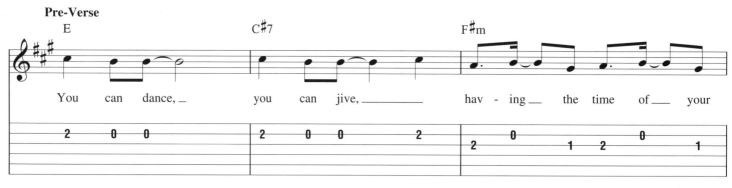

You can dance, __ you can jive, __ hav-ing __ the time of __ your

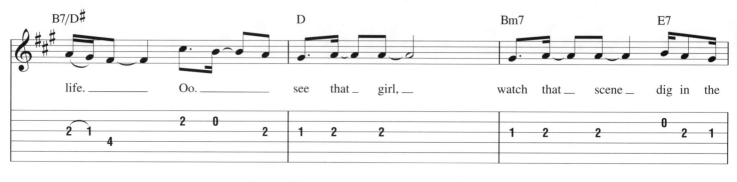

life. _____ Oo. _____ see that _ girl, __ watch that _ scene _ dig in the

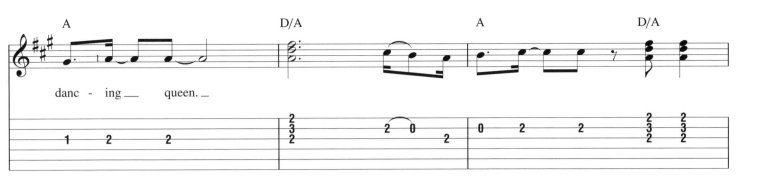

danc - ing ___ queen. ___

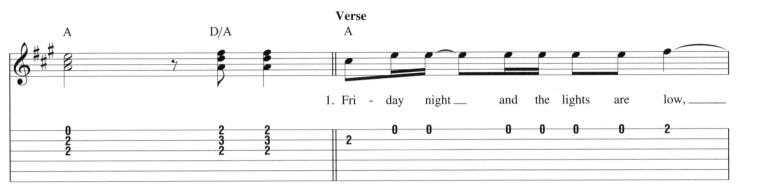

Verse

1. Fri - day night ___ and the lights are low, ___

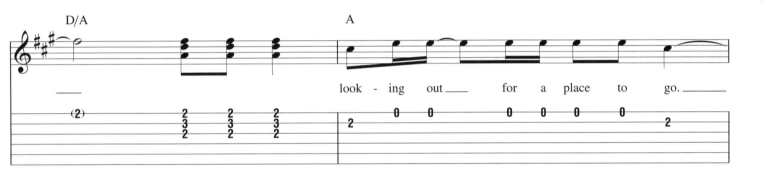

look - ing out ___ for a place to go.

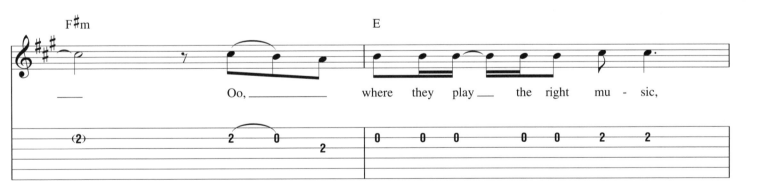

Oo, ___ where they play ___ the right mu - sic,

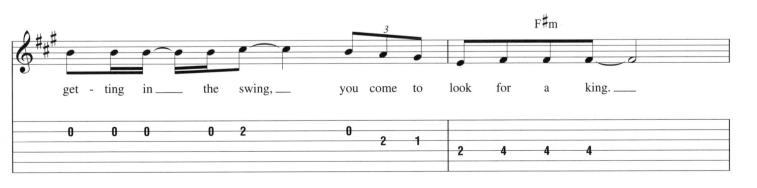

get - ting in ___ the swing, ___ you come to look for a king. ___

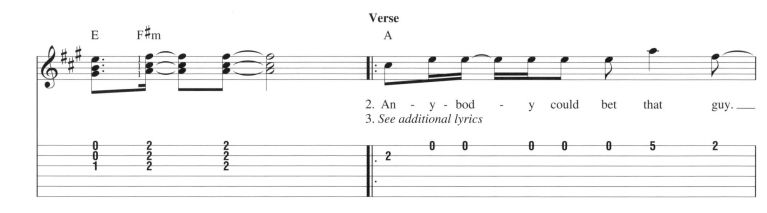

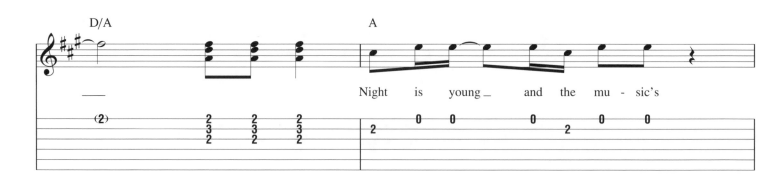

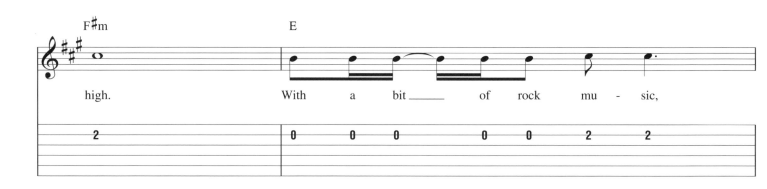

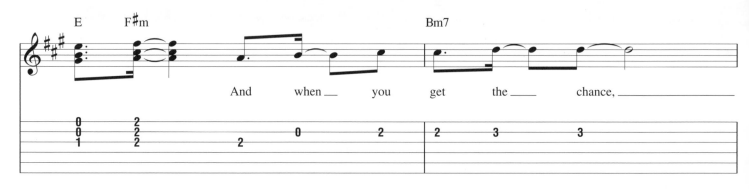

66

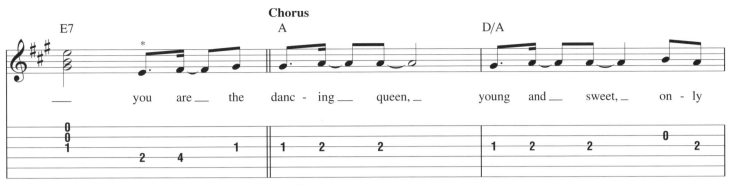

Chorus

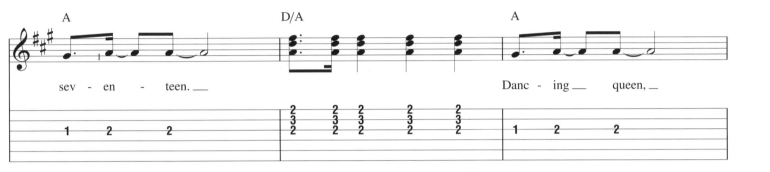

*Sung one octave higher throughout Chorus.

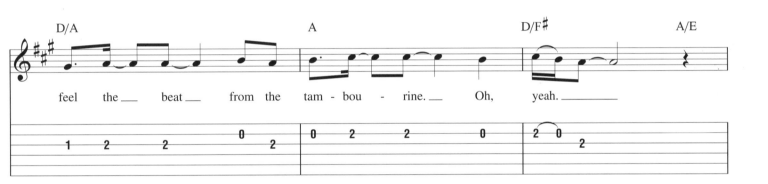

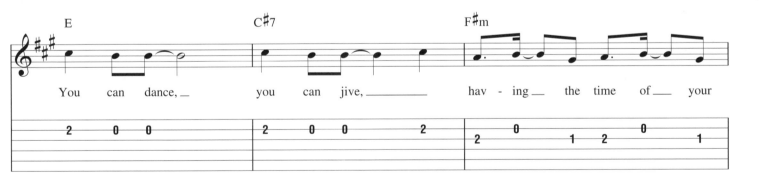

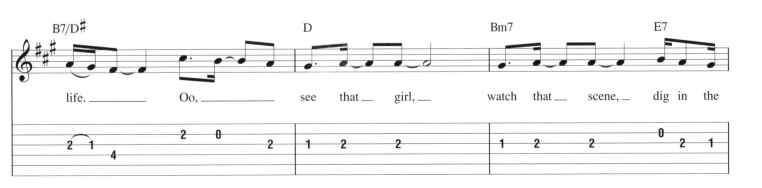

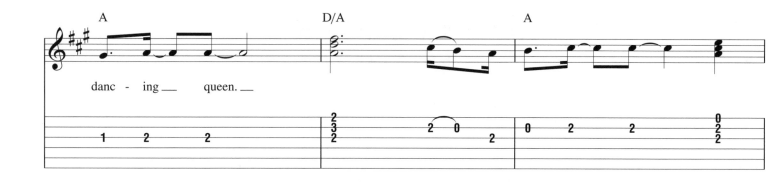

danc - ing ___ queen. ___

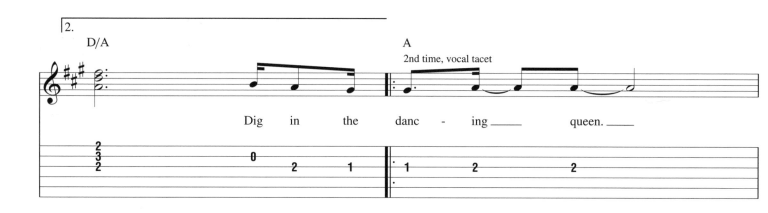

Dig in the danc - ing ___ queen. ___

2nd time, vocal tacet

Repeat and fade

Additional Lyrics

3. You're a teaser, you turn 'em on.
Leave 'em burning and then you're gone.
Looking out for another, anyone will do.
You're in the mood for a dance.

Don't Speak

Words and Music by Eric Stefani and Gwen Stefani

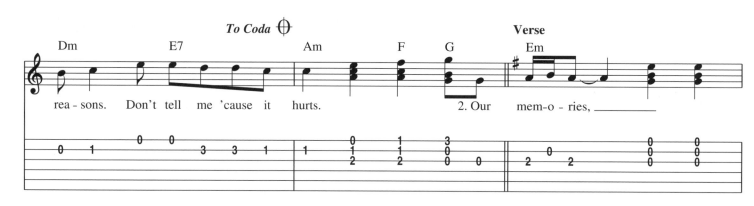

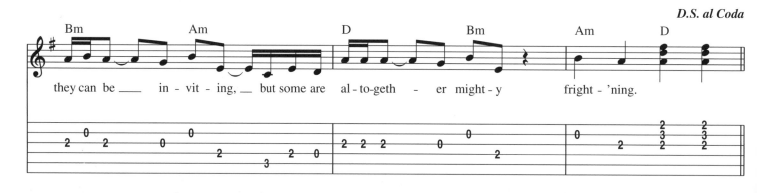

Additional Lyrics

Pre-Chorus As we die, both you and I,
With my head in my hands I sit and cry.

Do You Really Want to Hurt Me

Words and Music by George O'Dowd, Jon Moss, Michael Craig and Roy Hay

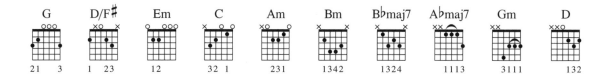

*Strum Pattern: 1
*Pick Pattern: 2

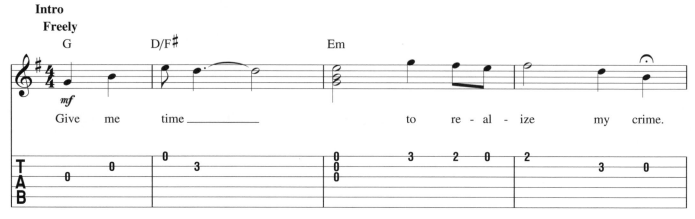

*Use Pattern 10 for 2/4 meas.

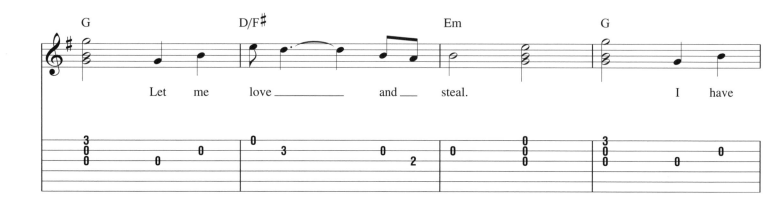

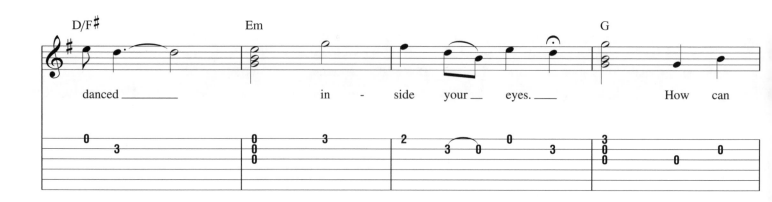

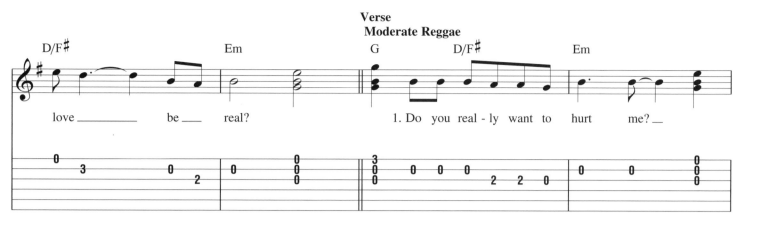

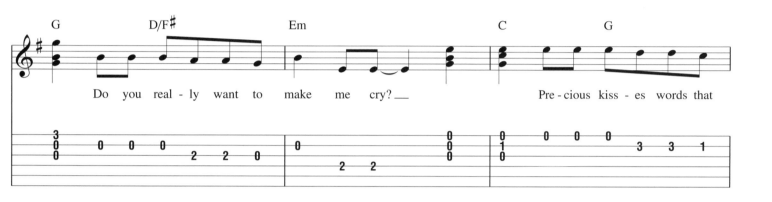

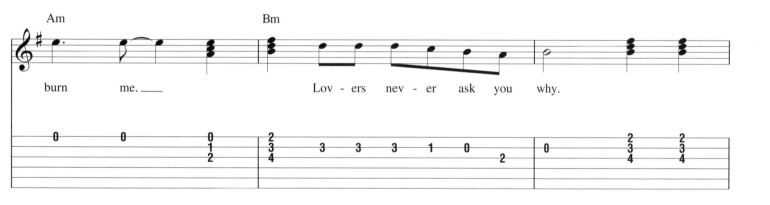

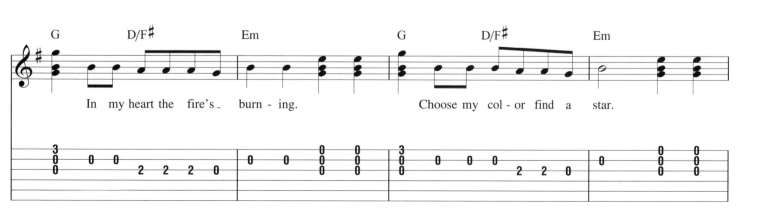

73

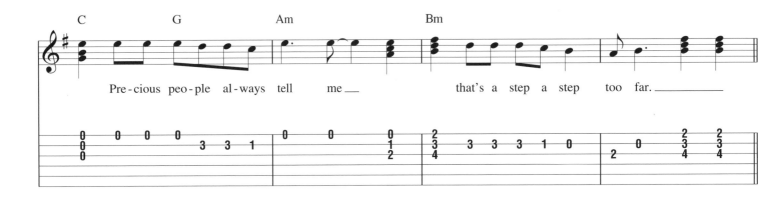

Pre - cious peo - ple al - ways tell me ___ that's a step a step too far. ___

𝄋 Chorus

Do you real - ly want to hurt me? ___ Do you real - ly want to

make me cry? ___ Do you real - ly want to hurt me? ___

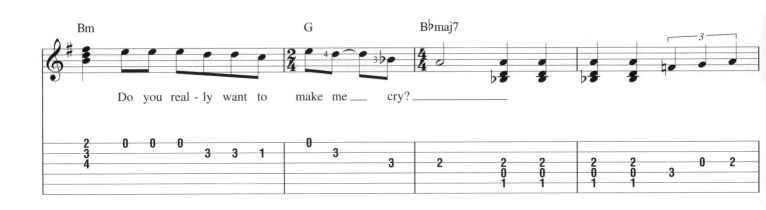

Do you real - ly want to make me ___ cry? ___

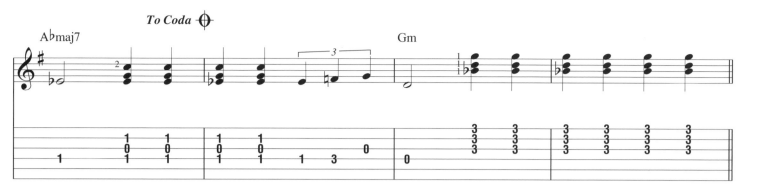

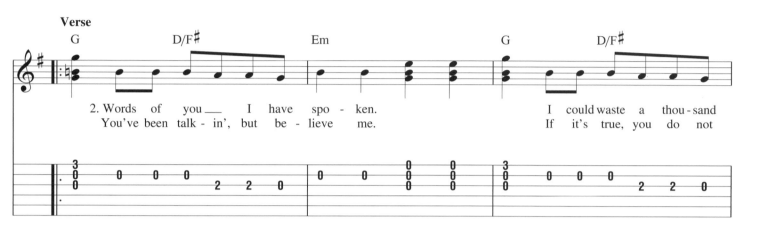

2. Words of you ___ I have spo - ken. | I could waste a thou - sand
You've been talk - in', but be - lieve me. | If it's true, you do not

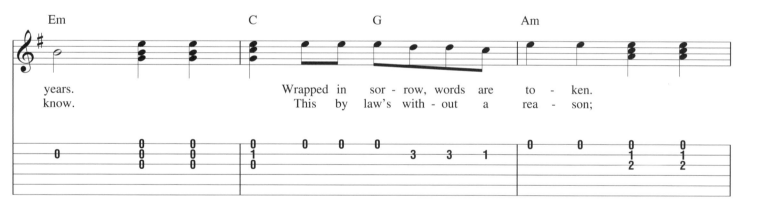

years. | Wrapped in sor - row, words are to - ken.
know. | This by law's with - out a rea - son;

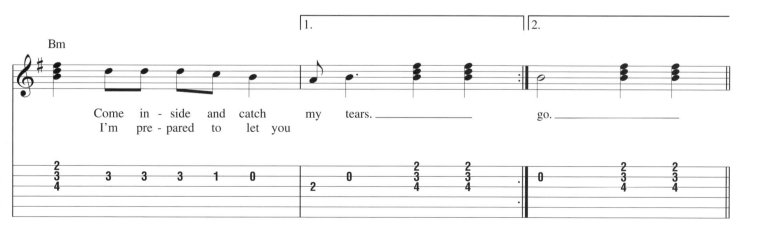

Come in - side and catch my tears. ___ | go. ___
I'm pre - pared to let you

Bridge

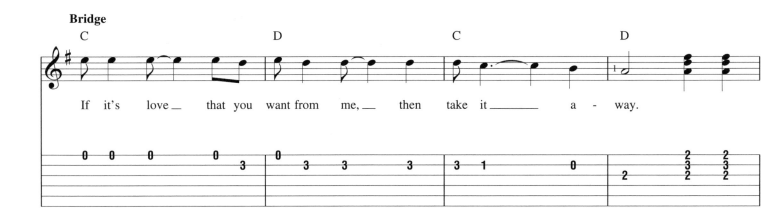

If it's love_ that you want from me, _ then take it _____ a - way.

D.S. al Coda

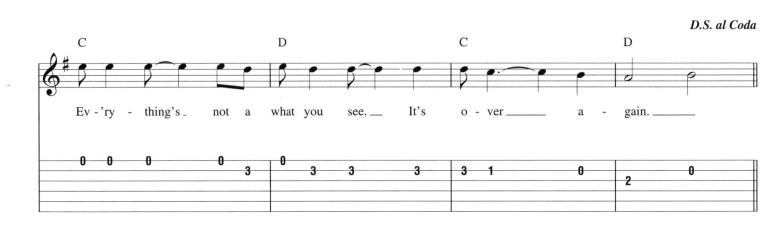

Ev - 'ry - thing's_ not a what you see._ It's o - ver_____ a - gain. _____

 Coda

Interlude

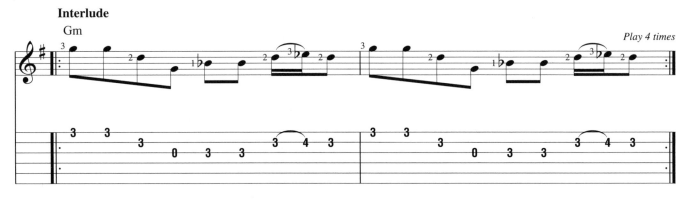

Play 4 times

Outro

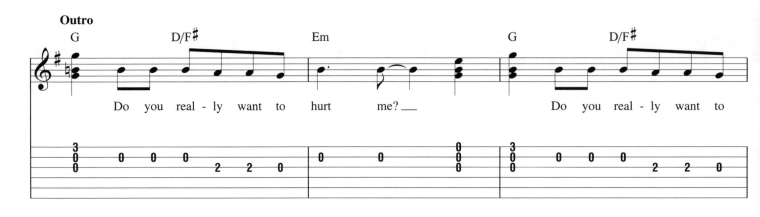

Do you real - ly want to hurt me? _ Do you real - ly want to

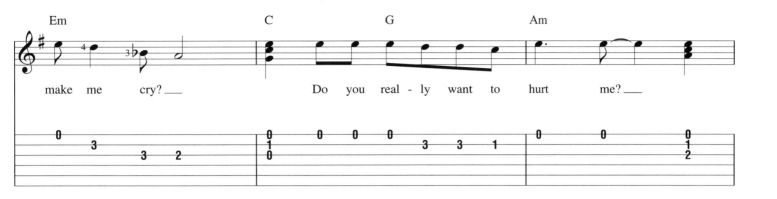

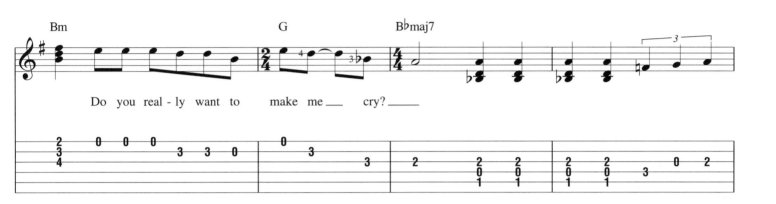

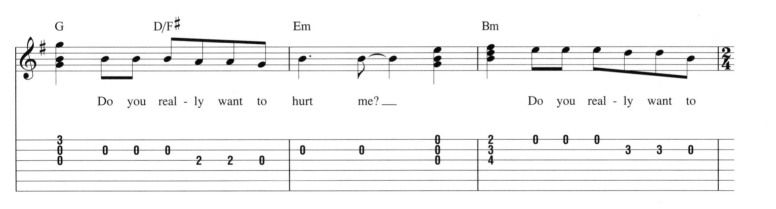

(Sittin' On)
The Dock of the Bay

Words and Music by Steve Cropper and Otis Redding

Strum Pattern: 2
Pick Pattern: 2

Additional Lyrics

2. I left my home in Georgia,
   Headed for the Frisco bay.
   I have nothin' to live for,
   Look like nothin's gonna come my way.

3. Sittin' here restin' my bones,
   And this loneliness won't leave me alone.
   Two thousand miles I roam,
   Just to make this dock my home.

Don't You Want Me

Words and Music by Phil Oakey, Adrian Wright and Jo Callis

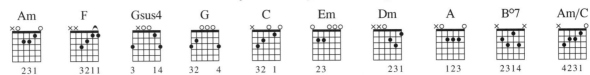

Strum Pattern: 2
Pick Pattern: 4

Intro
Moderately fast

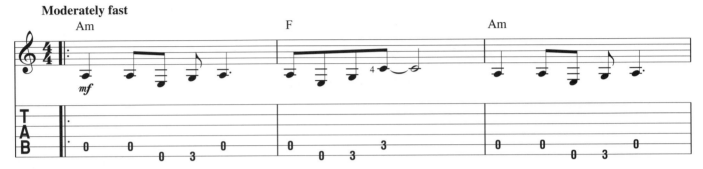

Male: 1. You were work-ing as a wait-ress in a
2. *See additional lyrics*

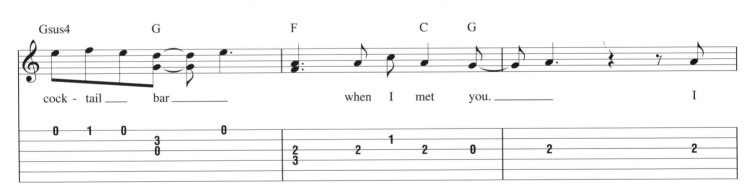

cock - tail bar when I met you. I

picked you out, I shook you up and turned you a - round,

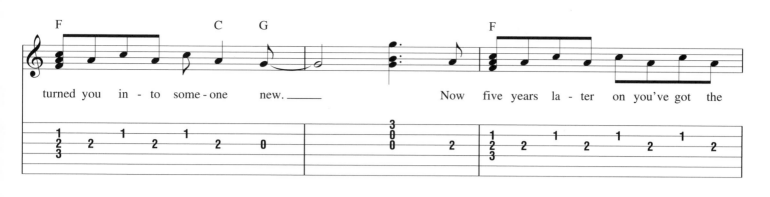

turned you in-to some-one new. _____ Now five years la-ter on you've got the

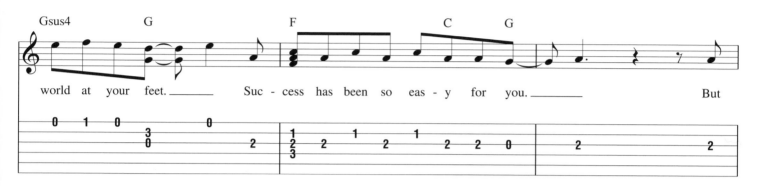

world at your feet. _____ Suc-cess has been so eas-y for you. _____ But

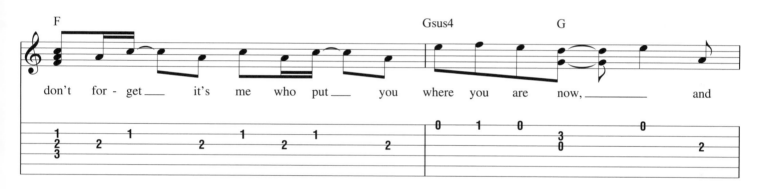

don't for-get ___ it's me who put ___ you where you are now, _____ and

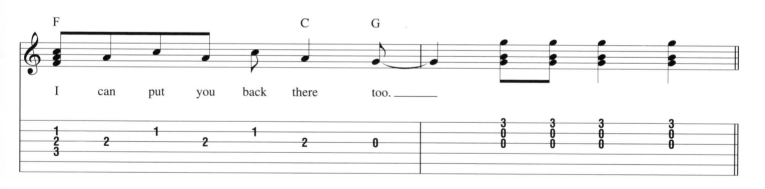

I can put you back there too. _____

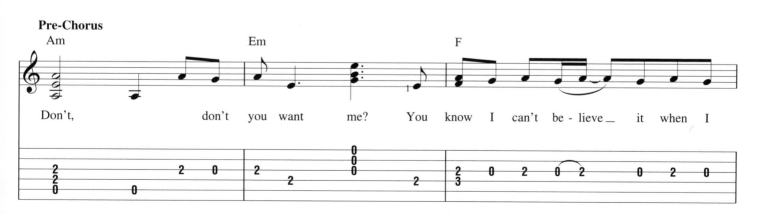

Pre-Chorus

Don't, don't you want me? You know I can't be-lieve ___ it when I

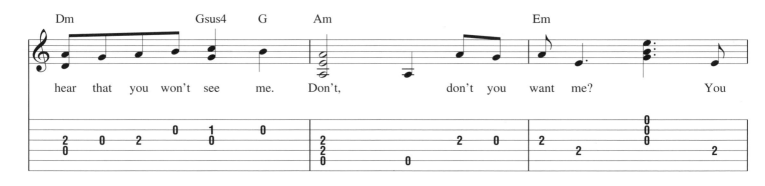

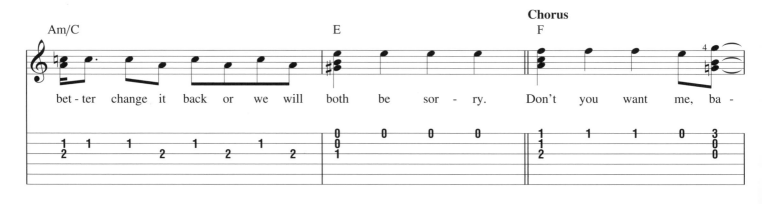

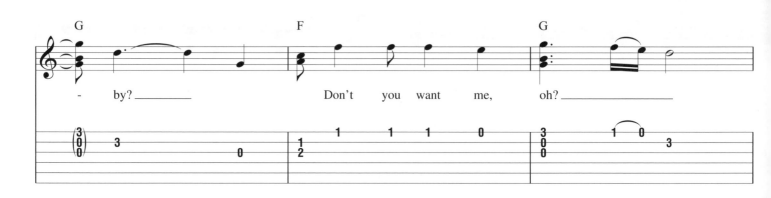

Additional Lyrics

Female: 2. I was working as a waitress in a cocktail bar,
That much is true.
But even then I knew I'd find a much better place
Either with or without you.
The five years we have had have been such good times,
I still love you.
But now I think it's time I live my life on my own.
I guess it's just what I must do.

Every Breath You Take

Music and Lyrics by Sting

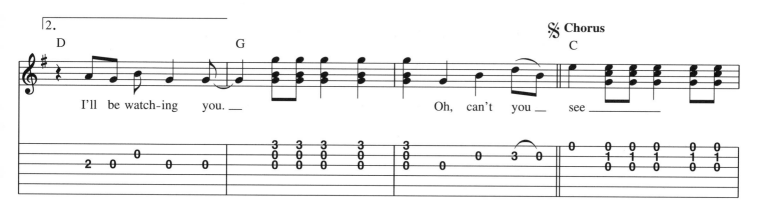

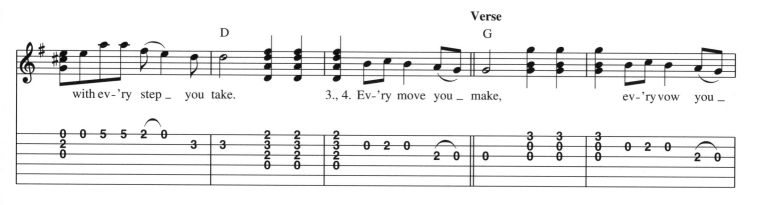

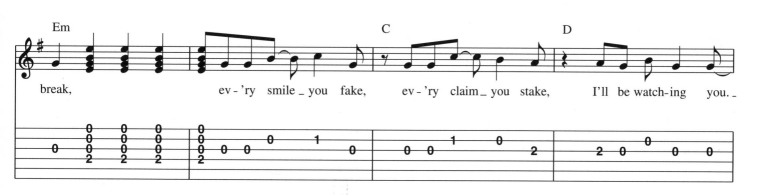

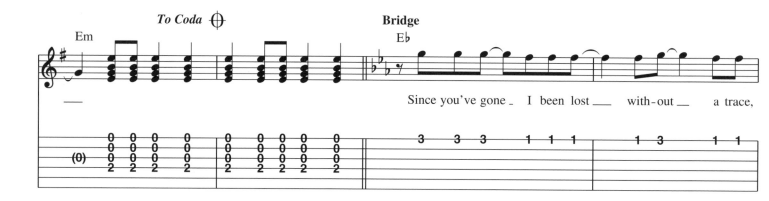

Since you've gone __ I been lost __ with-out __ a trace,

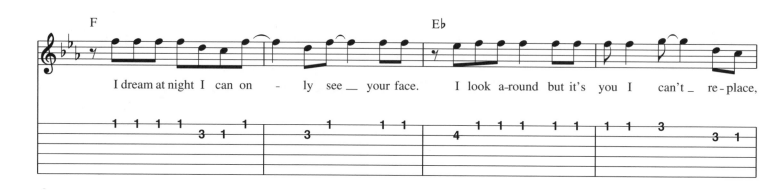

I dream at night I can on - ly see __ your face. I look a-round but it's you I can't __ re - place,

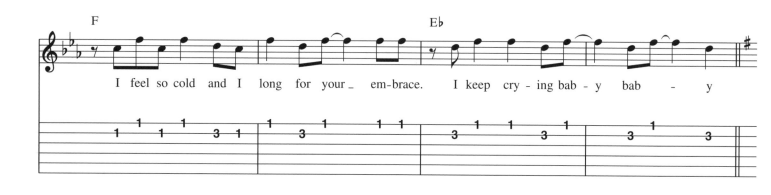

I feel so cold and I long for your __ em-brace. I keep cry - ing bab - y bab - y

please. _____

Oh can't you __

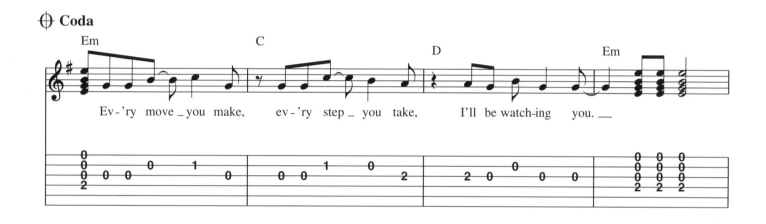

Ev-'ry move __ you make, ev-'ry step __ you take, I'll be watch-ing you. __

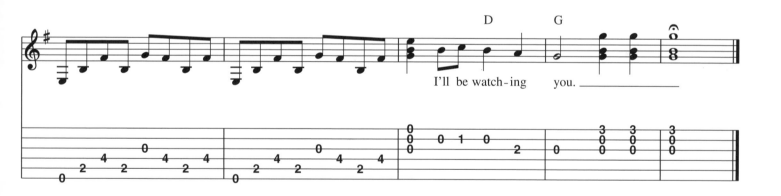

I'll be watch-ing you. _____

Additional Lyrics

2. Ev'ry single day, ev'ry word you say,
   Ev'ry game you play, ev'ry night you stay,
   I'll be watching you.

Faith

Words and Music by George Michael

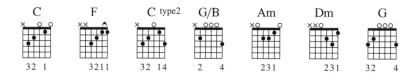

Strum Pattern: 6
Pick Pattern: 6

§ Verse

Bright Rock

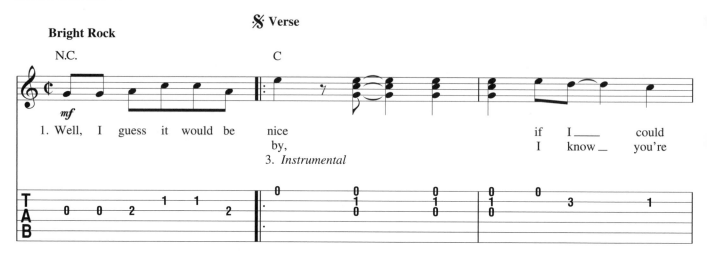

1. Well, I guess it would be nice if I ___ could
   by,
3. *Instrumental* I know ___ you're

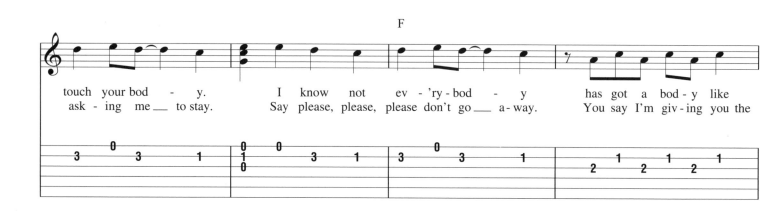

touch your bod - y. I know not ev - 'ry - bod - y has got a bod - y like
ask - ing me ___ to stay. Say please, please, please don't go ___ a - way. You say I'm giv - ing you the

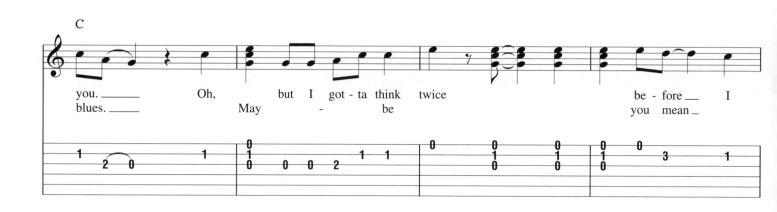

you. ___ Oh, but I got - ta think twice be - fore ___ I
blues. ___ May - be you mean ___

give my heart a - way. And I know all the games __ you play be-cause I play them
ev - 'ry word __ you say. Can't help but think of yes - ter - day and an - oth-er who

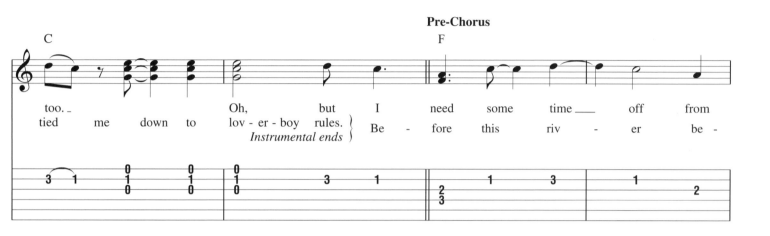

too. __ Oh, but I need some time __ off from
tied me down to lov - er - boy rules. Be - fore this riv - er be -
Instrumental ends

Pre-Chorus

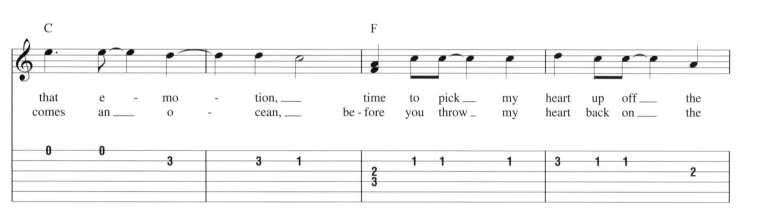

that e - mo - tion, __ time to pick __ my heart up off __ the
comes an __ o - cean, __ be - fore you throw __ my heart back on __ the

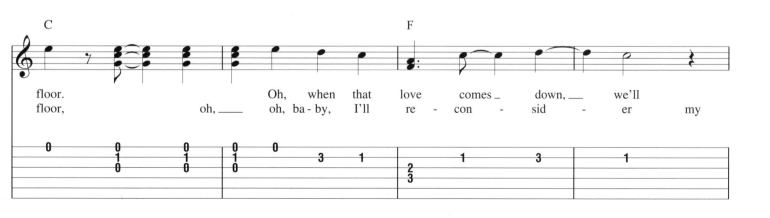

floor. Oh, when that love comes __ down, __ we'll
floor, oh, __ oh, ba - by, I'll re - con - sid - er my

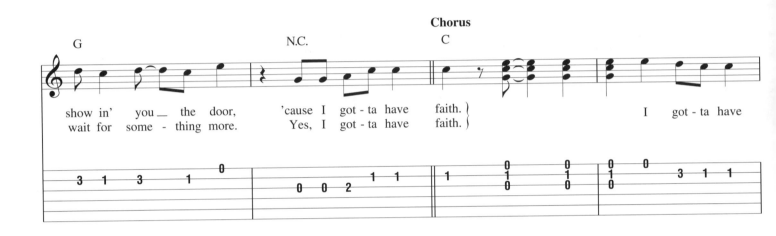

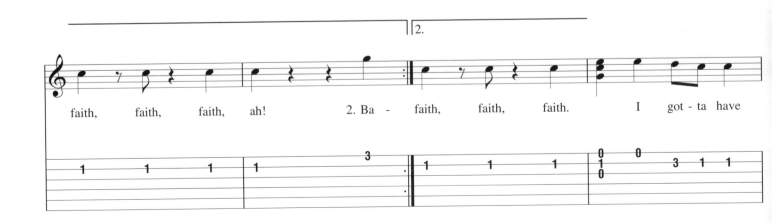

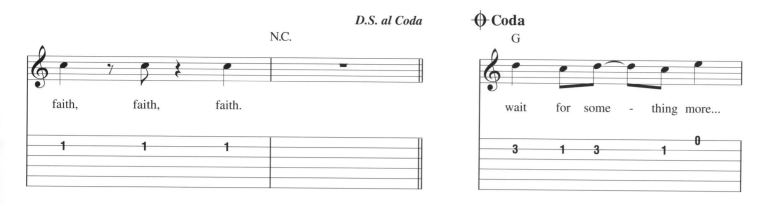

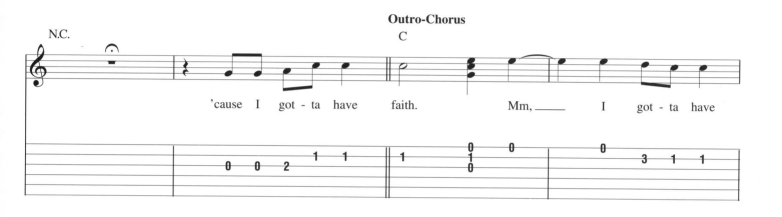

Free Fallin'

Words and Music by Tom Petty and Jeff Lynne

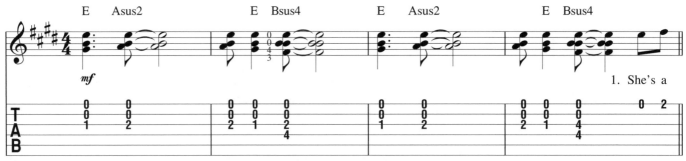

Strum Pattern: 6
Pick Pattern: 6

Intro
Moderate Rock

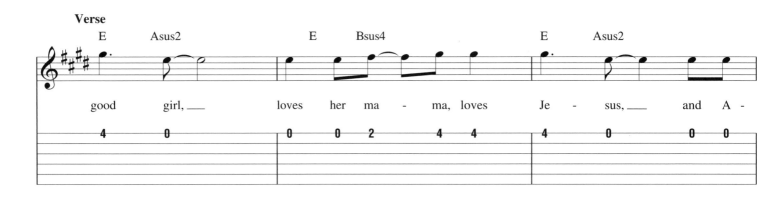

1. She's a

Verse

good girl, ___ loves her ma - ma, loves Je - sus, ___ and A -

mer - i - ca, too. ___ She's a good girl, ___ cra - zy 'bout El - vis, loves

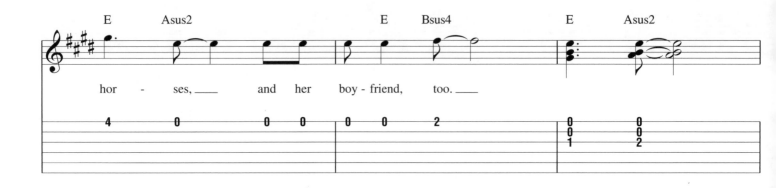

hor - ses, ___ and her boy - friend, too. ___

Interlude

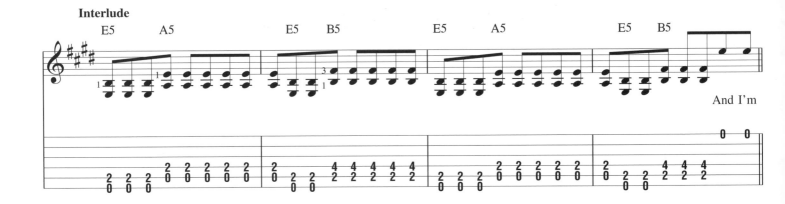

And I'm

Outro-Chorus

free,　　　　　　　　　　free fall - in'. _____　　　　　　Yeah, I'm

Repeat and fade

free,　　　　　　　　　　free fall - in'. _____　　　　　　And I'm

Additional Lyrics

3. All the vampires walkin' through the valley
   Move west down Ventura Boulevard.
   And all the bad boys are standing in the shadows.
   And the good girls are home with broken hearts.

4. Wanna glide down over Mulholland.
   I wanna write her name in the sky.
   I wanna free fall out into nothin'.
   Gonna leave this world for a while.

Go Your Own Way

Words and Music by Lindsey Buckingham

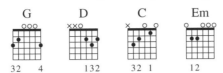

Strum Pattern: 2, 6
Pick Pattern: 2, 4

Intro
Moderately

Verse

1. Lov - ing you   is - 'nt the right _
2. *See additional lyrics*

_ thing _ to do.

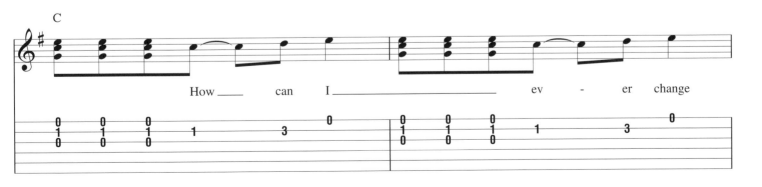

How _ can I _ ev - er change

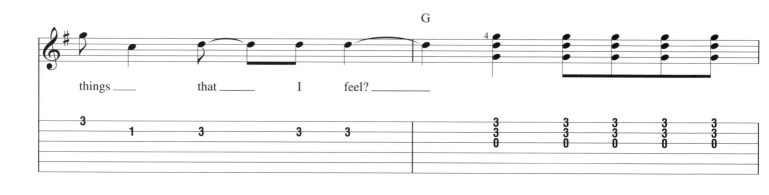

things _____ that _____ I feel? _____

If _____ I could, _____ may - be I'd give _____

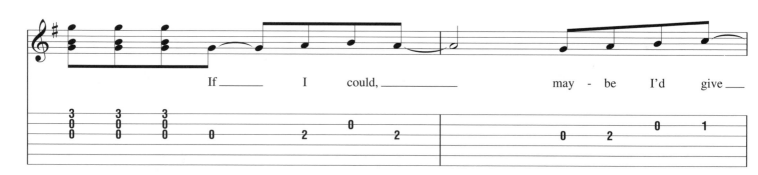

_____ you ___ my world. _____ How can I

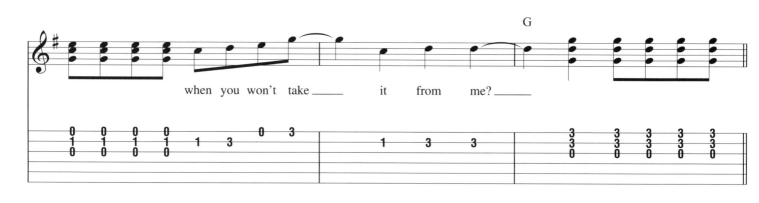

when you won't take _____ it from me? _____

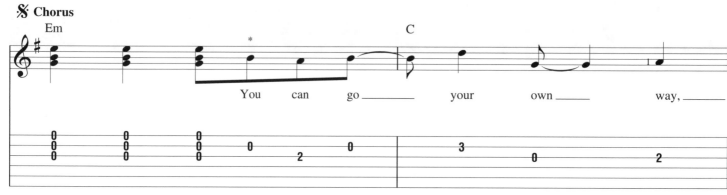

Chorus

You can go _____ your own _____ way, _____

*Sung one octave higher throughout Chorus.

96

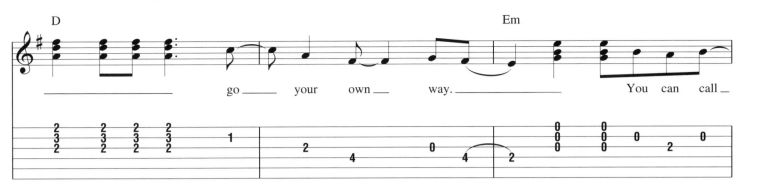

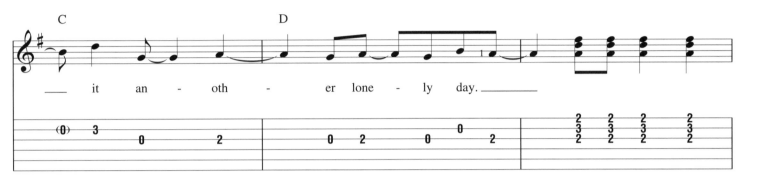

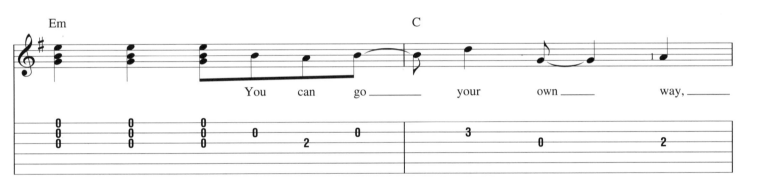

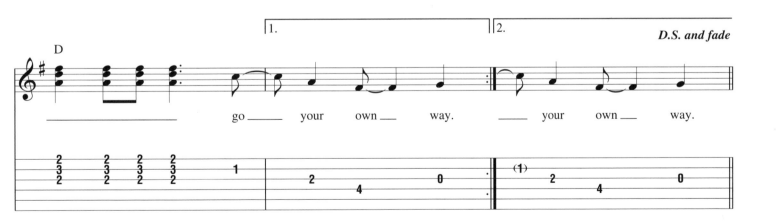

Additional Lyrics

2. Tell me why ev'rything turned around.
Packing up, shacking up is all you wanna do.
If I could, baby, I'd give you my world.
Open up, ev'rything's waiting for you.

Gone till November

Words and Music by Wyclef Jean

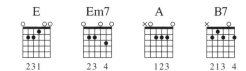

Strum Pattern: 3
Pick Pattern: 2

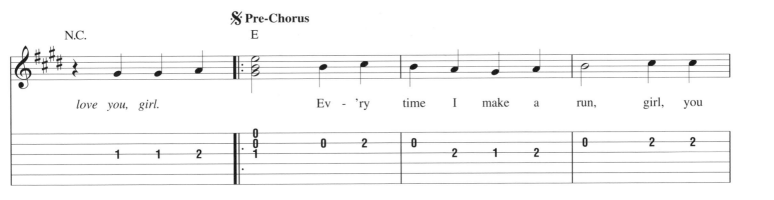

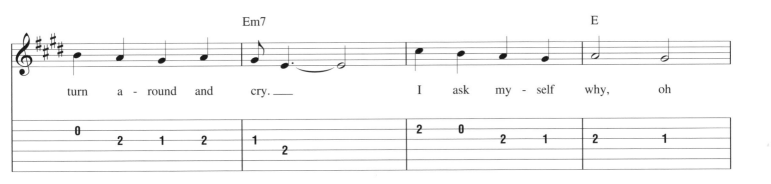

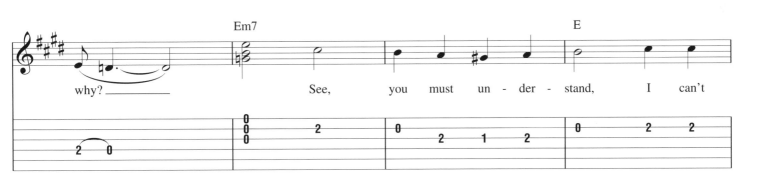

Chorus

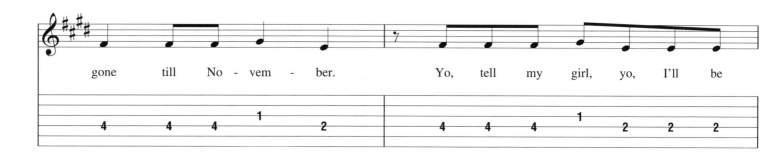

gone till No - vem - ber. Yo, tell my girl, yo, I'll be

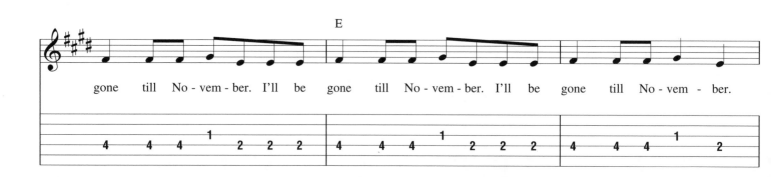

gone till No - vem - ber. I'll be gone till No - vem - ber. I'll be gone till No - vem - ber.

Yo, tell my girl, yo, I'll be gone till No - vem - ber. Jan - u - ar - y, Feb - ru - ar - y,

March, Ap - ril, May. I see you cry - in', but girl, I can't stay. I'll be

To Coda

gone till No - vem - ber. I'll be gone till No - vem - ber. { 1., 3. And } give a kiss to my moth - er { 2. Yo, }

Verse

1. Girl, I got - ta leave._____ Please don't cry _____
2. We had _____ mon - ey, I had to do some, so I'm

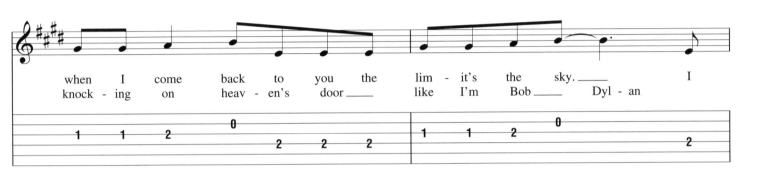

when I come back to you the lim - it's the sky. _____ I
knock - ing on heav - en's door ____ like I'm Bob ____ Dyl - an

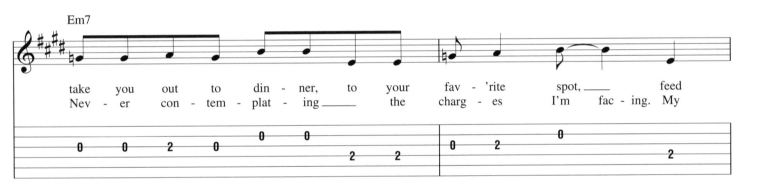

take you out to din - ner, to your fav - 'rite spot, ____ feed
Nev - er con - tem - plat - ing _____ the charg - es I'm fac - ing. My

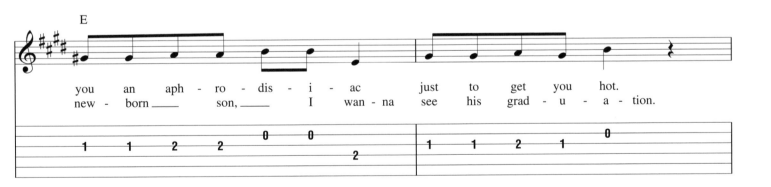

you an aph - ro - dis - i - ac just to get you hot.
new - born ____ son, ____ I wan - na see his grad - u - a - tion.

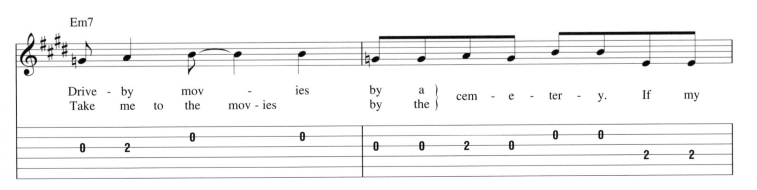

Drive - by mov - ies by a cem - e - ter - y. If my
Take me to the mov - ies by the cem - e - ter - y. If my

corpse can talk, _____ then I would tell { you } { him } I was sor - ry.

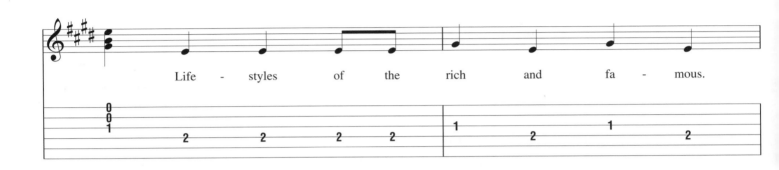

Life - styles of the rich and fa - mous.

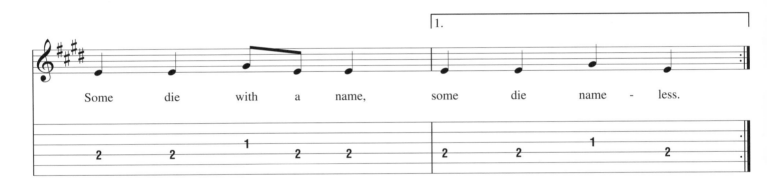

1.

Some die with a name, some die name - less.

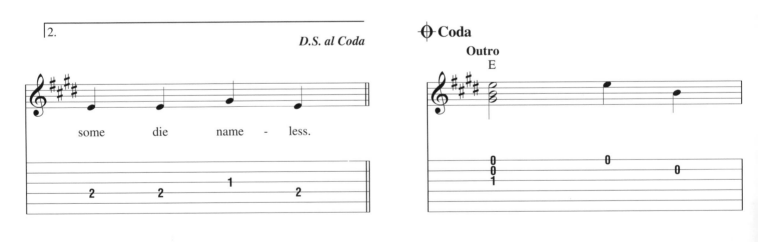

2.

D.S. al Coda

some die name - less.

Coda

Outro

E

Good Times

Words and Music by Nile Rodgers and Bernard Edwards

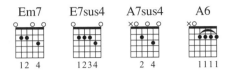

Strum Pattern: 1
Pick Pattern: 3

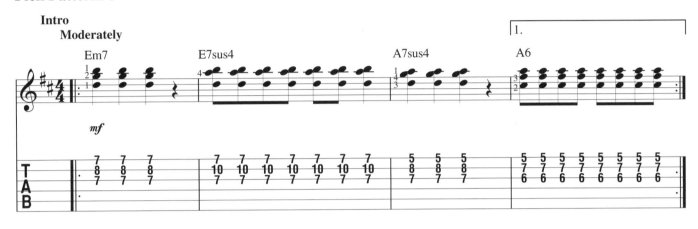

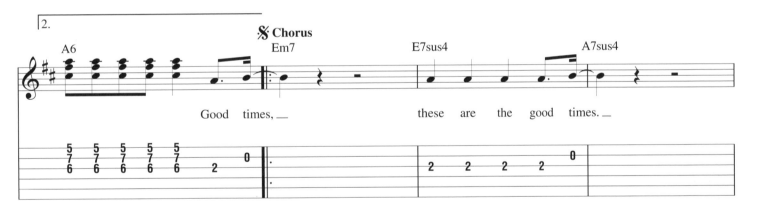

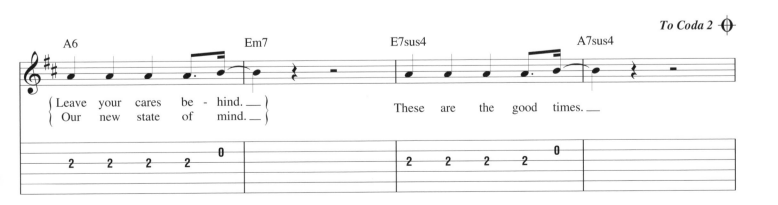

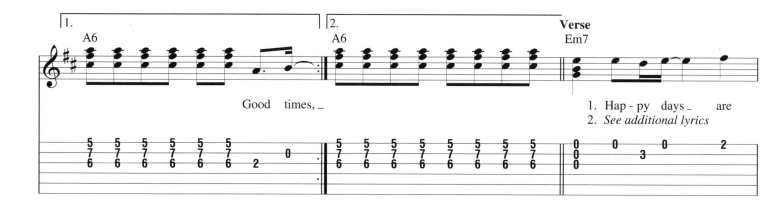

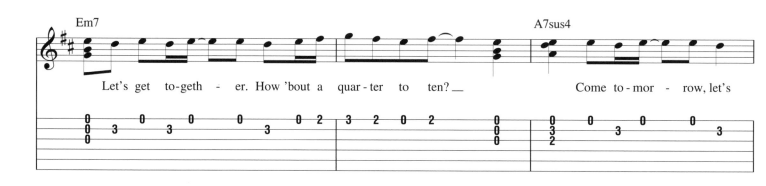

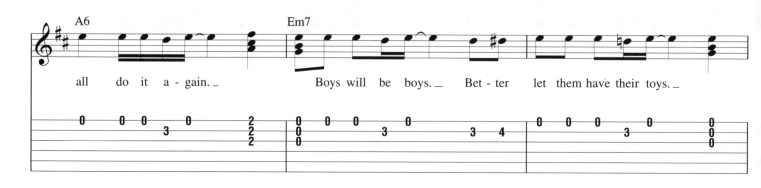

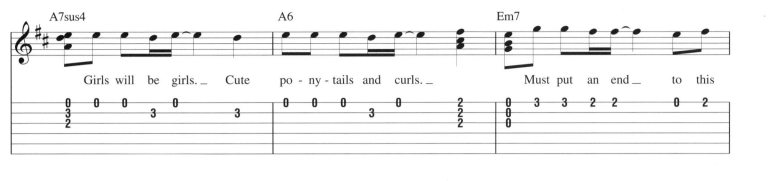

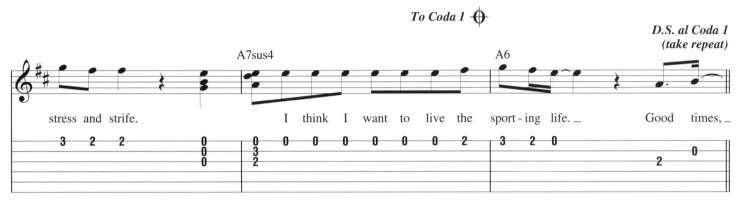

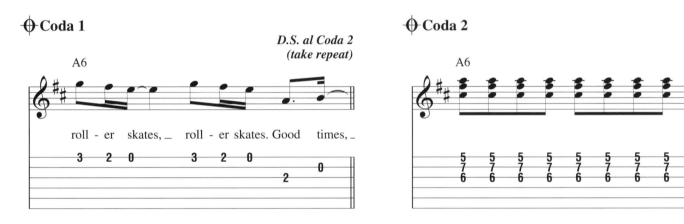

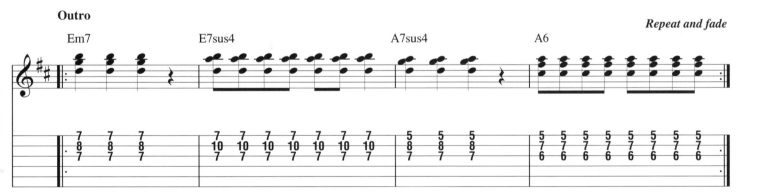

Additional Lyrics

2. A rumor has it that it's getting late.
   Time marches on; just can't wait.
   The clock keeps turnin'. Why hesitate?
   You silly fool, you can't change your fate.
   Let's cut the rug; little jive and jitterbug.
   We want the best. We won't settle for less.
   Don't be a drag. Participate.
   Clams on the half shell and roller skates, roller skates.

Good Vibrations

Words and Music by Brian Wilson and Mike Love

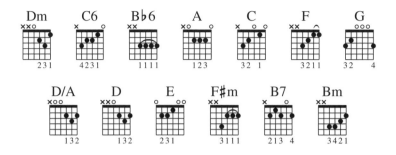

Strum Pattern: 4
Pick Pattern: 3

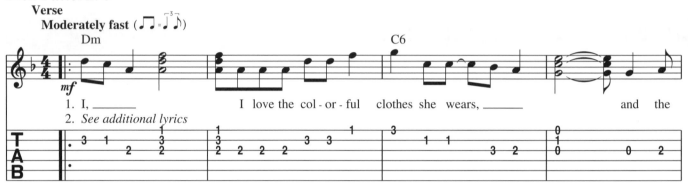

1. I, _____ I love the col-or-ful clothes she wears, _____ and the

2. *See additional lyrics*

way the sun-light plays up-on __ her hair. _____ I _____

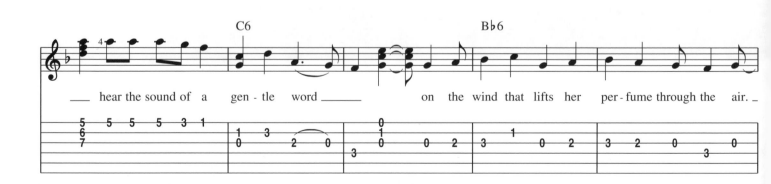

__ hear the sound of a gen-tle word _____ on the wind that lifts her per-fume through the air. _

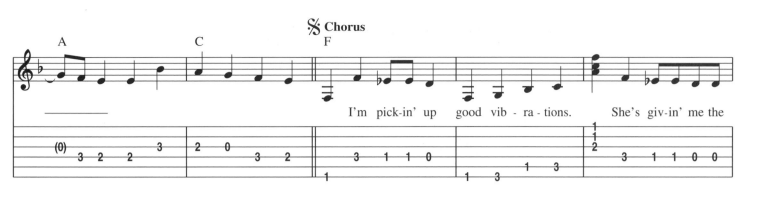

I'm pick-in' up good vib - ra - tions. She's giv-in' me the

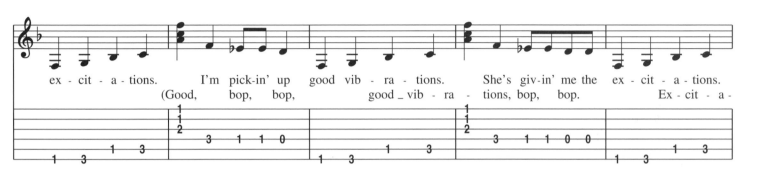

ex - cit - a - tions. I'm pick-in' up good vib - ra - tions. She's giv-in' me the ex - cit - a - tions.
(Good, bop, bop, good _ vib - ra - tions, bop, bop. Ex - cit - a -

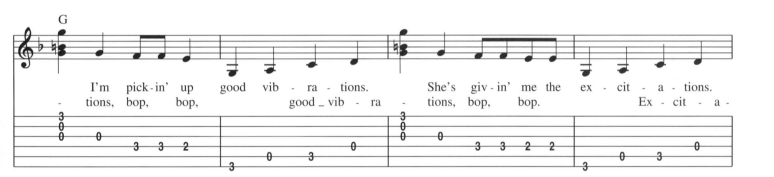

I'm pick-in' up good vib - ra - tions. She's giv-in' me the ex - cit - a - tions.
- tions, bop, bop, good _ vib - ra - tions, bop, bop. Ex - cit - a -

I'm pick-in' up good vib - ra - tions. She's giv-in' me the ex - cit - a - tions. ex - cit - a - tions.
- tions, bop, bop. Good _ vib - ra - tions, bop, bop.) (Ex - cit - a...)

Interlude

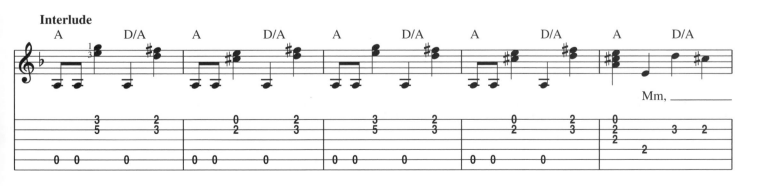

Mm, _____

107

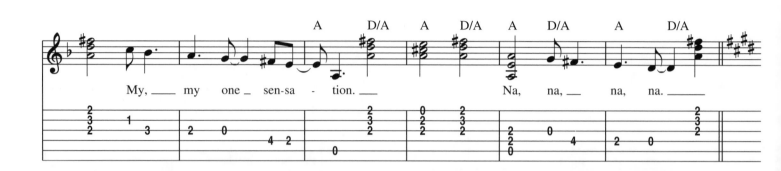

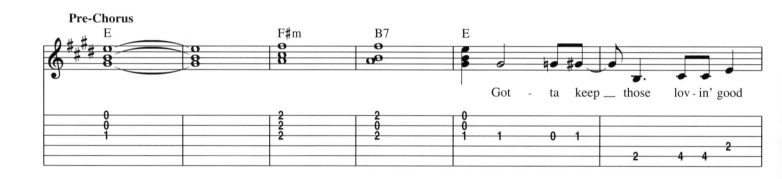

Chorus

I'm pick-in' up good vib - ra - tions. She's giv-in' me the ex - cit - a - tions. I'm pick-in' up
(Good, bop, bop. Good _ vib - ra - tions, bop, bop. Ex - cit - a - tions, bop, bop,

good vib - ra - tions. Na, __ na. _____
good _ vib - ra - tions.)

Breakdown

Na, na, na, na, na, na, na, na. _____ Na, na, na, na, na, na, na, na. _____

D.S. and fade

Na, na, na, na, na, na, na, na. _____ Na, na, na, na, na, na, na, na. _____

Additional Lyrics

2. Close my eyes, she's somehow closer now.
   Softly smile I know she must be kind.
   When I look in her eyes.
   She goes with me to a blossom room.

Hot Fun in the Summertime

Words and Music by Sylvester Stewart

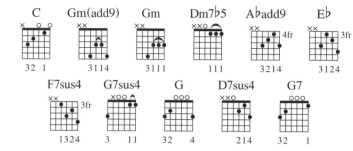

Strum Pattern: 3, 4
Pick Pattern: 2, 4

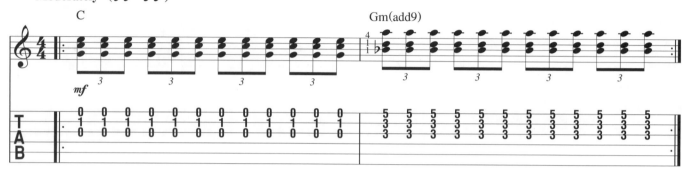

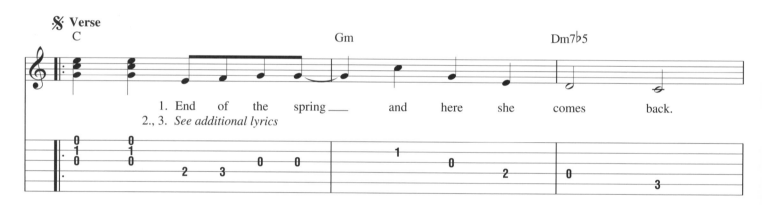

1. End of the spring ___ and here she comes back.
2., 3. *See additional lyrics*

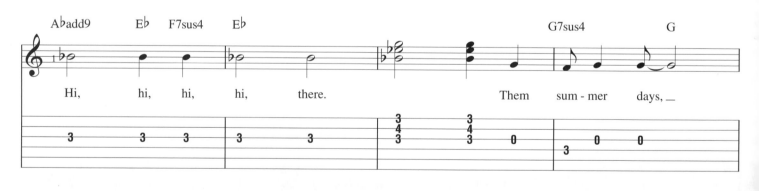

Hi, hi, hi, hi, there. Them sum-mer days, ___

those sum-mer days. ___

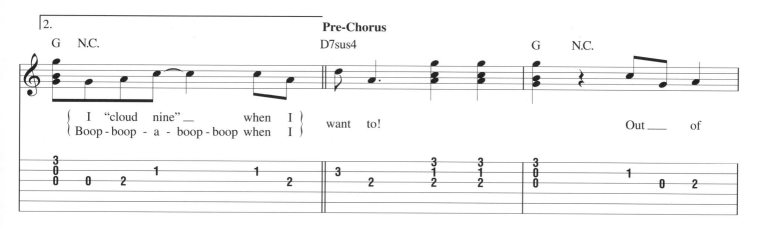

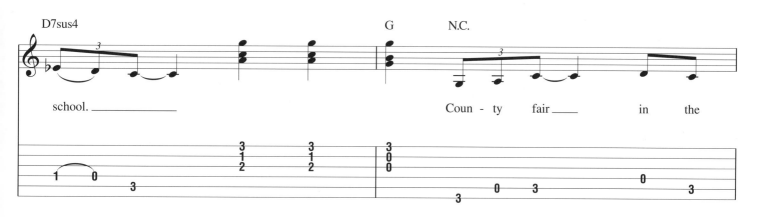

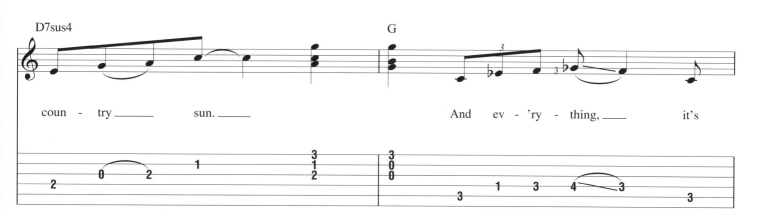

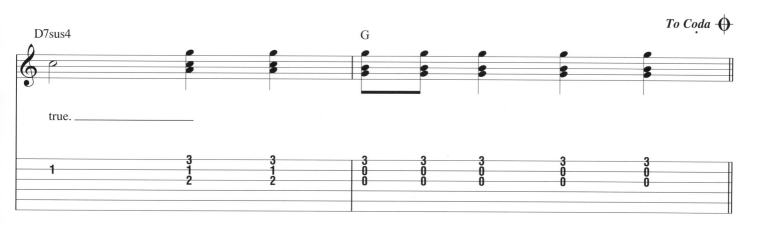

Chorus

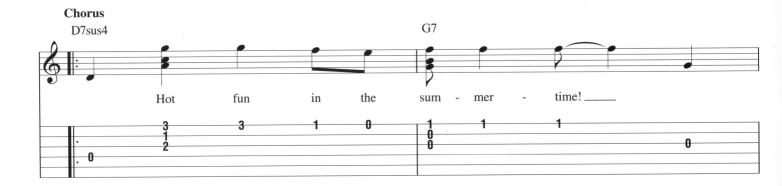

Hot fun in the sum-mer - time! _____

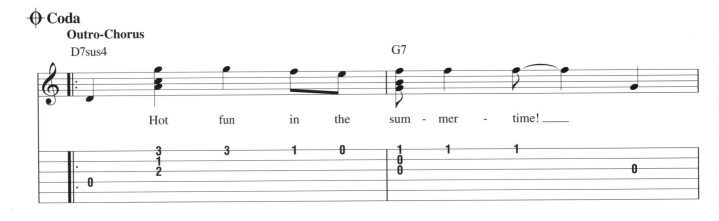

Hot fun in the sum-mer - time! __

sum-mer - time! __

D.S. al Coda
(take 2nd ending)

⊕ **Coda**

Outro-Chorus

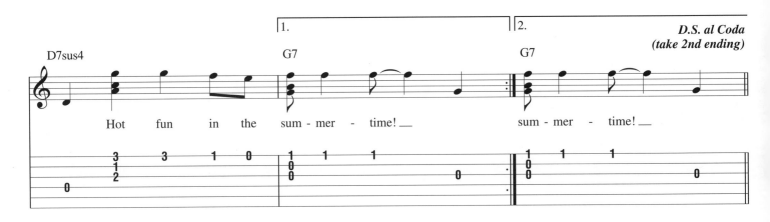

Hot fun in the sum-mer - time! _____

Repeat and fade

Hot fun in the sum-mer - time! _____

Additional Lyrics

2. That's when I had most of my fun, back.
   High, high, high, high there.
   Them summer days,
   Those summer days.

3. First of the fall and there she goes back.
   Bye, bye, bye, bye there.
   Them summer days,
   Those summer days.

Hotel California

Words and Music by Don Henley, Glenn Frey and Don Felder

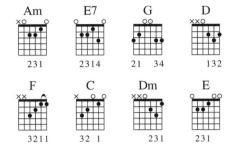

Strum Pattern: 3
Pick Pattern: 4

Intro
Moderate Rock

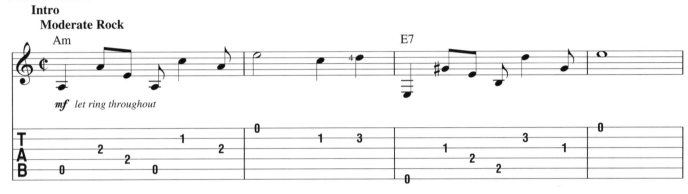

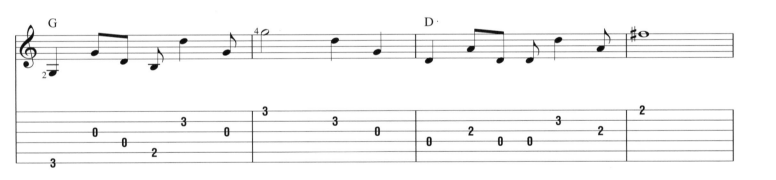

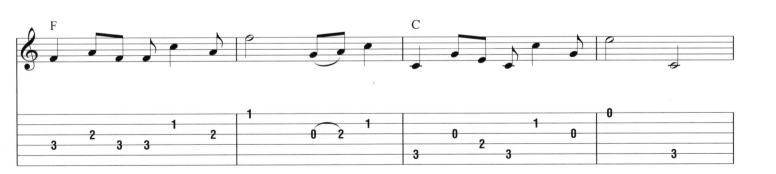

% **Verse**

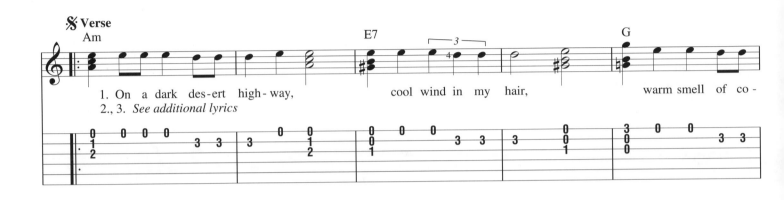

1. On a dark des-ert high-way,   cool wind in my hair,   warm smell of co-
2., 3. *See additional lyrics*

li-tas   ris-ing up through the air. _____   Up a-head in the

dis-   tance,   I saw a shim-mer-ing light.   My head grew heav-y and my

sight grew dim; __   I had to stop for the night.   There she stood in the

door - way;   I heard the mis - sion bell. _____   And I was think-ing

to my - self: _ this could be heav - en or this could be hell. _____   Then she lit up a

can - dle,   and she showed me the way.   There were voic-es down the

3rd time, to Coda **Chorus**

cor - ri - dor; _   I thought I heard them say: "Wel - come _ to the Ho -

- tel Cal - i - for - nia.   Such a love - ly place, _ (Such a

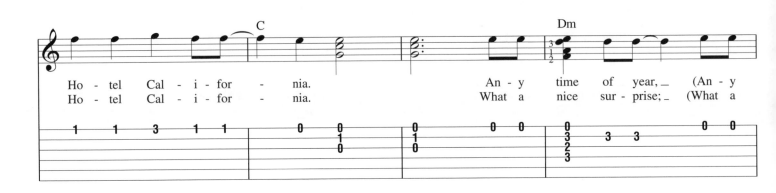

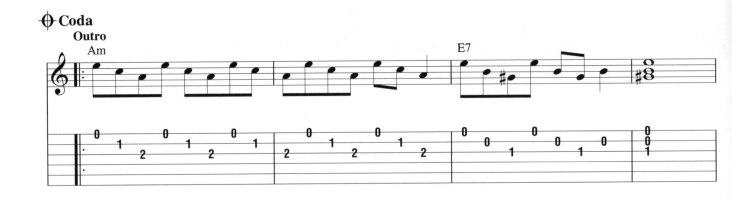

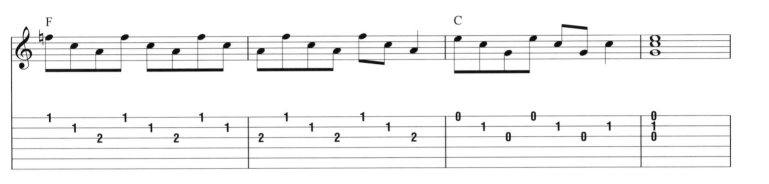

Repeat and fade

Additional Lyrics

2. Her mind is Tiffany twisted. She got the Mercedes bends.
   She got a lot of pretty, pretty boys that she calls friends.
   How they dance in the courtyard; sweet summer sweat.
   Some dance to remember; some dance to forget.
   So I called up the captain: "Please bring me my wine."
   He said, "We haven't had that spirit here since nineteen sixty-nine."
   And still those voices are calling from far away;
   Wake you up in the middle of the night just to hear them say:

3. Mirrors on the ceiling, the pink champagne on ice,
   And she said, "We are all just prisoners here of our own device."
   And in the master's chambers, they gathered for the feast.
   They stab it with their steely knives, but they just can't kill the beast.
   Last thing I remember, I was running for the door.
   I had to find the passage back to the place I was before.
   "Relax," said the night man. "We are programmed to receive.
   You can check out any time you like, but you can never leave."

I Need Love

Words and Music by James Todd Smith, Dwayne Simon, Bobby Erving, Darryl Pierce and Steven Ettinger

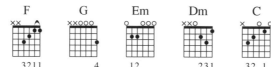

Strum Pattern: 2
Pick Pattern: 5

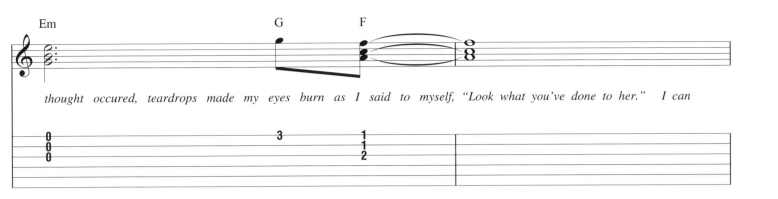

thought occured, teardrops made my eyes burn as I said to myself, "Look what you've done to her."   I can

feel it inside; I can't explain how it feels,   all I know is that I'll never dish another raw deal, playin'

make-believe, pretending that I'm true,   holding in my laugh as I say that I love you.

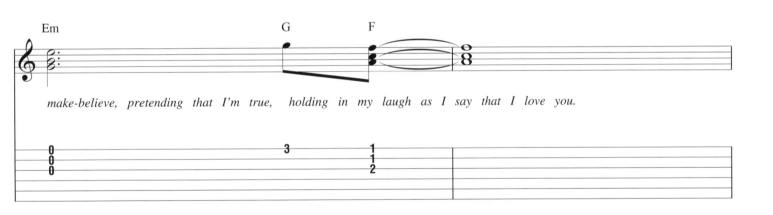

Saying, "Amour," kissing you on the ear, whispering, "I love you" and, "I'll always be here." Although I

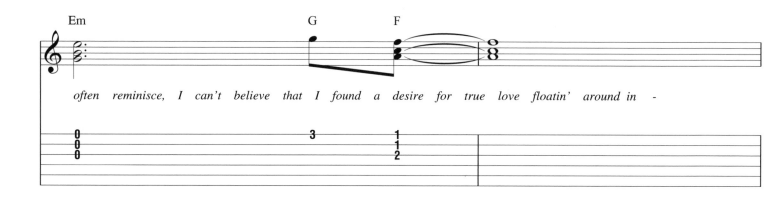

often reminisce, I can't believe that I found a desire for true love floatin' around in -

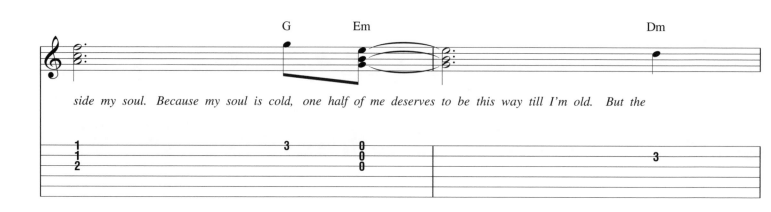

side my soul. Because my soul is cold, one half of me deserves to be this way till I'm old. But the

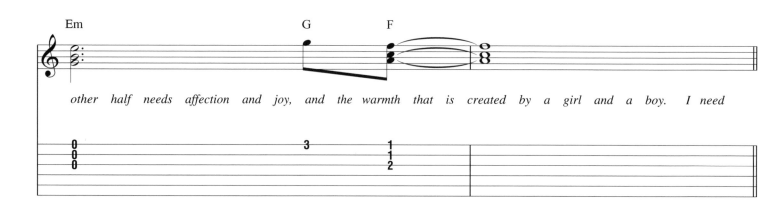

other half needs affection and joy, and the warmth that is created by a girl and a boy. I need

Chorus

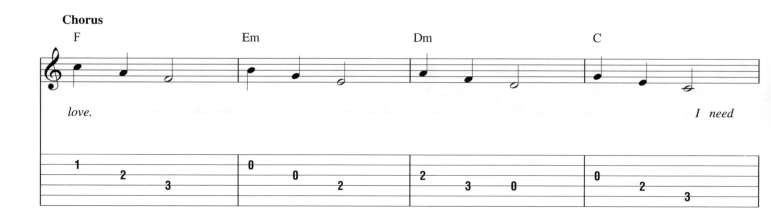

love.   *I need*

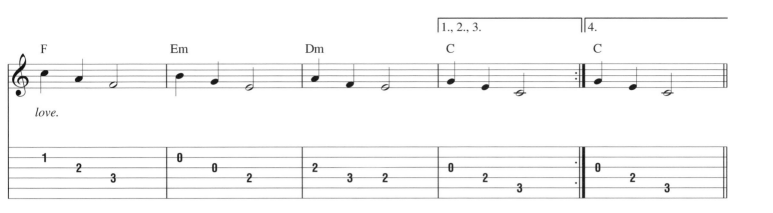

love.

Outro

Girl, listen to me. When I be sittin' in my room all alone, starin' at the wall, fantasies,

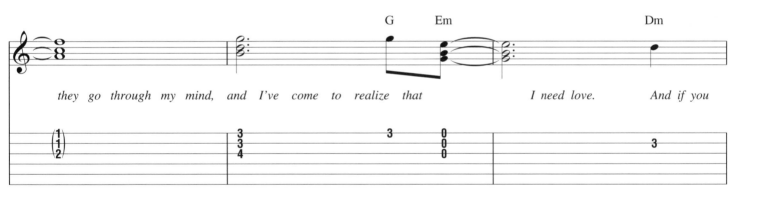

they go through my mind, and I've come to realize that I need love. And if you

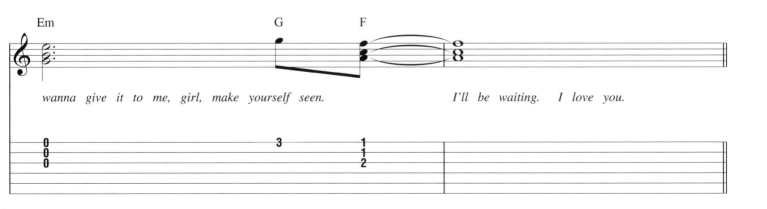

wanna give it to me, girl, make yourself seen. I'll be waiting. I love you.

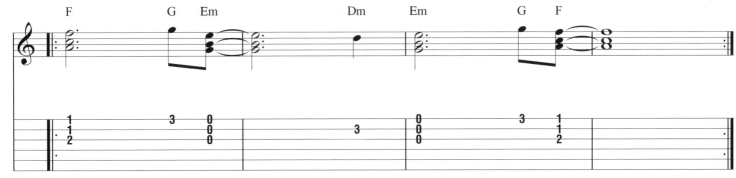

Additional Lyrics

2. *Romance, sheer delight, how sweet!*
   I gotta find me a girl to make my life complete.
   You could scratch my back; we'll get cozy and huddle.
   I'll lay down my jacket so you can walk over a puddle.
   I'd give you a rose, pull out your chair before we eat,
   Kiss you on the cheek and say, "Ooh, girl, you're so sweet."
   It's deja vu whenever I'm with you;
   I could go on forever tellin' you what I'd do.
   But where you at? You're neither here nor there.
   I swear I can't find you anywhere.
   Damn sure ain't in my closet, or under my rug.
   This love search is really makin' me bug.
   And if you know who you are, why don't you make yourself seen?
   Take a chance with my love, and you'll find out what I mean.
   Fantasies can run, but they can't hide.
   And when I find you, I'm gonna pour all my love inside.

3. *I wanna kiss you, hold you, never scold you, just love you,*
   Suck on your neck, carees you and rub you,
   Grind, moan, and never be alone.
   If you're not standin' next to me, you're on the phone.
   Can't you hear it in my voice? I need love bad.
   I got money, but love's somethin' I've never had.
   I need your ruby red lips, sweet face and all.
   I love you more than a man who's ten feet tall.
   I watch the sun rise in your eyes.
   We're so in love, when we hug, we become paralyzed.
   Our bodies explode in ecstasy unreal.
   You're as soft as a pillow and I'm as hard as steel.
   It's like a dreamland; I can't lie, I never been there.
   Maybe this is an experience that me and you can share.
   Clean and unsoiled, yet sweaty and wet.
   I swear to you, this is somethin' I'll never forget.

4. *See what I mean? I've changed; I'm no longer*
   A playboy on the run, I need somethin' that's stronger.
   Friendship, trust, honor, respect, admiration;
   This whole experience has been such a revelation.
   It's taught me love and how to be a real man,
   To always be considerate and do all I can,
   Protect you; you're my lady and you mean so much.
   My body tingles all over from the slightest touch
   Of your hand, and understand, I'll be frozen in time
   Till we meet face to face and you tell me your mind.
   If I find you, girl, I swear I'll always be a good man;
   I'm not gonna leave it in destiny's hands.
   I can't sit and wait for my princess to arrive;
   I've gotta struggle and fight to keep my dream alive.
   I'll search the whole world for that special girl;
   When I finally find you, watch our love unfurl.

I Want You Back

Words and Music by Freddie Perren, Alphonso Mizell, Berry Gordy and Deke Richards

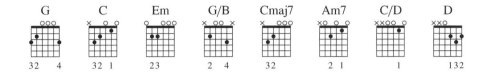

Intro
Moderately

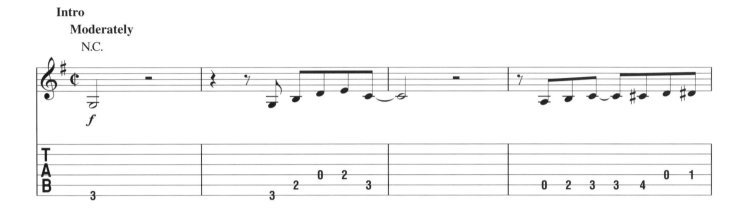

Strum Pattern: 4, 5
Pick Pattern: 3, 4

Verse

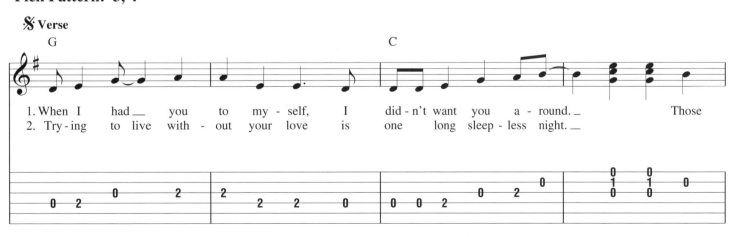

1. When I had __ you to my-self, I did-n't want you a-round. __ Those
2. Try-ing to live with-out your love is one long sleep-less night. __

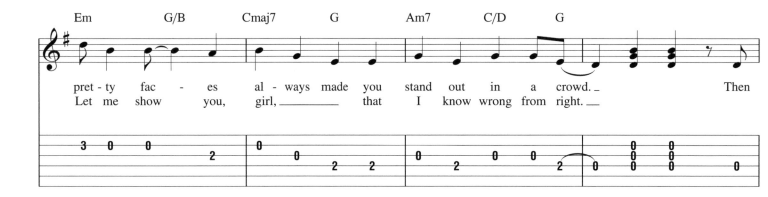

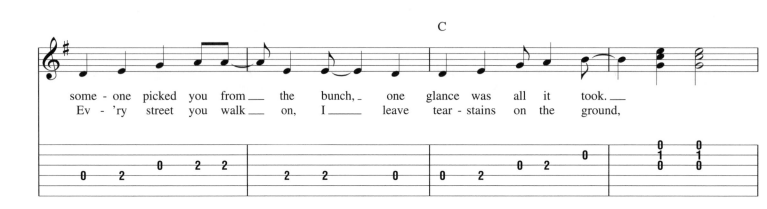

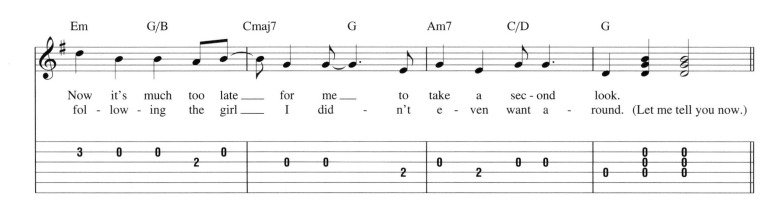

Chorus

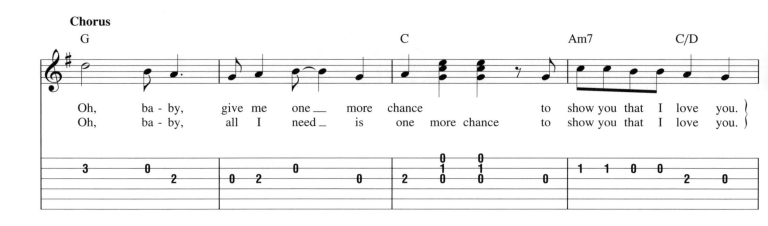

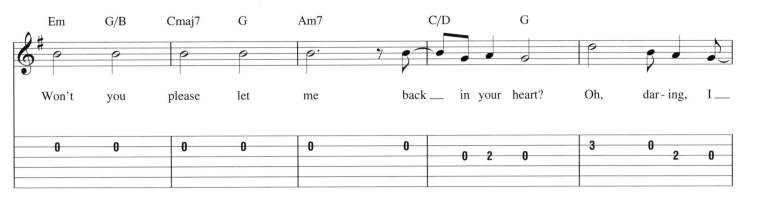

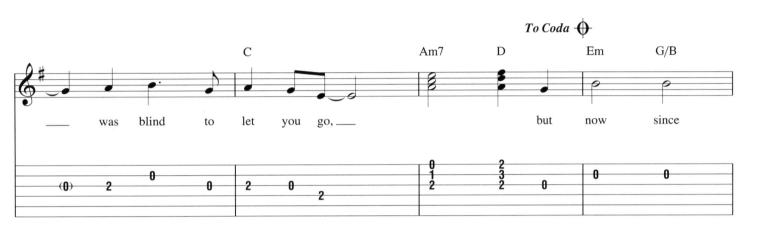

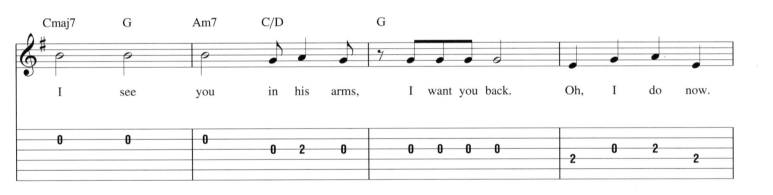

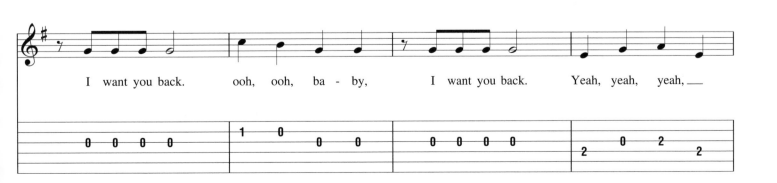

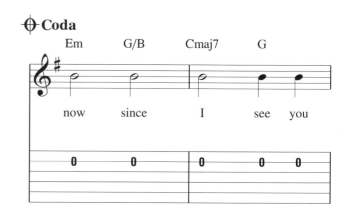

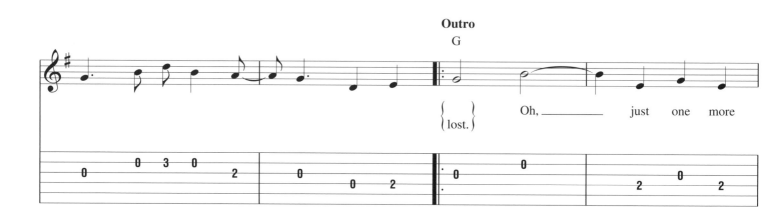

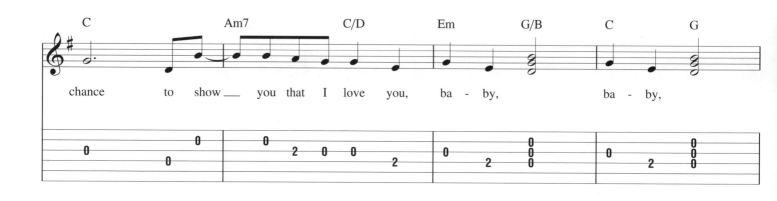

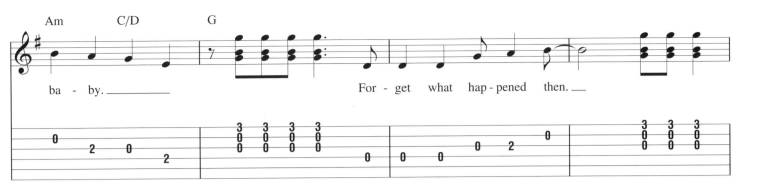

ba - by. _____ For - get what hap - pened then. _

Let me live a - gain. _ Oh, ba - by, I was blind _ to let _ you go, _____

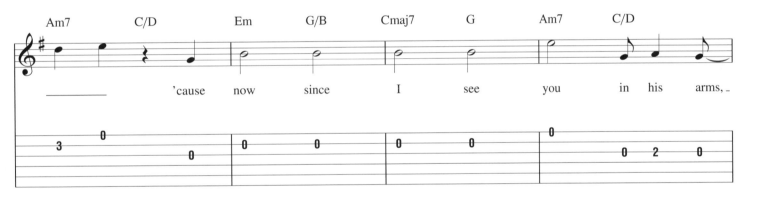

_____ 'cause now since I see you in his arms, _

Repeat and fade

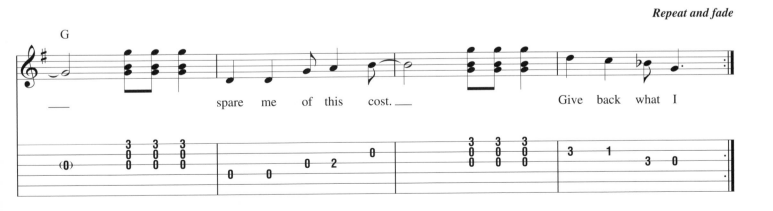

_ spare me of this cost. _ Give back what I

I Wanna Be Sedated

Words and Music by Jeffrey Hyman, John Cummings and Douglas Colvin

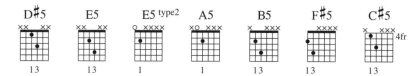

Strum Pattern: 1
Pick Pattern: 5

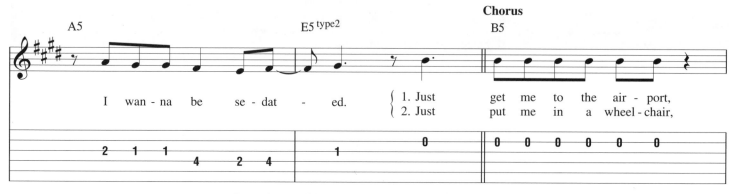

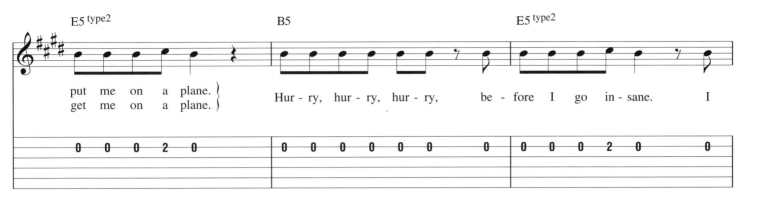

put me on a plane.
get me on a plane.
Hur - ry, hur - ry, hur - ry, be - fore I go in - sane. I

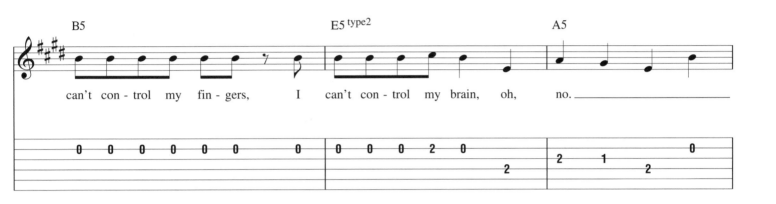

can't con - trol my fin - gers, I can't con - trol my brain, oh, no. _____

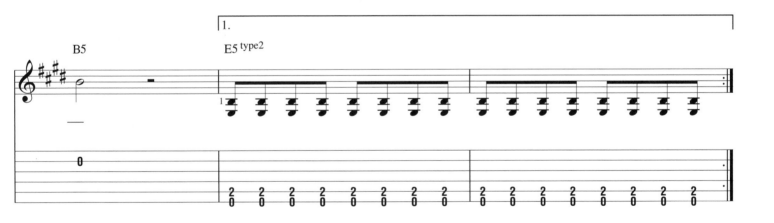

1.

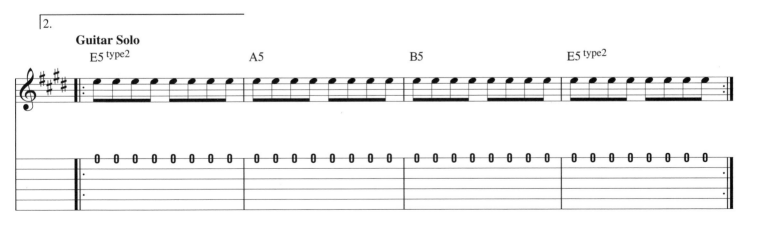

2.

Guitar Solo

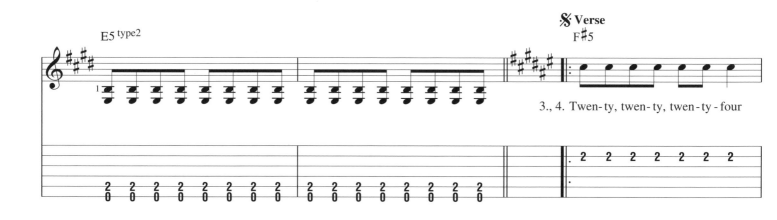

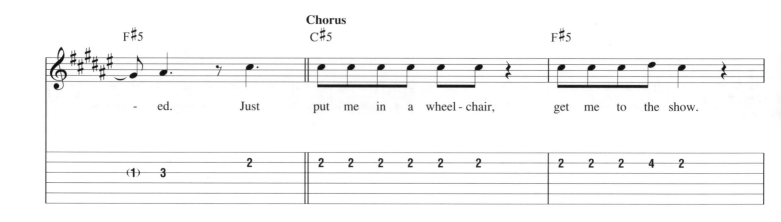

Hur - ry, hur - ry, hur - ry, be - fore I go lo - co. I can't con - trol my fin - gers, I

To Coda

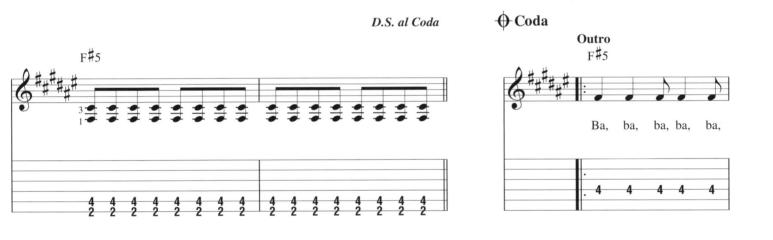

can't con - trol my toes, oh, no. _____

D.S. al Coda **Coda**

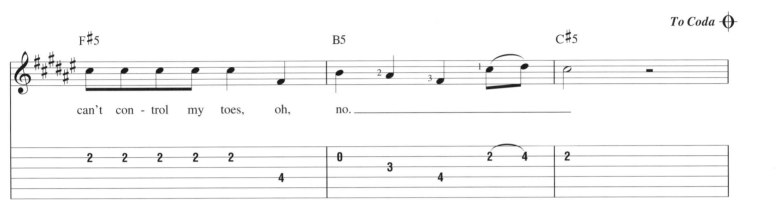

Outro

Ba, ba, ba, ba, ba,

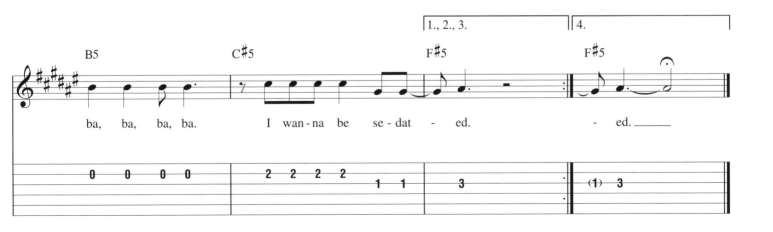

ba, ba, ba, ba. I wan - na be se - dat - ed. - ed. _____

1., 2., 3. | 4.

I Want It That Way

Words and Music by Martin Sandberg and Andreas Carlsson

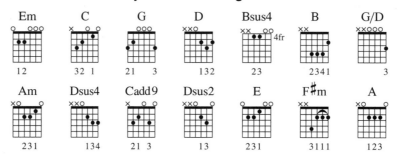

*Capo II

Strum Pattern: 1, 6
Pick Pattern: 2, 4

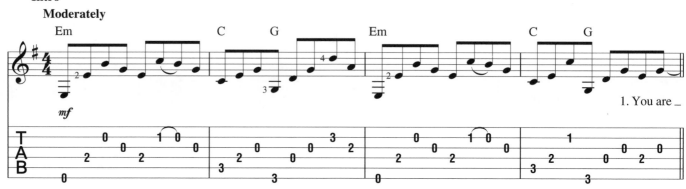

*Optional: To match recording, place capo at 2nd fret.

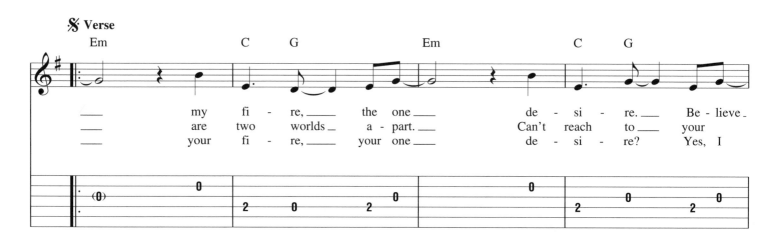

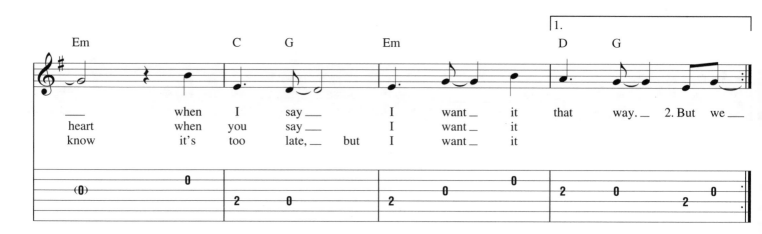

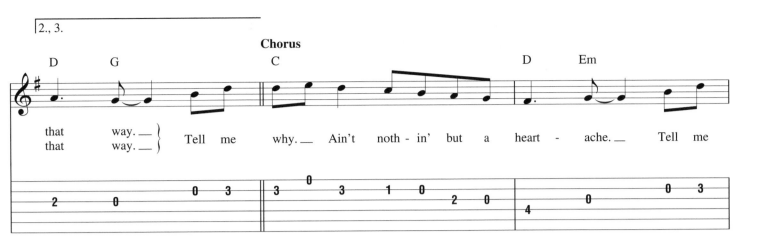

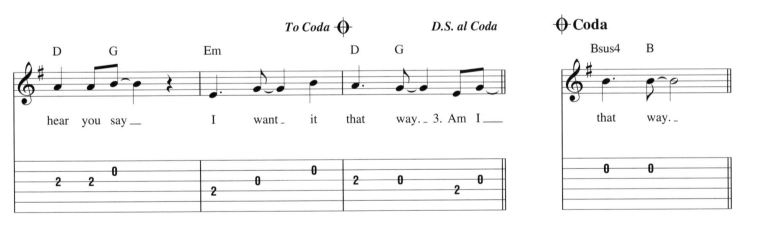

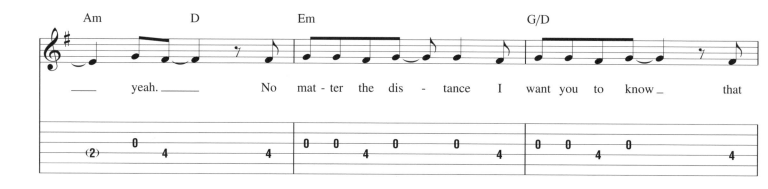

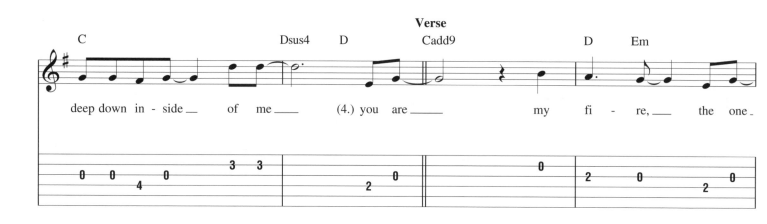

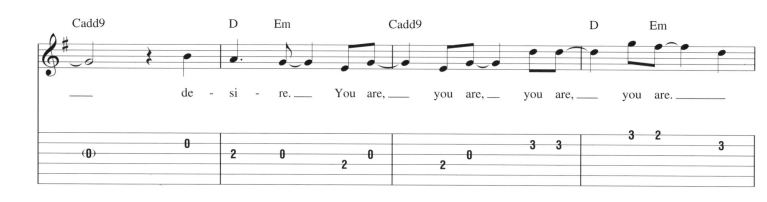

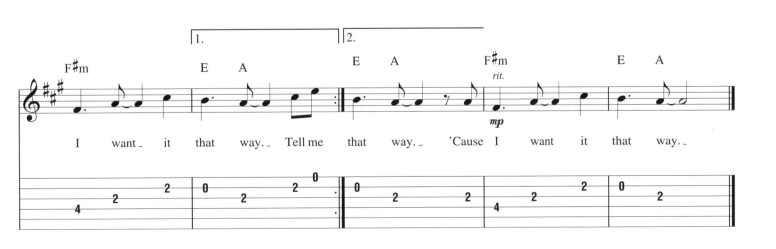

I Want to Hold Your Hand

Words and Music by John Lennon and Paul McCartney

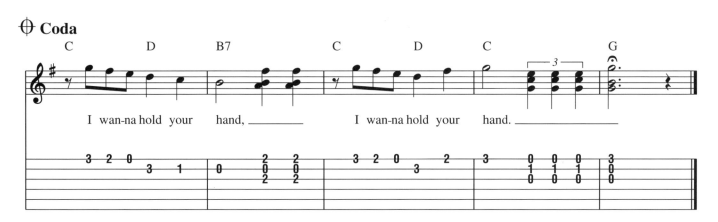

Additional Lyrics

2. Oh, please say to me
   You'll let me be your man.
   And please say to me
   You'll let me hold your hand.

3. Yeah, you got that somethin',
   I think you'll understand.
   When I {say/feel} that something,
   I wanna hold your hand.

I Want to Know What Love Is

Words and Music by Mick Jones

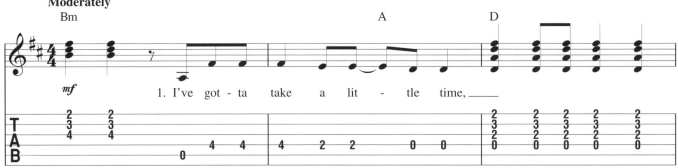

Strum Pattern: 3
Pick Pattern: 1

Verse
Moderately

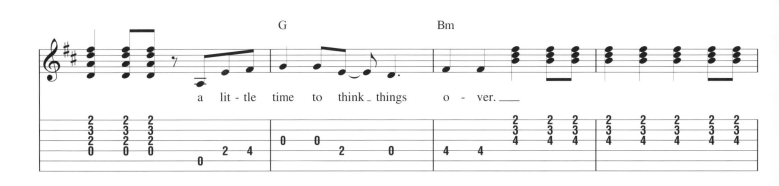

1. I've got - ta take a lit - tle time, _____

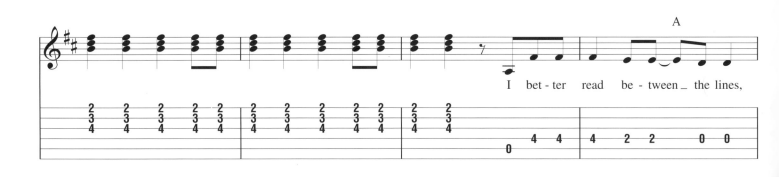

a lit - tle time to think _ things o - ver. _____

I bet - ter read be - tween _ the lines,

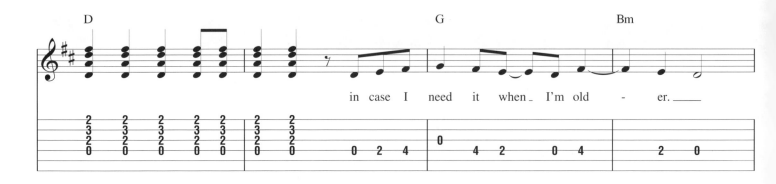

in case I need it when _ I'm old - er. _____

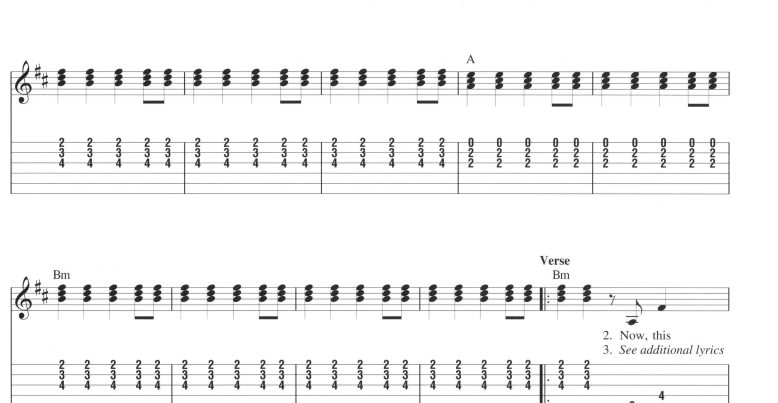

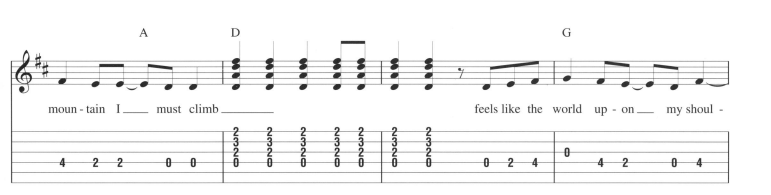

2. Now, this
3. *See additional lyrics*

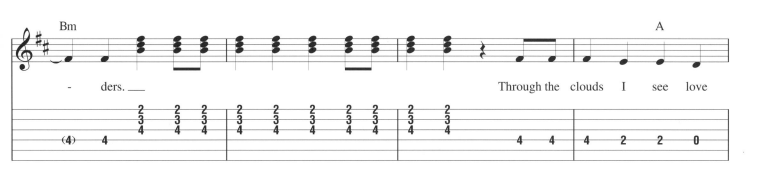

moun - tain I ___ must climb _____ feels like the world up - on ___ my shoul -

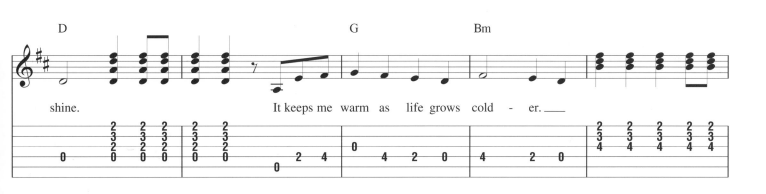

- ders. ___ Through the clouds I see love shine.

It keeps me warm as life grows cold - er. ___

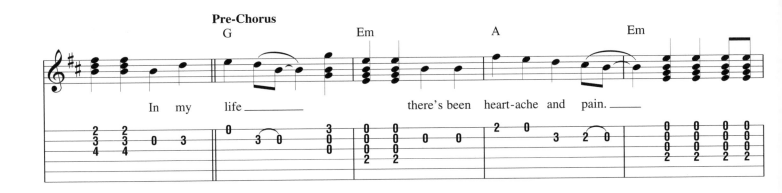

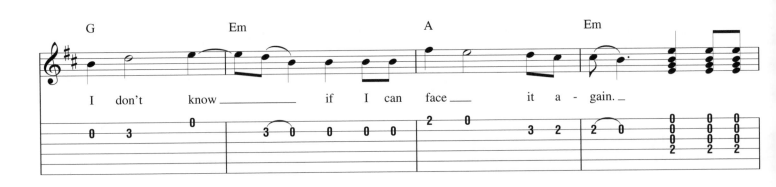

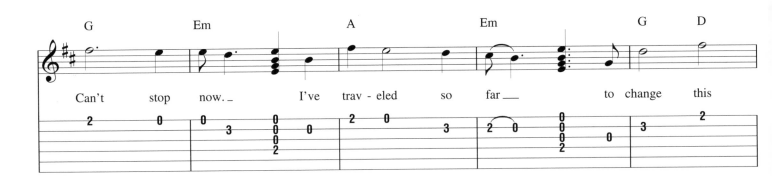

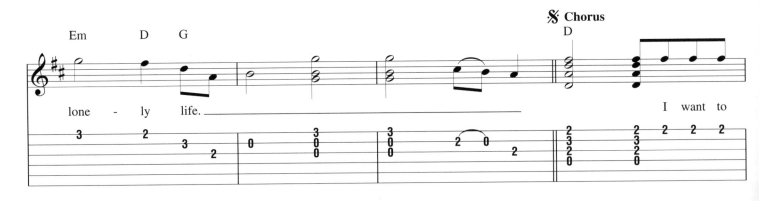

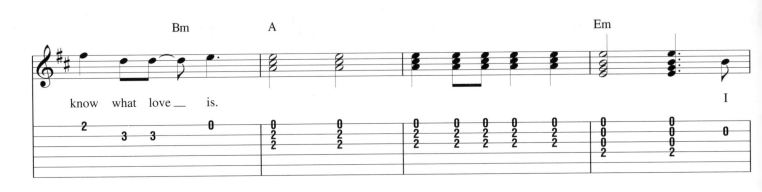

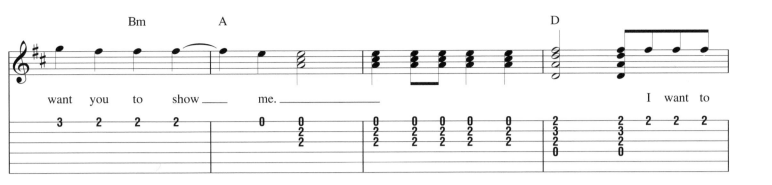

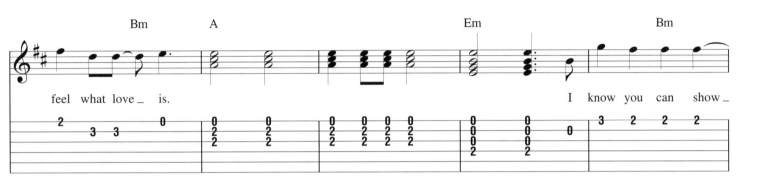

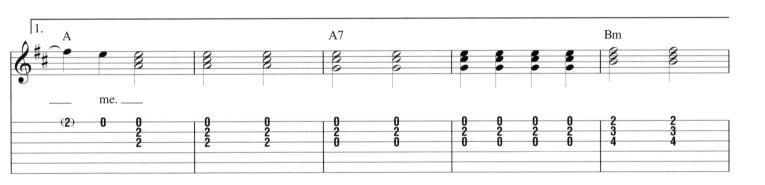

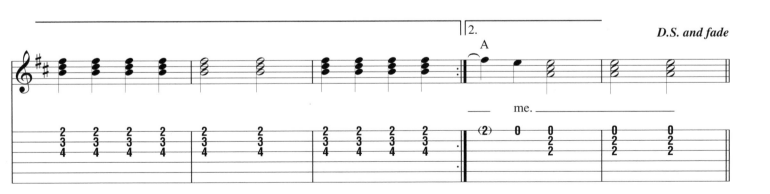

Additional Lyrics

3. I'm gonna take a little time,
   A little time to look around me.
   I've got nowhere left to hide.
   It looks like love has fin'lly found me.

I Will Always Love You

Words and Music by Dolly Parton

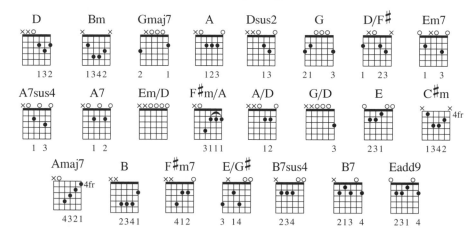

Strum Pattern: 3, 4
Pick Pattern: 4, 5

Verse
Freely

1. If __ I should __ stay, I would on - ly be in your

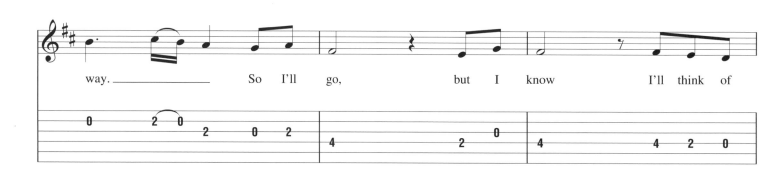

way. _____ So I'll go, but I know I'll think of

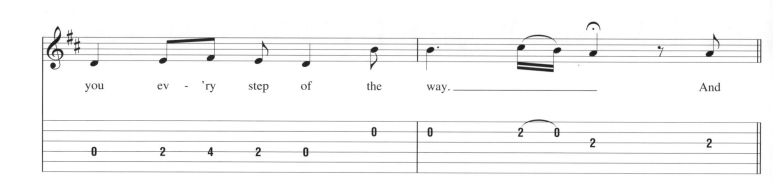

you ev - 'ry step of the way. _____ And

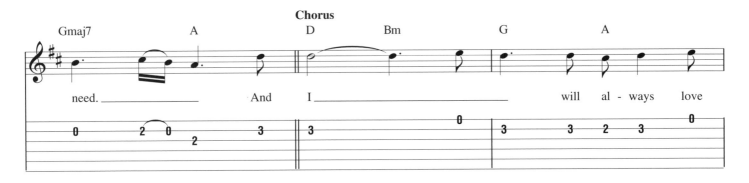

Chorus

need._____ And I_____ will al - ways love

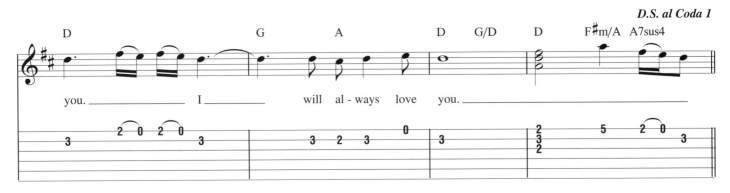

D.S. al Coda 1

you._____ I____ will al - ways love you._____

✠ Coda 1

D.S. al Coda 2

4. I____

✠ Coda 2

love._____ And

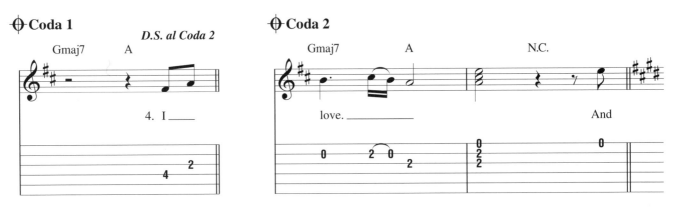

Outro-Chorus

I_____ will al - ways love you._____ I___ will

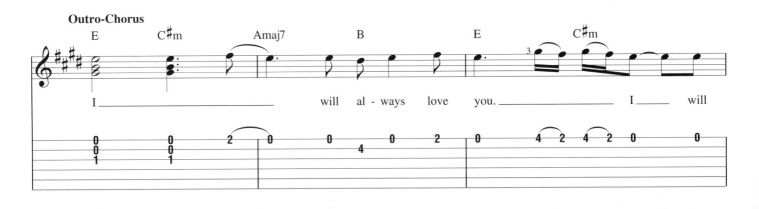

al - ways__ love you. I____ will al - ways__ love

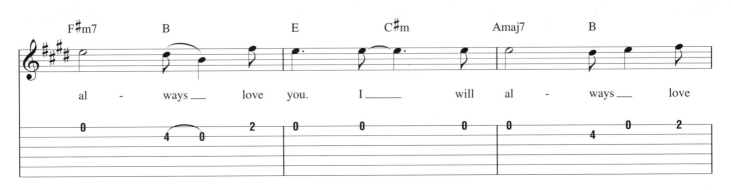

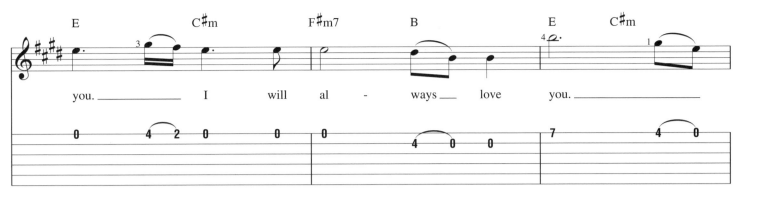

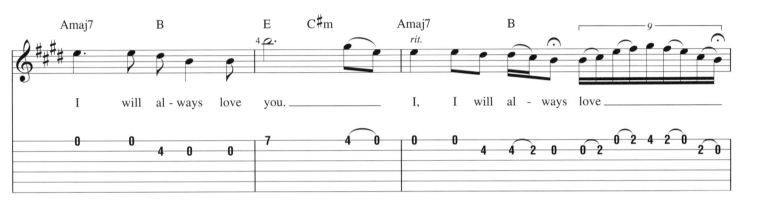

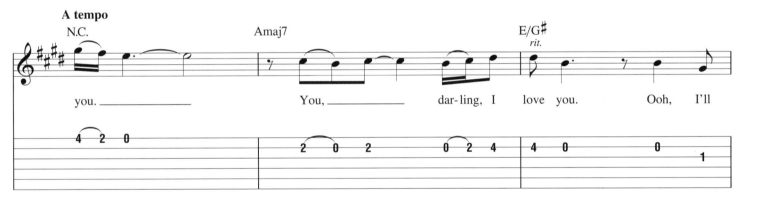

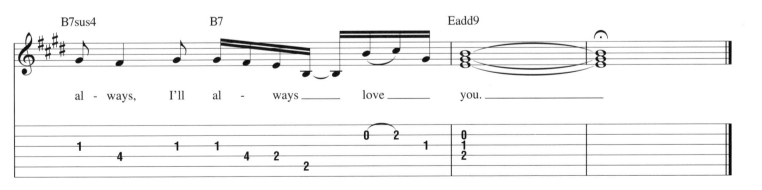

Additional Lyrics

4. I hope life treats you kind.
   And I hope you have all you've dreamed of.
   And I wish to you, joy and happiness.
   But above all this, I wish you love.

I Will Survive

Words and Music by Dino Fekaris and Frederick J. Perren

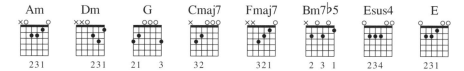

Strum Pattern: 2
Pick Pattern: 5

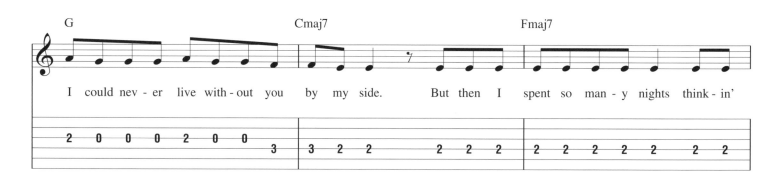

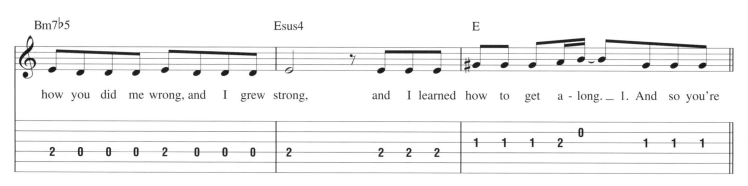

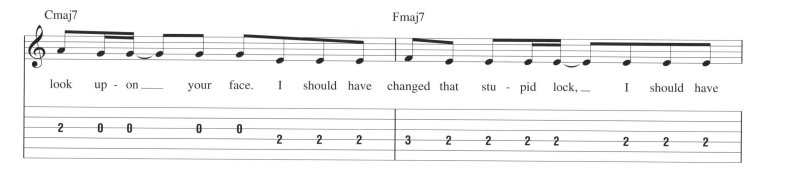

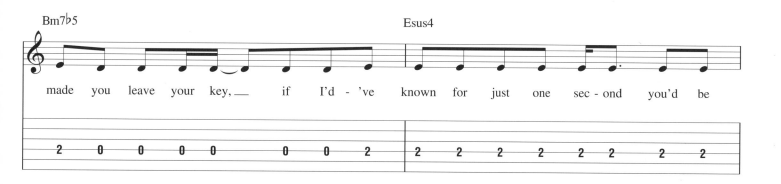

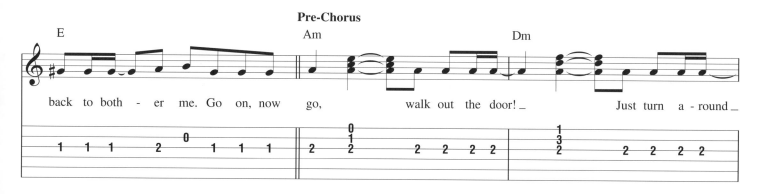

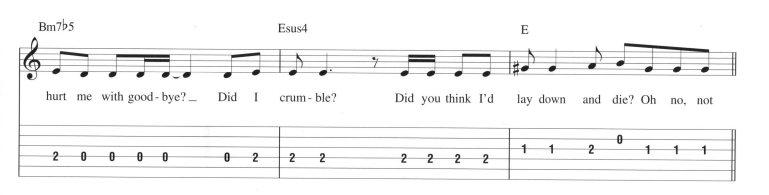

Chorus

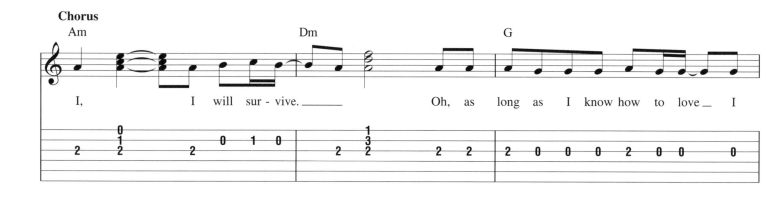

I, I will sur-vive._____ Oh, as long as I know how to love_ I

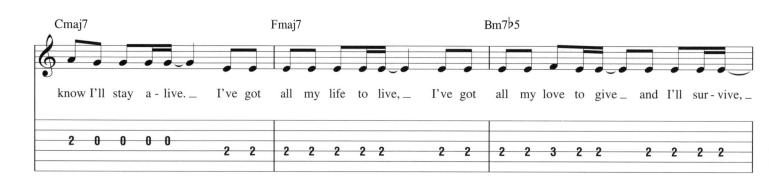

know I'll stay a-live._ I've got all my life to live,_ I've got all my love to give_ and I'll sur-vive,

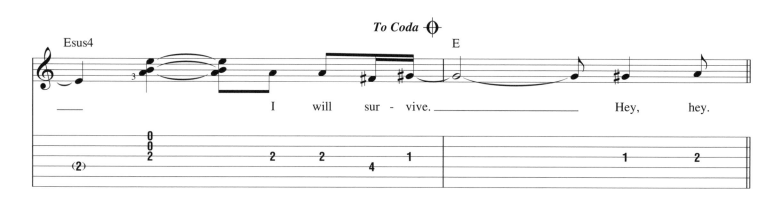

_____ I will sur-vive._____ Hey, hey.

Interlude

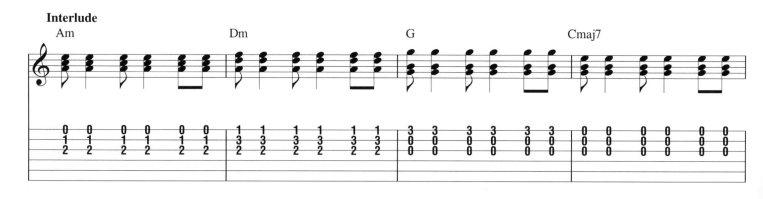

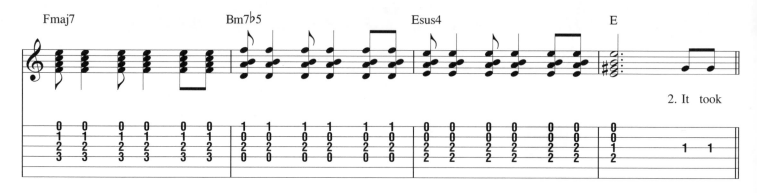

2. It took

148

Verse

all the strength_ I had not to fall a - part, _____ kept try - in' hard to mend_ the piec - es of my

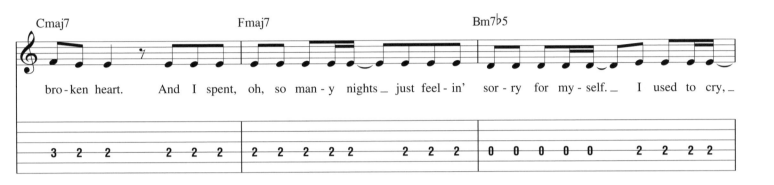

bro - ken heart. And I spent, oh, so man - y nights_ just feel - in' sor - ry for my - self._ I used to cry, _

D.S. al Coda

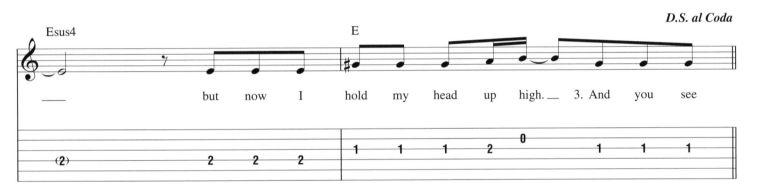

_ but now I hold my head up high._ 3. And you see

Coda

I'll sur - vive. ___

Additional Lyrics

3. And you see me, somebody new,
   I'm not that chained up little person still in love with you.
   And so you feel like droppin' in and you expected me to be free.
   Now I'm savin' all my lovin' for someone who's lovin' me.

Imagine

Words and Music by John Lennon

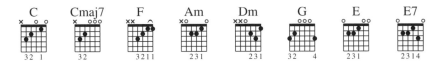

Strum Pattern: 1
Pick Pattern: 2

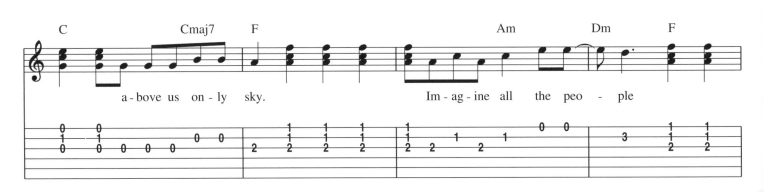

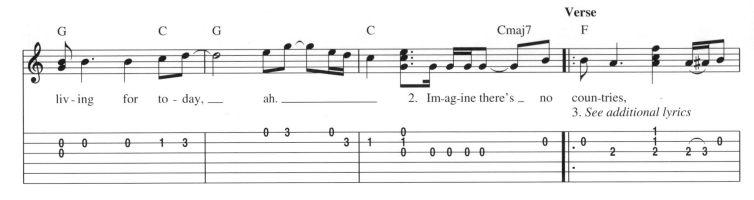

Additional Lyrics

3. Imagine no possessions,
   I wonder if you can;
   No need for greed or hunger,
   A brotherhood of man.
   Imagine all the people sharing all the world.

In My Life

Words and Music by John Lennon and Paul McCartney

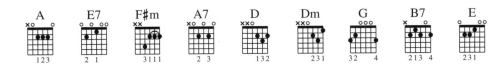

Strum Pattern: 6
Pick Pattern: 5

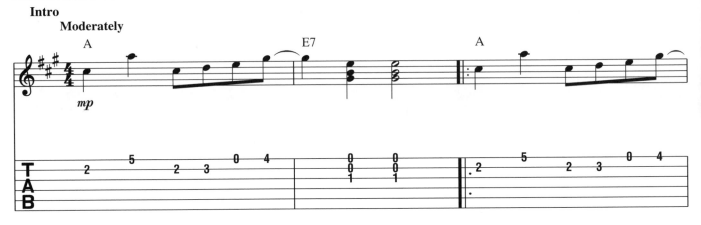

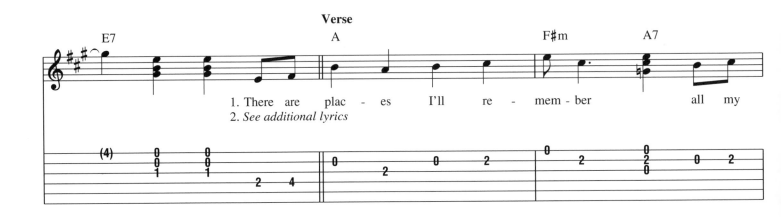

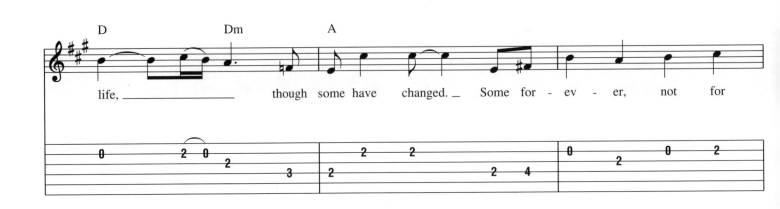

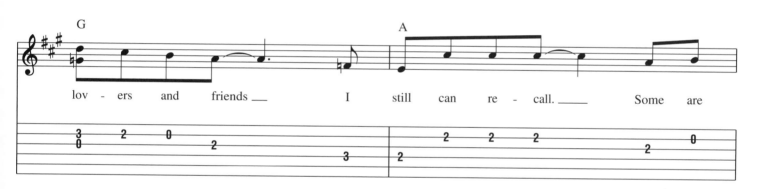

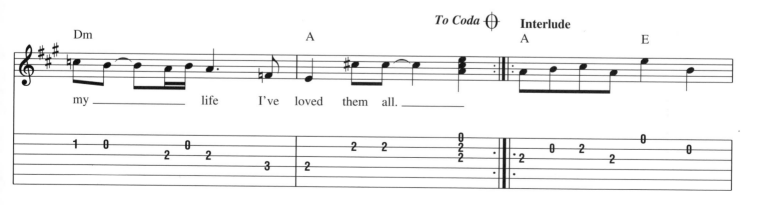

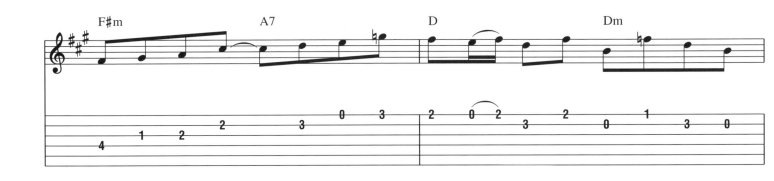

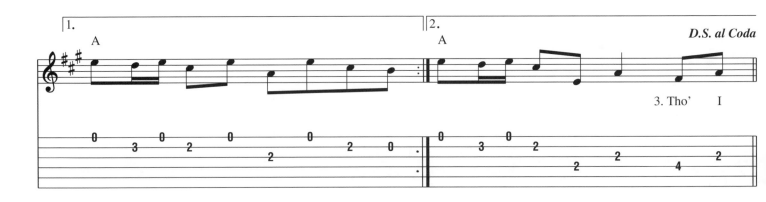

Coda

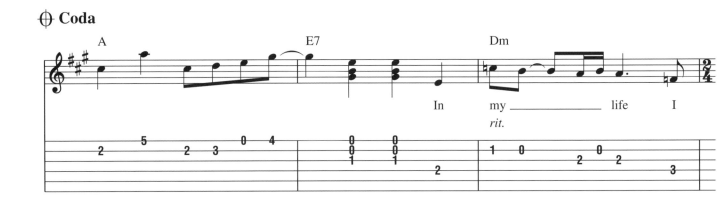

In my _____ life I
rit.

A Tempo

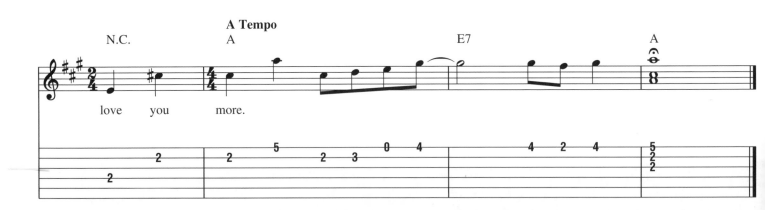

love you more.

Additional Lyrics

2. But of all these friends and lovers,
   There is no one compares with you.
   And these mem'ries lose their meaning
   When I think of love as something new.

Bridge 2., 3. Tho' I know I'll never lose affection
   For people and things that went before.
   I know I'll often stop and think about them,
   In my life I'll love you more.

Just a Friend

Words and Music by Biz Markie

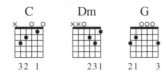

Strum Pattern: 5
Pick Pattern: 5

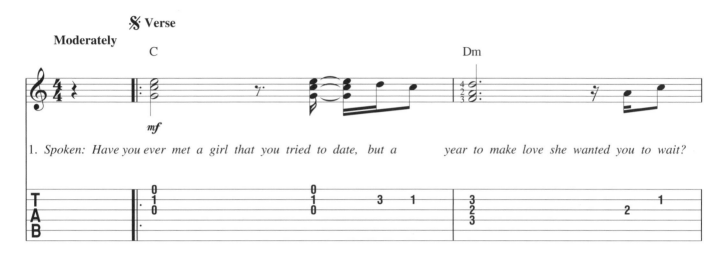

1. Spoken: Have you ever met a girl that you tried to date, but a year to make love she wanted you to wait?

Let me tell you a story of my situation: I was talkin' to this girl from the U.S. nation. The

way that I met her, was on tour at our concert. She had long hair and a short mini skirt. I

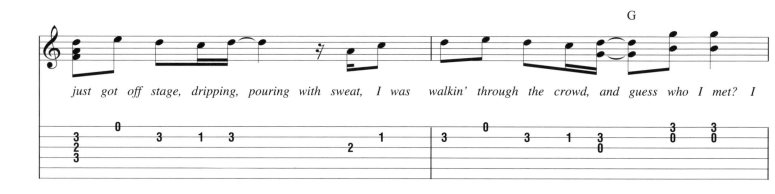

just got off stage, dripping, pouring with sweat, I was walkin' through the crowd, and guess who I met? I

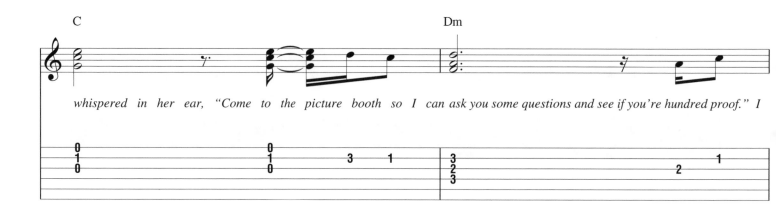

whispered in her ear, "Come to the picture booth so I can ask you some questions and see if you're hundred proof." I

asked her her name, and she said, "Blah, blah, blah." She had nine ten pants and a very big bra. I

took a coupla flicks and she was enthused... I said, "How did you like the show?" She said, "I was very amused." I

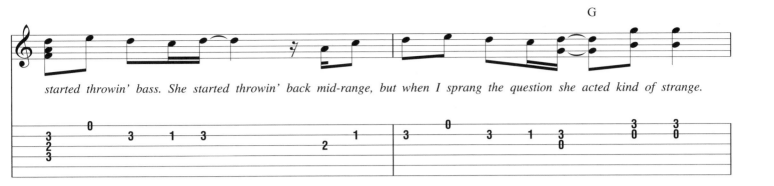

started throwin' bass. She started throwin' back mid-range, but when I sprang the question she acted kind of strange.

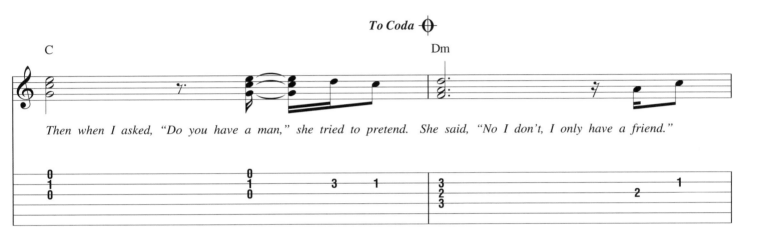

To Coda ⊕

Then when I asked, "Do you have a man," she tried to pretend. She said, "No I don't, I only have a friend."

Tsk, come on,   I'm not even   goin' for it. This is what I'm gonna sing:

Chorus

Sung: You,   you got _ what I   need, ___   but you   say   he   just   a   friend, _   but you

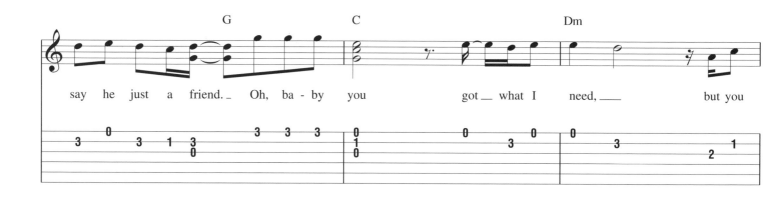

say he just a friend. _ Oh, ba - by you got _ what I need, ___ but you

say he just a friend, _ but you say he just a friend. _ Oh, ba - by you got _ what I

1.

need, ___ but you say he just a friend, _ but you say he just a friend. 2. *Spoken: So I*

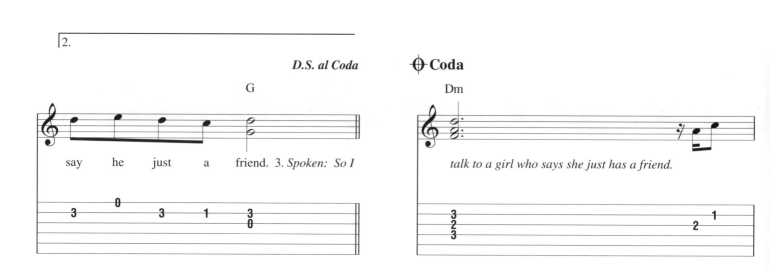

2.

D.S. al Coda   ⊕ **Coda**

say he just a friend. 3. *Spoken: So I*   *talk to a girl who says she just has a friend.*

Additional Lyrics

2. So I took Blah Blah's word for it at this time.
   I thought just havin' a friend couldn't be no crime.
   'Cause I have friends, and that's a fact.
   Like Agnes, Agatha, Jermaine and Jack.
   Forget about that, let's go into the story
   About a girl named Blah Blah Blah that adore me.
   So we started talkin', gettin' familiar,
   Spendin' a lot of time so we can build a relationship
   Or some understanding how it's gonna be in the future we was plannin'.
   Everything sounded so dandy and sweet
   I had no idea I was in for a treat.
   After this was established, everything was cool.
   The tour was over and she went back to school.
   I called every day to see how she was doin',
   Every time that I call her, it seemed something was brewin'.
   I called her room, a guy picked up and then I called again.
   I said, "Yo, who is that?" Oh, he's just a friend.
   Tsk, don't give me that. Don't even give me that. Just watch this.

3. So I came to her college on a surprise visit,
   To see my girl that is so exquisite.
   It was a school day, I knew she was there,
   The first semester of the school year.
   I went to a gate to ask where was her dorm,
   This guard made me fill out a visitor's form.
   He told me where it was, and I was on my way,
   To see my baby doll, I was happy to say.
   I arrived in front of the dormitory.
   Yo, could you tell me where is door three?
   They showed me where it was for the moment.
   I didn't know I was in for such an event.
   So I came to her room and opened the door.
   Oh, snap. Guess what I saw?
   A fella tongue kissin' my girl in the mouth.
   I was so in shock, my heart went down south.
   So please listen to the message that I send, don 't ever
   Talk to a girl who says she just has a friend.

Iris

Words and Music by John Rzeznik

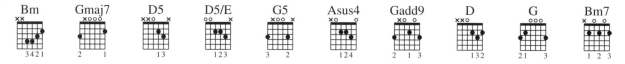

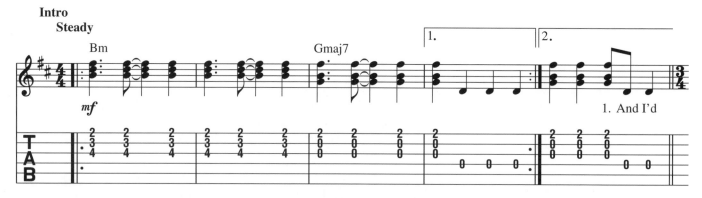

Strum Pattern: 3
Pick Pattern: 4

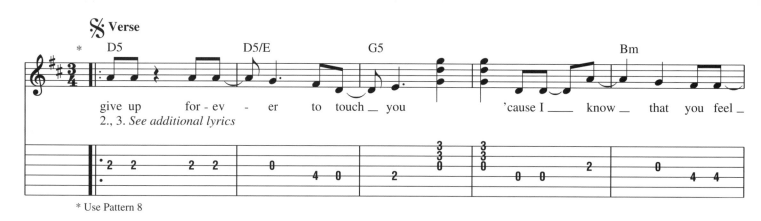

1. And I'd

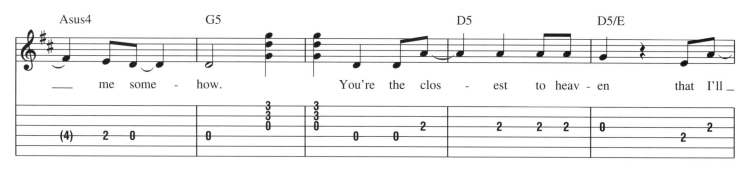

give up   for - ev - er   to touch __ you   'cause I ____ know __ that you feel __
2., 3. *See additional lyrics*

* Use Pattern 8

__ me some - how.   You're the clos - est to heav - en   that I'll

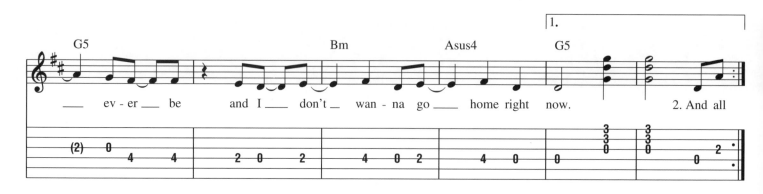

__ ev - er __ be   and I ___ don't __ wan - na go __ home right   now.   2. And all

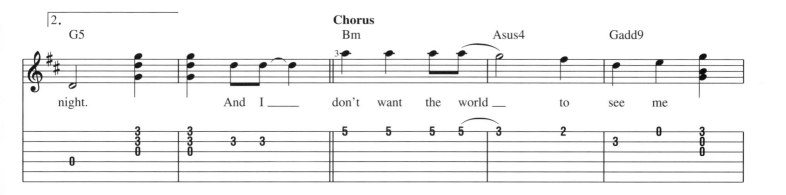

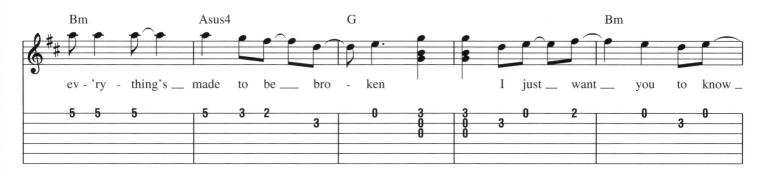

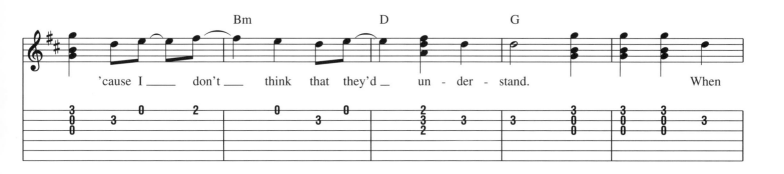

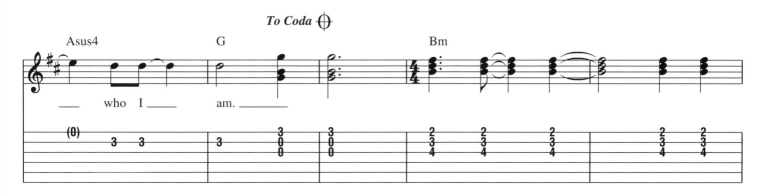

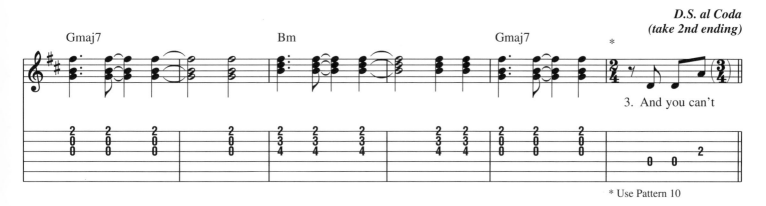

* Use Pattern 10

⊕ Coda

Interlude

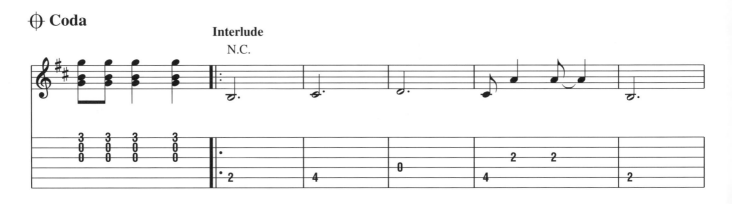

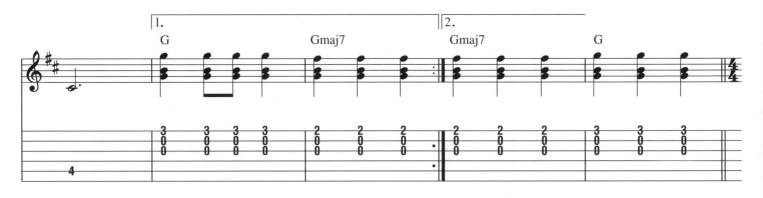

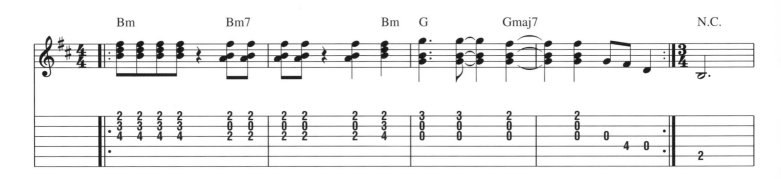

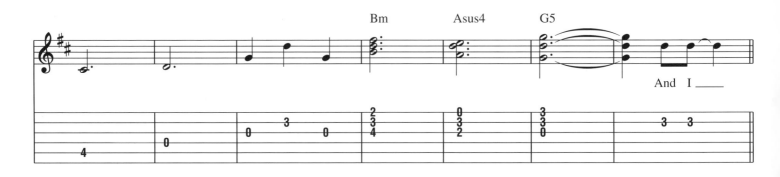

Chorus

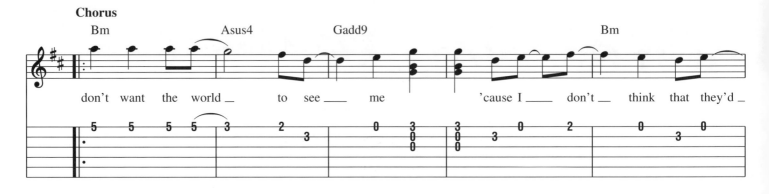

don't want the world _ to see __ me   'cause I ____ don't __ think that they'd _

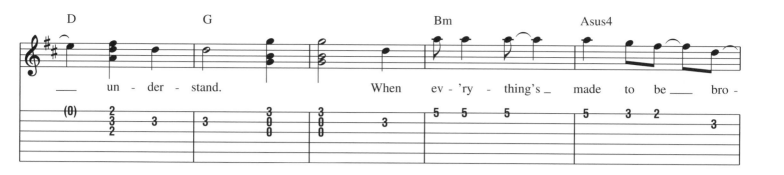

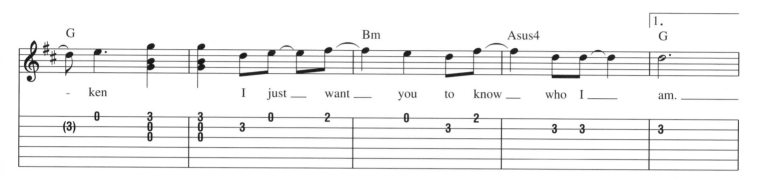

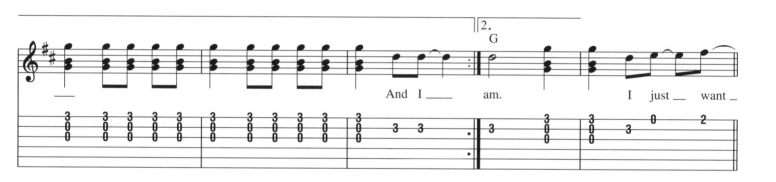

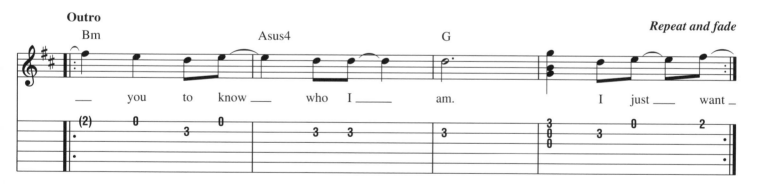

Additional Lyrics

2. And all I could taste is this moment,
   And all I can breathe is your life.
   And sooner or later it's over.
   I just don't wanna miss you tonight.

3. And you can't fight the tears that ain't coming,
   Or the moment of truth in your lies.
   When ev'rything feels like the movies,
   Yeah, you bleed just to know you're alive.

Jump

Words and Music by David Lee Roth, Edward Van Halen, Alex Van Halen and Michael Anthony

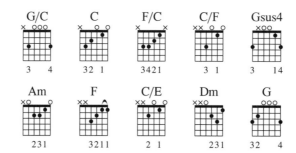

Strum Pattern: 1
Pick Pattern: 2

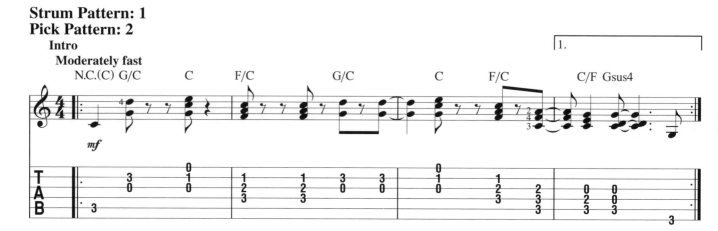

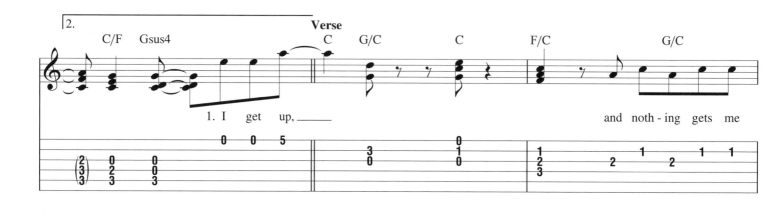

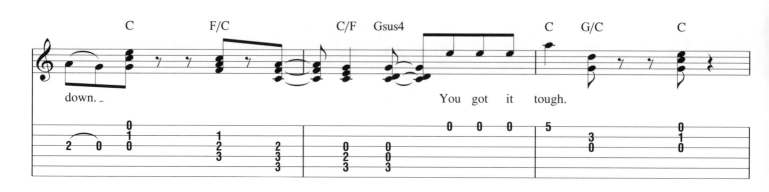

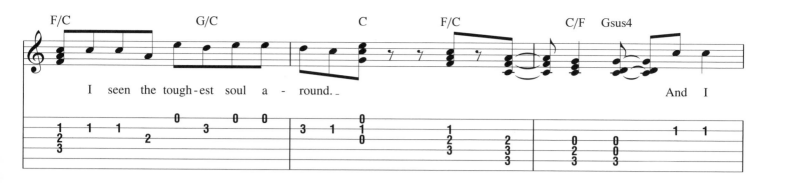

I seen the tough-est soul a - round. And I

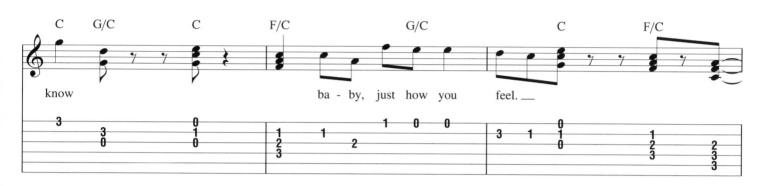

know ba - by, just how you feel.

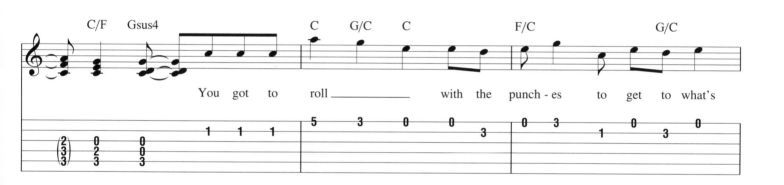

You got to roll _____ with the punch - es to get to what's

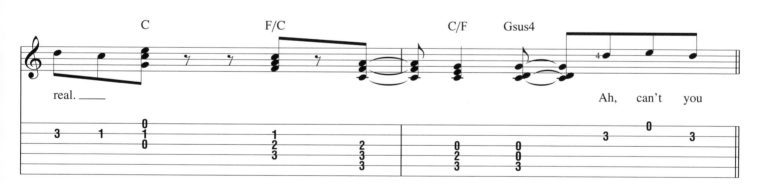

real. _____ Ah, can't you

𝄋 Pre-Chorus

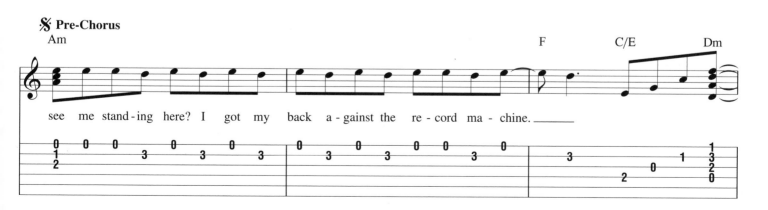

see me stand-ing here? I got my back a - gainst the re - cord ma - chine. _____

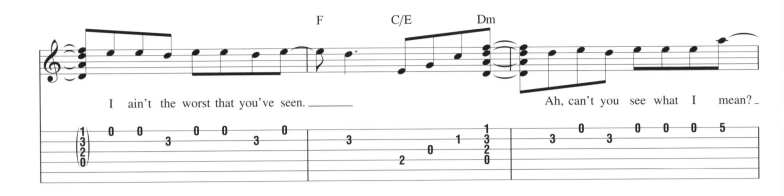

I ain't the worst that you've seen. _____ Ah, can't you see what I mean? _

To Coda ⊕

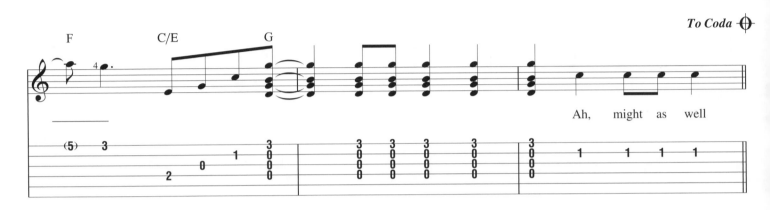

_____ Ah, might as well

Chorus

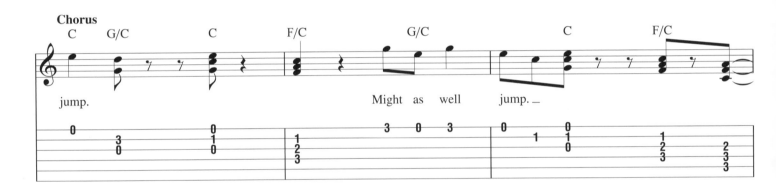

jump. Might as well jump. _

Go a - head and jump. _____

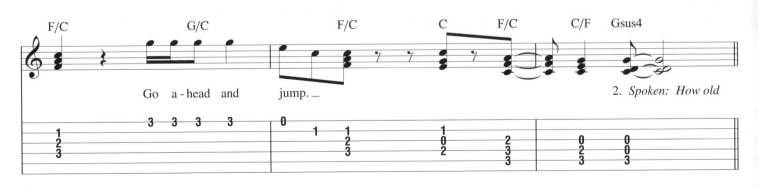

Go a - head and jump. _ 2. *Spoken: How old*

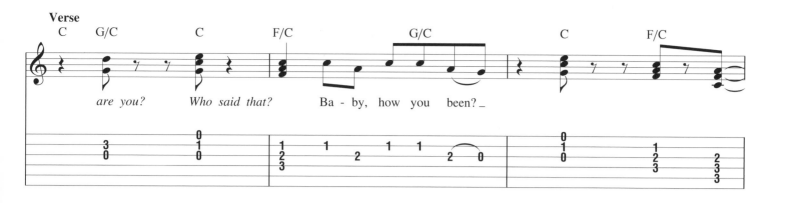

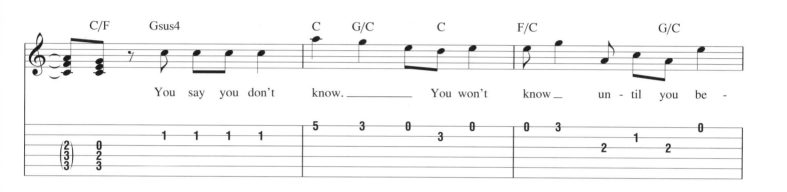

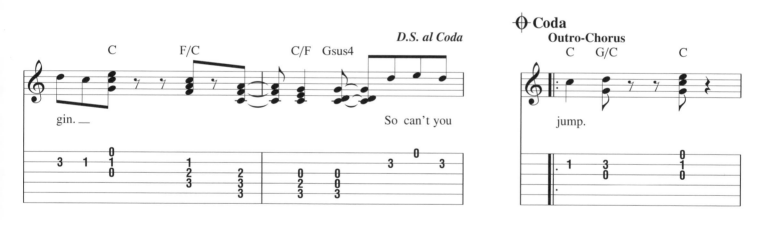

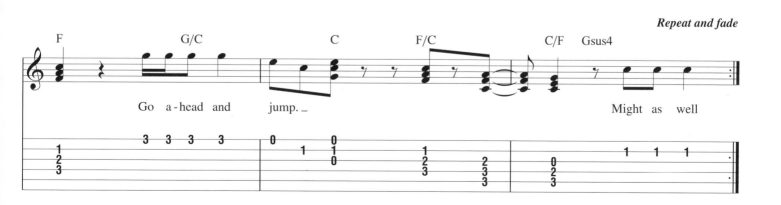

Just Can't Get Enough

Words and Music by Vince Clark

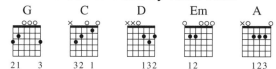

Strum Pattern: 2
Pick Pattern: 2

Intro
Moderately

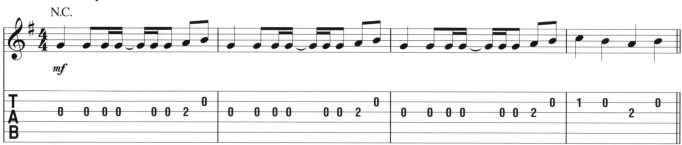

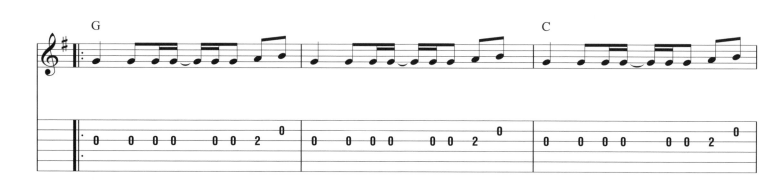

1. When I'm with you ba - by,
2., 3. *See additional lyrics*

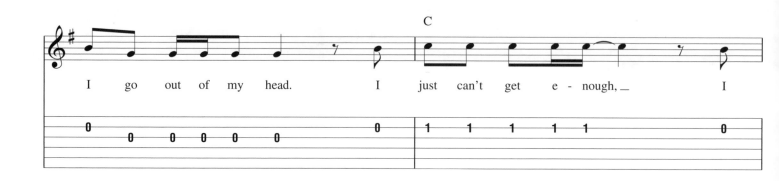

I go out of my head. I just can't get e - nough, ___ I

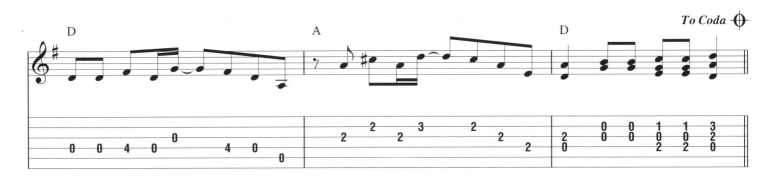

Interlude

Just can't get e - nough, _ I just can't get e - nough, _ I just can't get e - nough, _ I

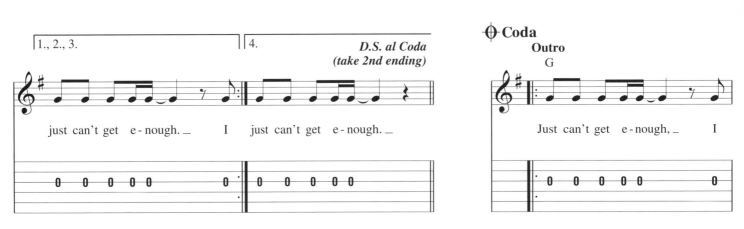

just can't get e - nough. _ I just can't get e - nough. _

Just can't get e - nough, _ I

just can't get e - nough, _ I just can't get e - nough, _ I just can't get e - nough. _ I

Additional Lyrics

2. We walk together, we're walking down the street.
   I just can't get enough, I just can't get enough.
   Ev'ry time I think of you, I know we have to meet.
   I just can't get enough, I just can't get enough.
   It's getting hotter, it's our burning love.
   And I just can't seem to get enough, ahhh!

3. And when it rains, you're shining down for me.
   I just can't get enough, I just can't get enough.
   Just like a rainbow, you know you set me free.
   I just can't get enough, I just can't get enough.
   You're like an angel and you give me your love.
   And I just can't seem to get enough, ahhh!

Just My Imagination (Running Away with Me)

Words and Music by Norman J. Whitfield and Barrett Strong

Strum Pattern: 2
Pick Pattern: 4

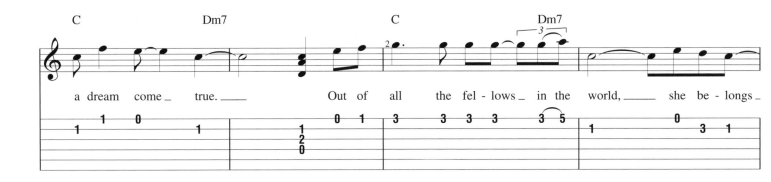

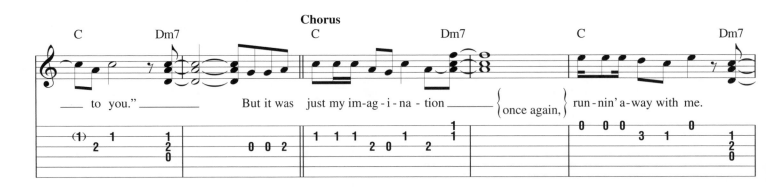

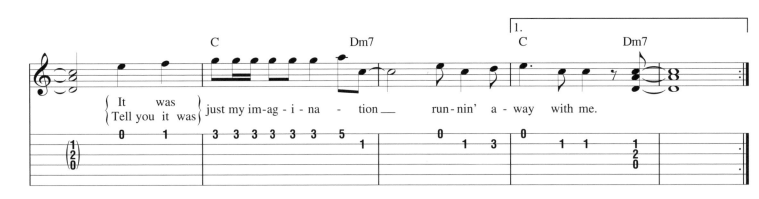

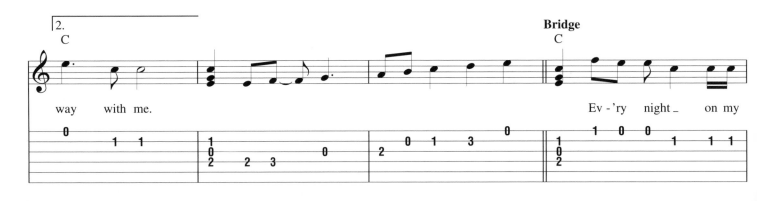

Additional Lyrics

2. Soon we'll be married and raise a family.
   A cozy little home out in the country,
   With two children, maybe three.
   I tell you, I can visualize it all.
   This couldn't be a dream,
   Far too real it all seems.

Just the Way You Are

Words and Music by Billy Joel

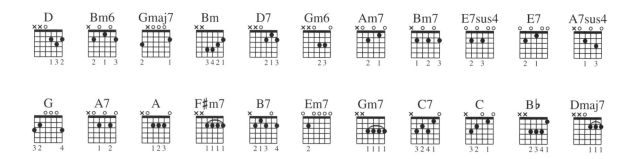

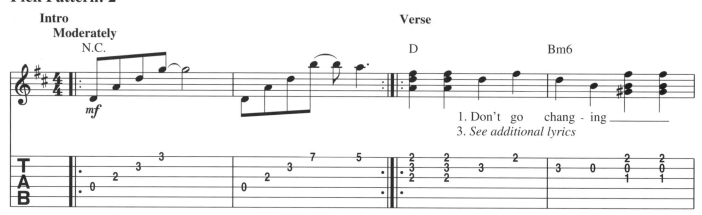

Strum Pattern: 1
Pick Pattern: 2

1. Don't go chang - ing _____
3. *See additional lyrics*

to try and please me, _____ you nev - er let me down _ be -

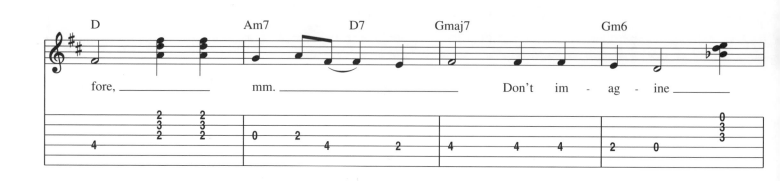

fore, _____ mm. _____ Don't im - ag - ine _____

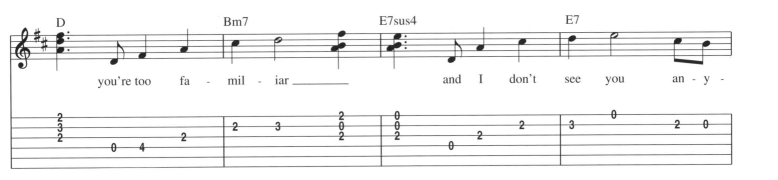

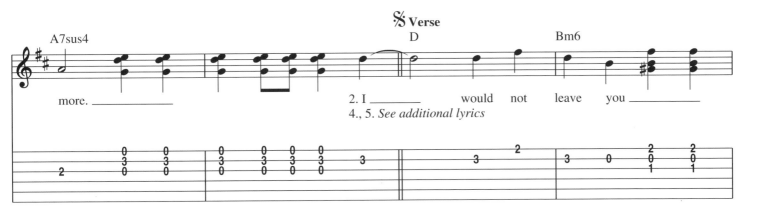

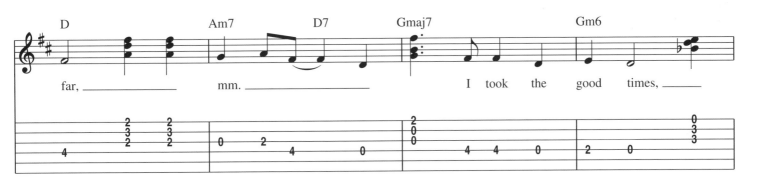

are.

Bridge

I need to know that you will al - ways be _____

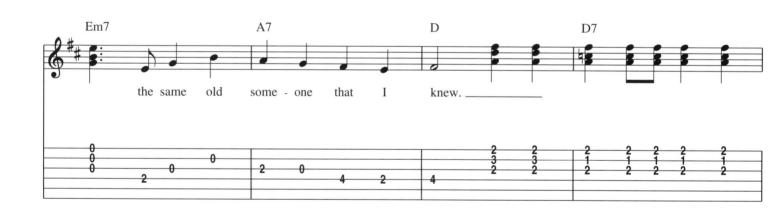

the same old some - one that I knew. _____

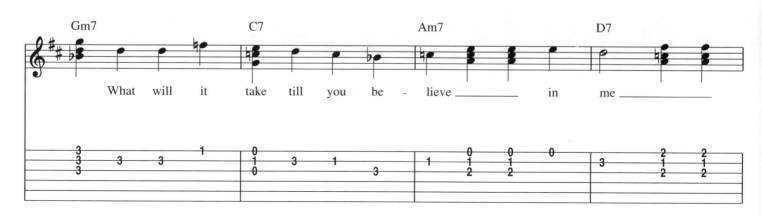

What will it take till you be - lieve _____ in me _____

x

176

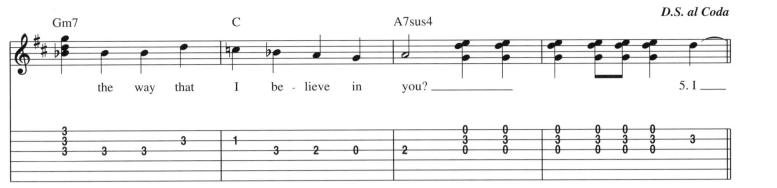

the way that I be-lieve in you? _____ 5. I _____

⊕ Coda

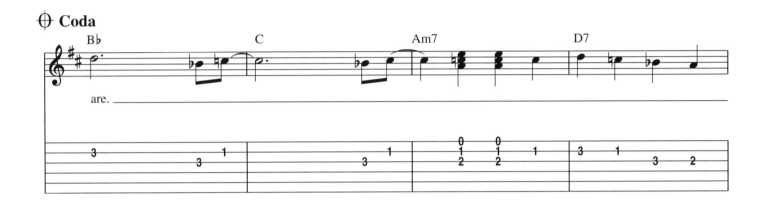

are. _____

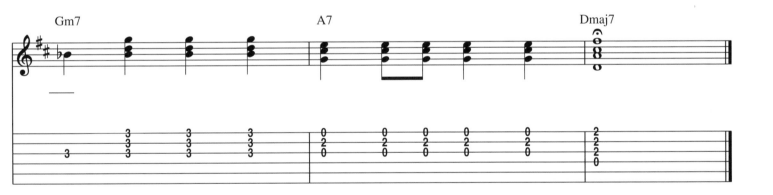

Additional Lyrics

3. Don't go trying some new fashion,
   Don't change the color of your hair, mm.
   You always have my unspoken passion,
   Although I might not seem to care.

4. I don't want clever conversation,
   I never want to work that hard, mm.
   I just want someone that I can talk to;
   I want you just the way you are.

5. I said I love you and that's forever,
   And this I promise from the heart, mm.
   I could not love you any better,
   I love you just the way you are.

Just What I Needed

Words and Music by Ric Ocasek

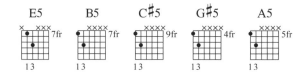

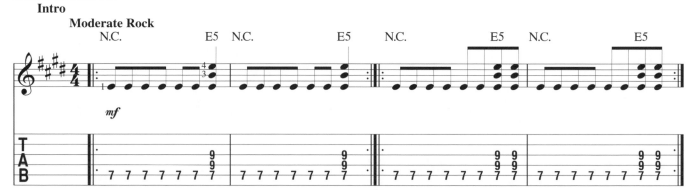

Strum Pattern: 1
Pick Pattern: 2

Intro
Moderate Rock

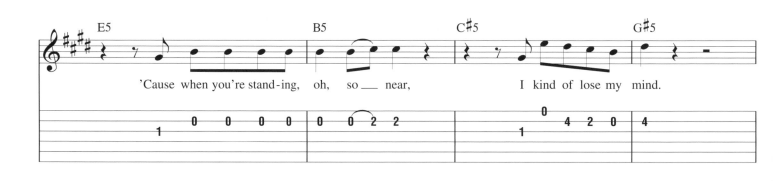

1., 3. I don't mind you com-ing here,
2. See additional lyrics
wast-ing all my time.

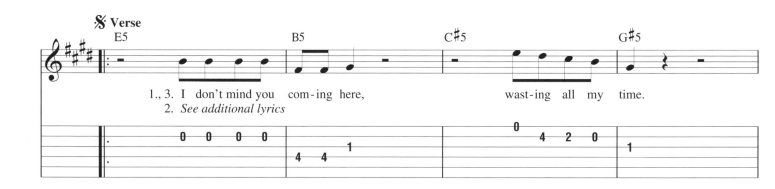

'Cause when you're stand-ing, oh, so ___ near, I kind of lose my mind.

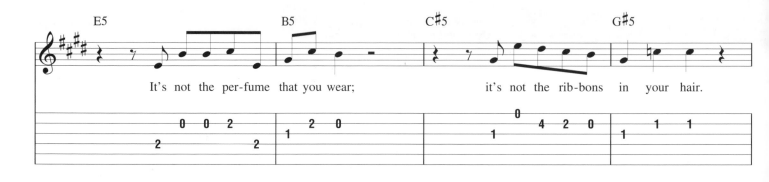

It's not the per-fume that you wear; it's not the rib-bons in your hair.

179

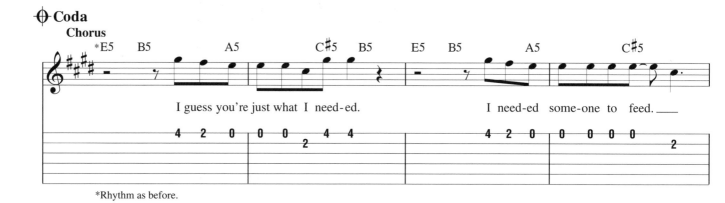

Coda
Chorus

*Rhythm as before.

I guess you're just what I need-ed.

I need-ed some-one to feed. ____

I guess you're just what I need-ed.

I need-ed some-one to bleed. __

Outro

____

Spoken: So bleed me.

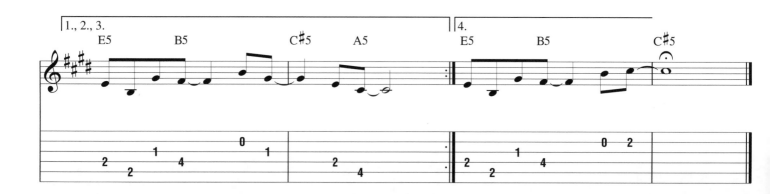

1., 2., 3.

4.

Additional Lyrics

2. I don't mind you hangin' out
   And talking in your sleep.
   It doesn't matter where you've been
   As long as it was deep.
   You always knew to wear it well.
   And you look so fancy, I can tell.
   I don't mind you hangin' out
   And talking in your sleep.

Let's Stay Together

Words and Music by Al Green, Willie Mitchell and Al Jackson, Jr.

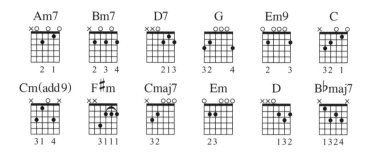

*Tune down 1 step:
(low to high) D–G–C–F–A–D

Strum Pattern: 3, 4
Pick Pattern: 4, 5

Intro
Moderately

Whispered: Let's stay together.

*Optional: To match recording, tune down 1 step.

Verse

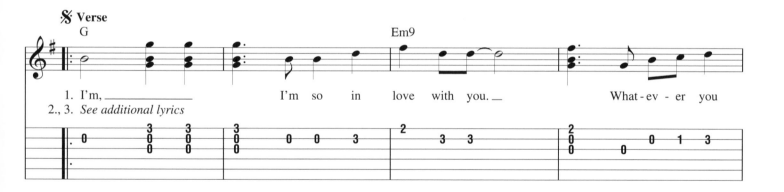

1. I'm, _____ I'm so in love with you. ___ What-ev-er you

2., 3. *See additional lyrics*

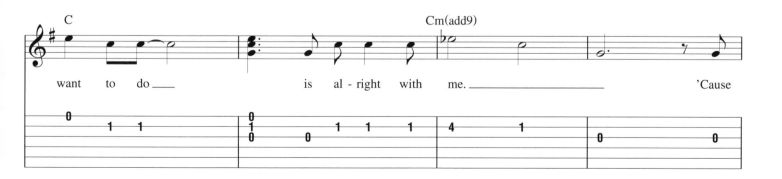

want to do ___ is al-right with me. _____ 'Cause

you ___ make me feel so ___ brand new, ___ and

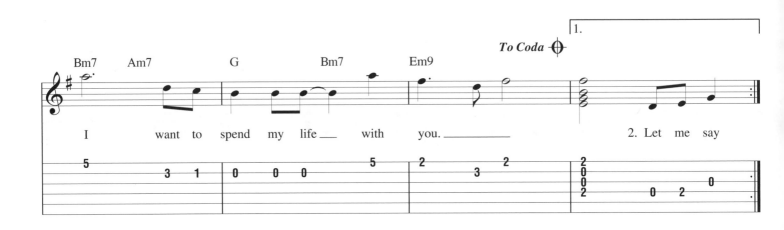

I want to spend my life ___ with you. ___ 2. Let me say

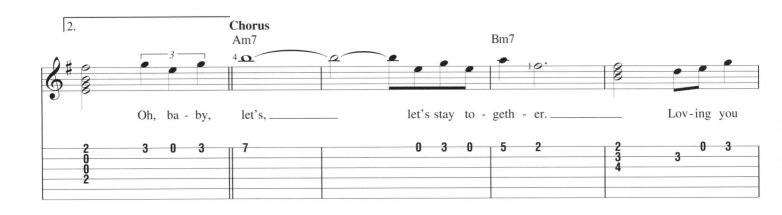

Oh, ba - by, let's, ___ let's stay to - geth - er. ___ Lov-ing you

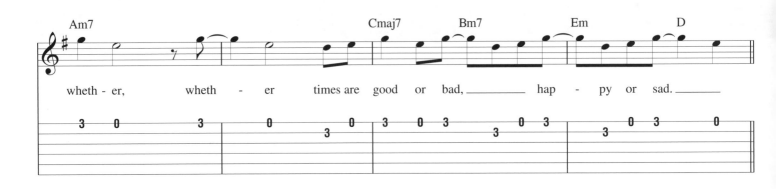

wheth - er, wheth - er times are good or bad, ___ hap - py or sad. ___

Interlude

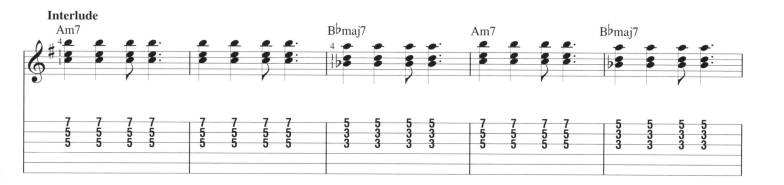

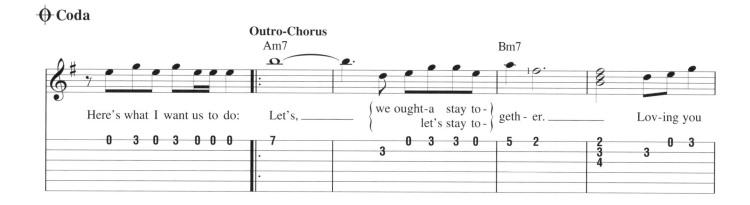

Weth-er times are good or bad, _____ hap - py or sad. _____

D.S. al Coda

⊕ Coda

Outro-Chorus

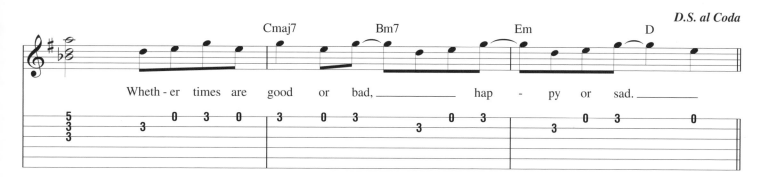

Here's what I want us to do: Let's, _____ { we ought-a stay to- / let's stay to- } geth - er. _____ Lov-ing you

Repeat and fade (2nd lyrics)

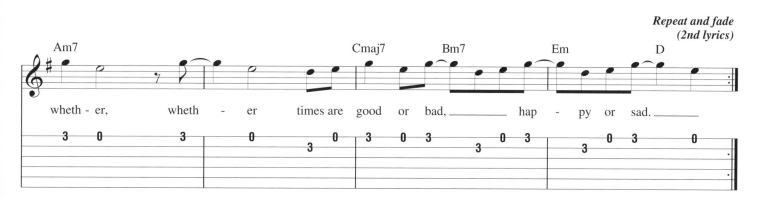

weth - er, weth - er times are good or bad, _____ hap - py or sad. _____

Additional Lyrics

2. Let me say since, baby, since we've been together,
   Ooh, lovin' you forever is what I need.
   Let me be the one you come runnin' to.
   I'll never be untrue.

3. Why, somebody, why people break up,
   Oh, and turn around and make up, I just can't see.
   You'd never do that to me, would you, baby?
   So being around you is all I see.

Like a Rolling Stone

Words and Music by Bob Dylan

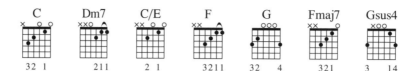

Strum Pattern: 4
Pick Pattern: 3

Intro
Moderately fast

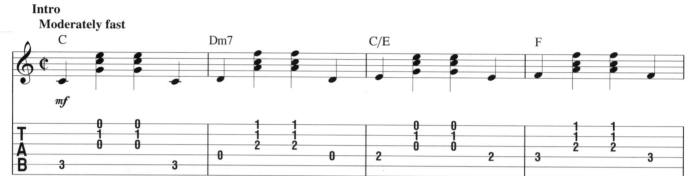

Verse

1. Once up - on ___ a time you dressed so fine, ___ you threw the bums a dime
2., 3., 4. *See additional lyrics*

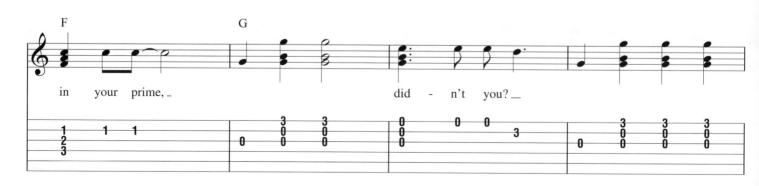

in your prime, ___ did - n't you? ___

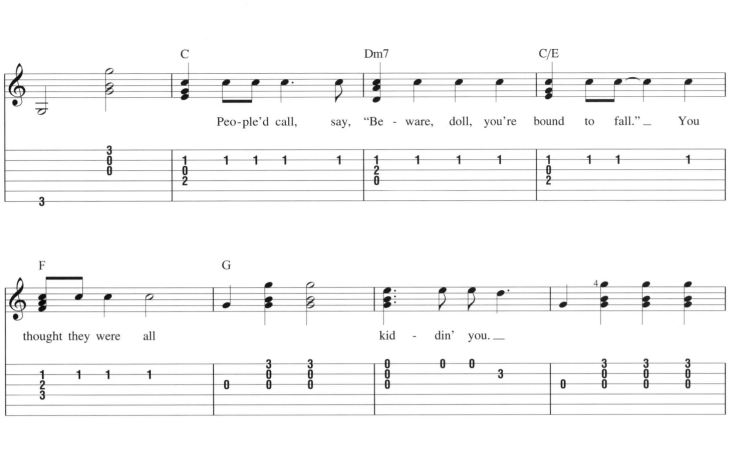

Peo-ple'd call, say, "Be - ware, doll, you're bound to fall." __ You

thought they were all

kid - din' you. __

You used to

laugh a - bout __

ev - ry - bod - y that was

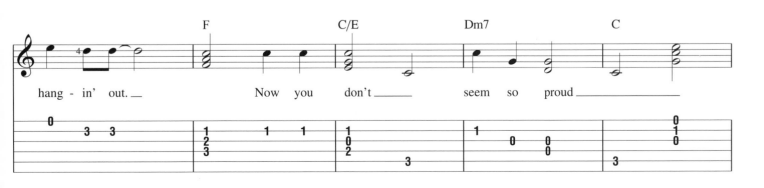

hang - in' out. __

Now you don't ____ seem so proud ____

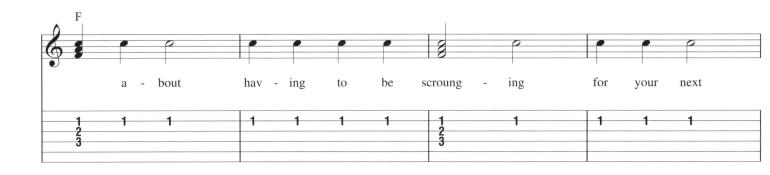

a - bout hav - ing to be scroung - ing for your next

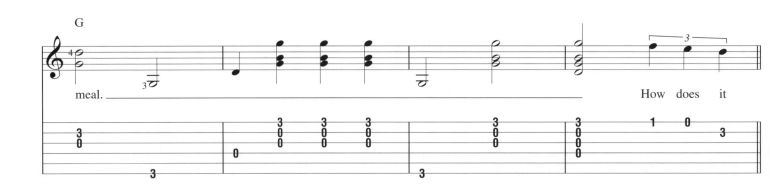

meal. How does it

Chorus

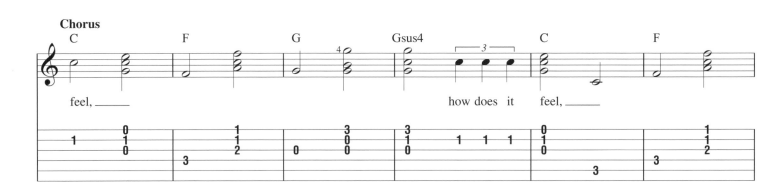

feel, how does it feel,

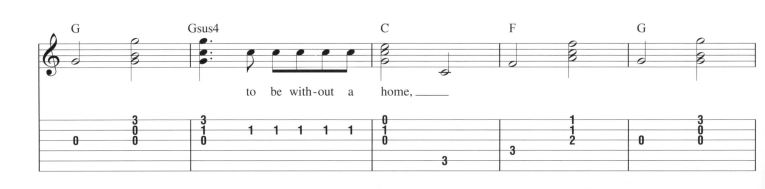

to be with-out a home,

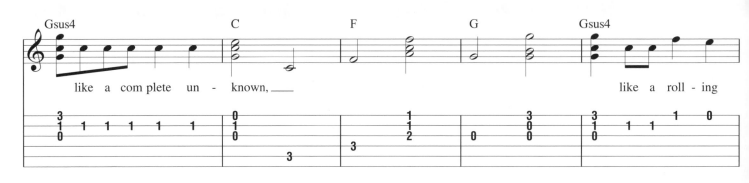

like a com - plete un - known, like a roll - ing

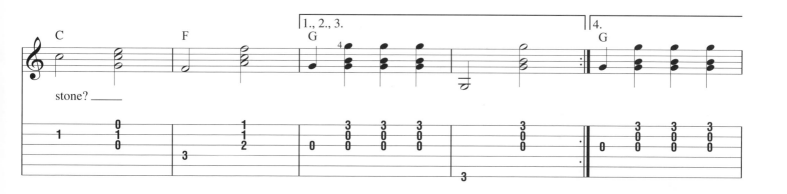

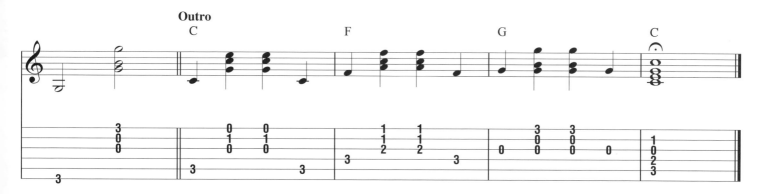

Additional Lyrics

2. You've gone to the finest school all right Miss Lonely,
   But you know you only used to get
   Juiced in it.
   And nobody's ever taught you how to live on the street
   And now you're gonna have to get
   Used to it.
   You said you'd never compromise
   With the mystery tramp, but now you realize
   He's not selling any alibis
   As you stare into the vacuum of his eyes
   And ask him, do you want to
   Make a deal?

3. You never turned around to see the frowns on the jugglers and the clowns
   When they all come down
   And did tricks for you.
   You never understood that it ain't no good,
   You shouldn't let other people
   Get your kicks for you.
   You used to ride on the chrome horse with your diplomat
   Who carried on his shoulder a Siamese cat.
   Ain't it hard when you discovered that
   He really wasn't where it's at
   After he took from you everything
   He could steal?

4. Princess on the steeple
   And all the pretty people're drinkin', thinkin'
   That they got it made.
   Exchanging all kinds of precious gifts and things,
   But you'd better lift your diamond ring,
   You'd better pawn it babe.
   You used to be so amused
   At Napoleon in rags and the language that he used.
   Go to him now, he calls you, you can't refuse.
   When you got nothing, you got nothing to lose.
   You're invisible now; you got no secrets
   To conceal.

Like a Virgin

Words and Music by Billy Steinberg and Tom Kelly

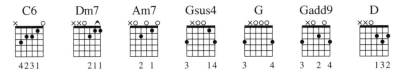

Strum Pattern: 1, 6
Pick Pattern: 2, 4

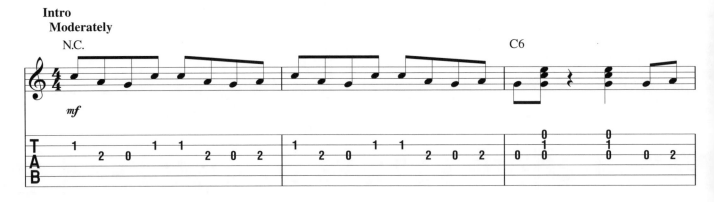

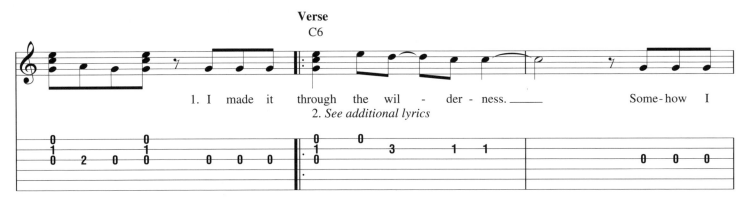

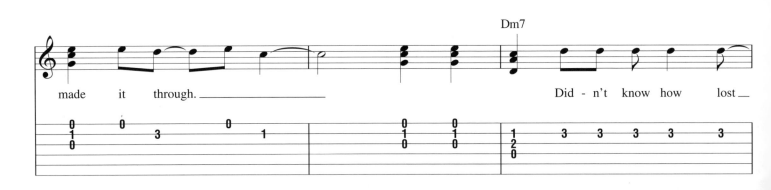

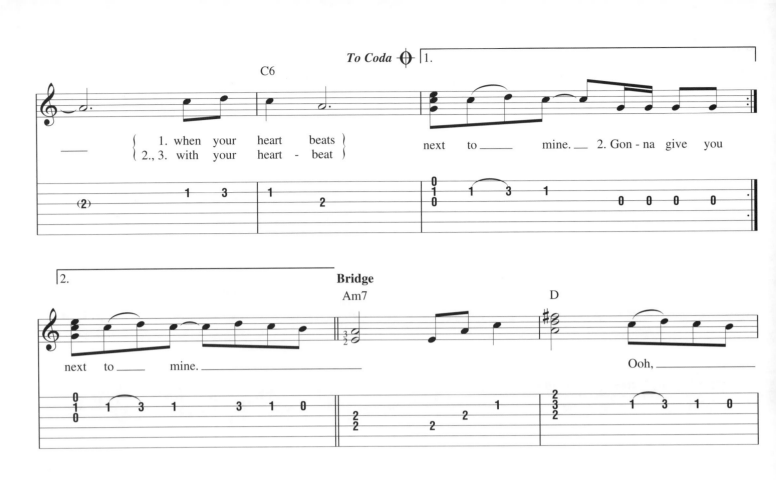

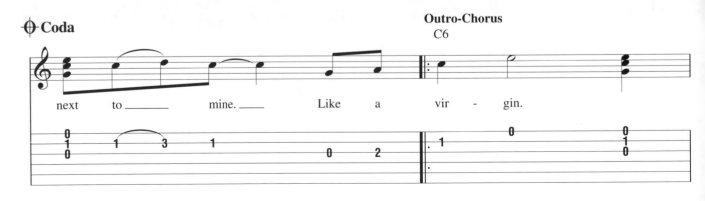

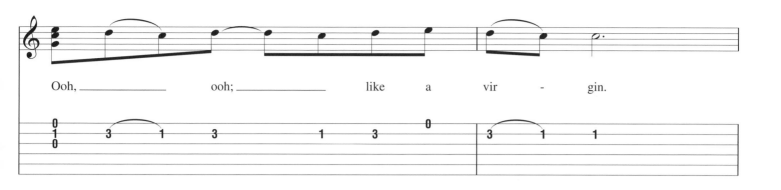

Ooh, _____ ooh; _____ like a vir - gin.

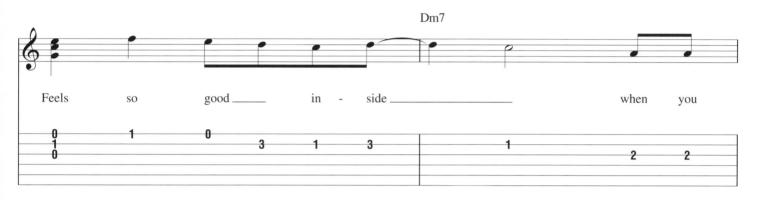

Feels so good _____ in - side _____ when you

Repeat and fade

hold me _____ and your heart beats _____ and you love me. Like a

Additional Lyrics

2. Gonna give you all my love, boy.
   My fear is fadin' fast.
   Been savin' it all for you,
   'Cause only love can last.

Pre-Chorus 2. You're so fine, and you're mine.
   Make me strong. Yeah, you make me bold.
   Oh, your love thawed out what was scared and cold.

Pre-Chorus 3. You're so fine, and you're mine.
   I'll be yours till the end of time.
   'Cause you made me feel,
   Yeah, you made me feel I've nothin' to hide.

Longview

Words by Billie Joe
Music by Billie Joe, Tre Cool and Mike Dirnt

Strum Pattern: 1, 5
Pick Pattern: 1

1. I sit a-round __ and watch the tube, __ but no-thing's on. __
2., 3. *See additional lyrics*

I change the chan - nels for an hour __ or two.

Twid - dle my thumbs just for a bit, I'm sick of all __ the same old

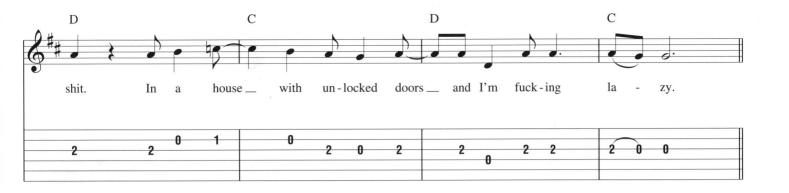

shit. In a house __ with un-locked doors __ and I'm fuck-ing la - zy.

Chorus

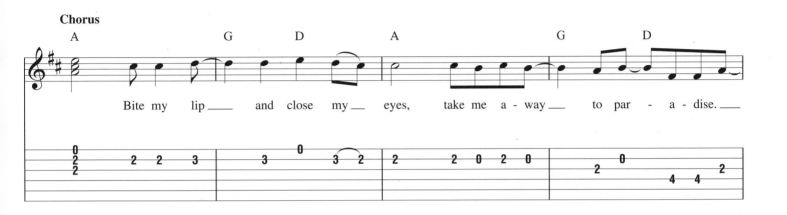

Bite my lip __ and close my __ eyes, take me a - way __ to par - a - dise. __

To Coda ⊕

|1.

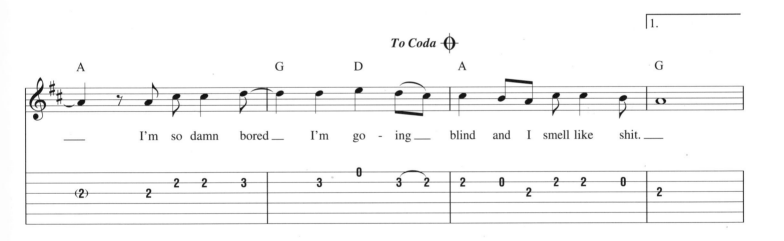

__ I'm so damn bored __ I'm go - ing __ blind and I smell like shit. __

|2.

Bridge

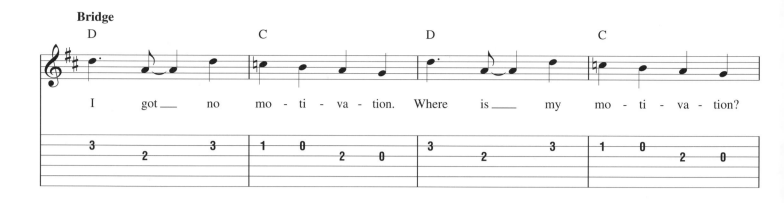

I got ___ no mo - ti - va - tion. Where is ___ my mo - ti - va - tion?

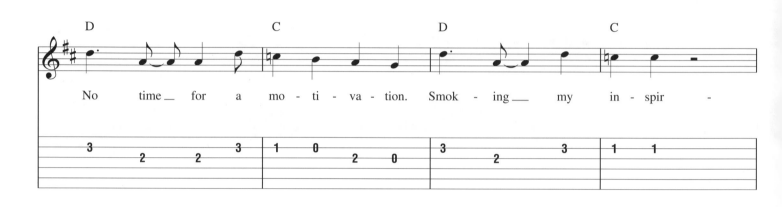

No time ___ for a mo - ti - va - tion. Smok - ing ___ my in - spir -

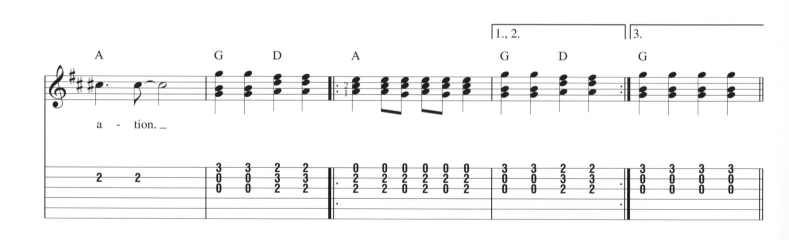

a - tion. ___

Interlude

D.S. al Coda

Coda

blind and lone-li - ness ___ has to ___ suf - fice. ___ Bite my lip ___ and close my ___

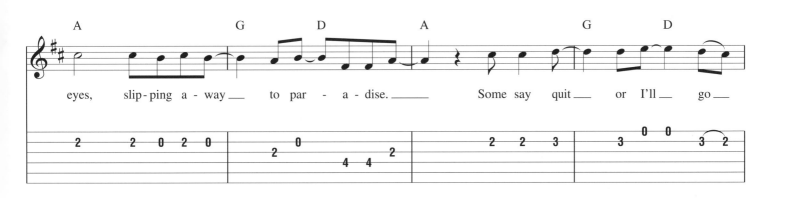

eyes, slip - ping a - way ___ to par - a - dise. ___ Some say quit ___ or I'll ___ go ___

Outro

Repeat and fade

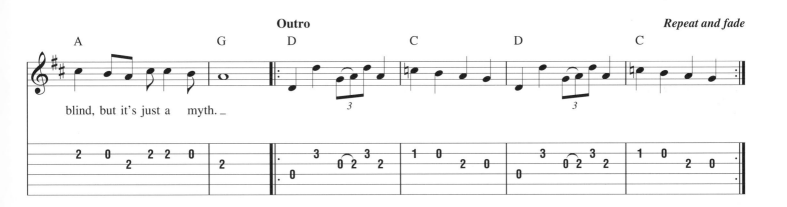

blind, but it's just a myth. _

Additional Lyrics

2. Peel me off this velcro seat and get me moving.
   I sure as hell can't do it by myself.
   I'm feeling like a dog in heat,
   Barred indoors from the summer street.
   I locked the door to my own cell and I lost the key.

3. I sit around and watch the phone, but no one's calling.
   Call me pathetic, call me what you will.
   My mother says to get a job,
   But she don't like the one she's got.
   When masturbation's lost it's fun, you're fucking lonely.

Losing My Religion

Words and Music by Bill Berry, Peter Buck, Mike Mills, Michael Stipe

Strum Pattern: 2
Pick Pattern: 4

Intro

Moderate Rock

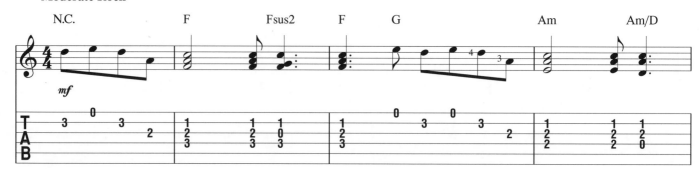

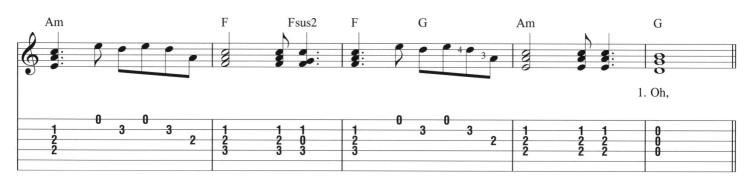

Verse

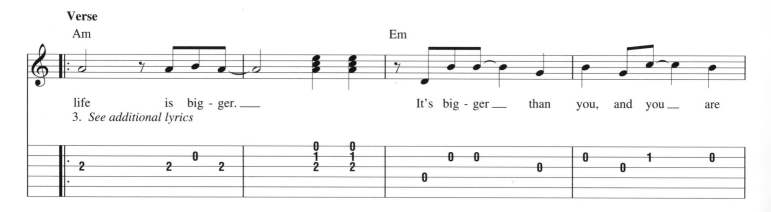

life is big-ger. ___ It's big-ger ___ than you, and you ___ are
3. *See additional lyrics*

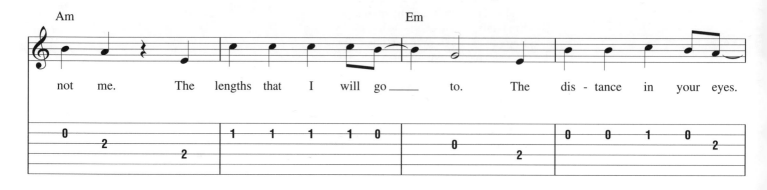

not me. The lengths that I will go ___ to. The dis-tance in your eyes.

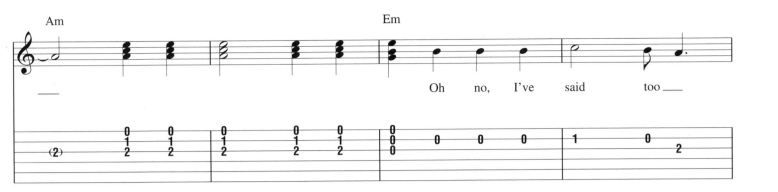

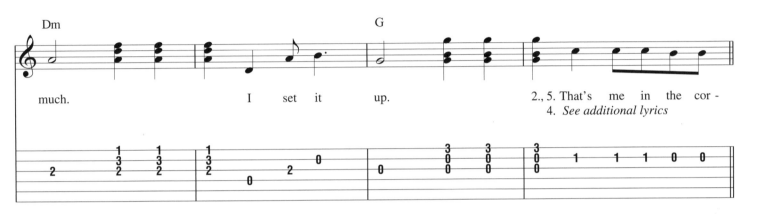

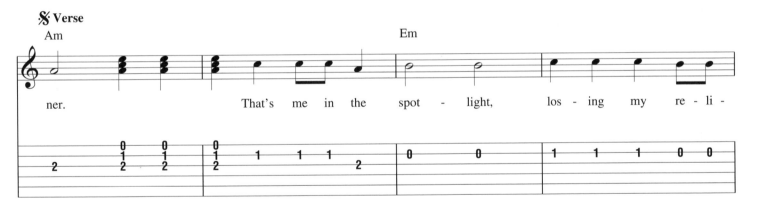

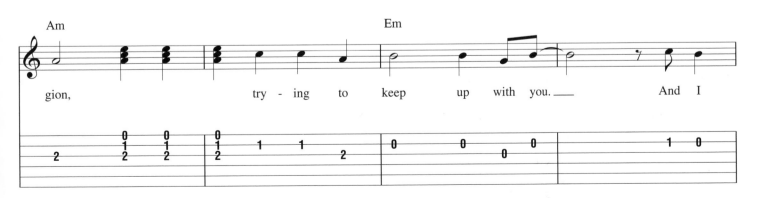

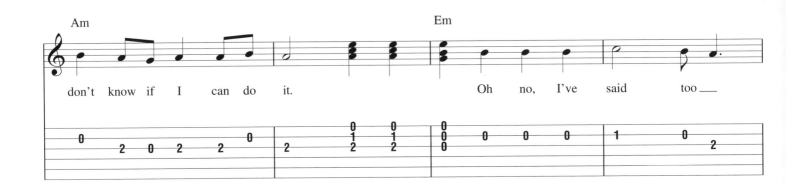

don't know if I can do it. Oh no, I've said too

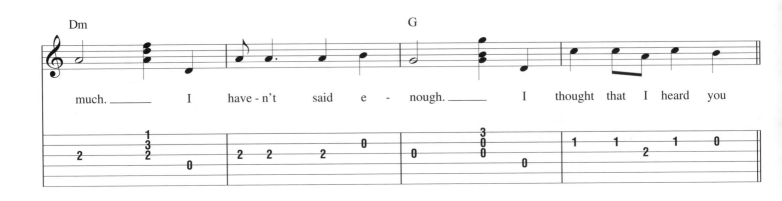

much. I have-n't said e - nough. I thought that I heard you

Chorus

laugh-ing. I thought that I heard you sing. I

1.

To Coda ⊕

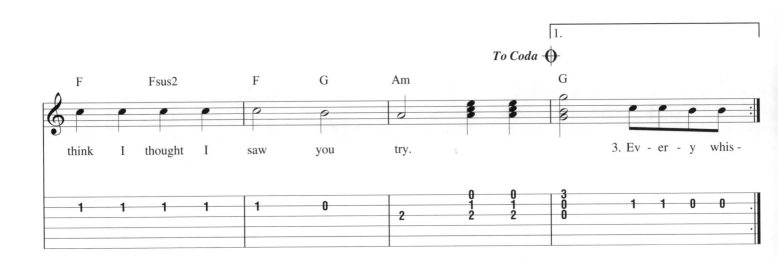

think I thought I saw you try. 3. Ev - er - y whis-

198

*Play chords once and let ring, next 8 meas.

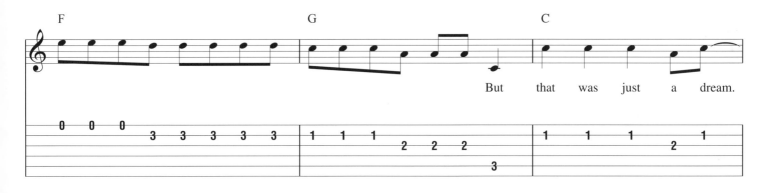

D.S. al Coda

199

Why try? __ That was just a dream, __ just a dream, __ just a dream,

Outro

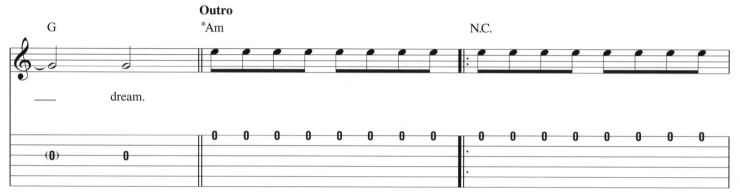

__ dream.

*Play chord once and let ring.

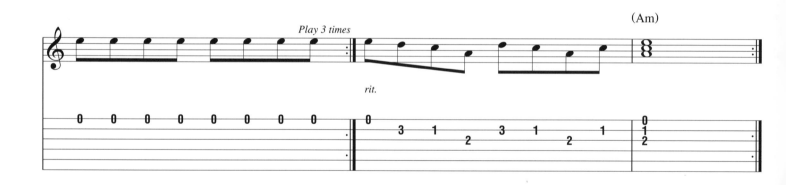

Play 3 times

rit.

Additional Lyrics

2. Every whisper of ev'ry waking hour
   I'm choosing my confessions, trying to keep an eye on you,
   Like a hurt, lost and blind fool, fool.
   Oh no, I've said too much. I set it up.
   Consider this. Consider this, the hint of the century.
   Consider this, the slip that brought me to my knees, failed.
   What if all these fantasies come flailing around?
   Now I've said too much.

Maybe I'm Amazed

Words and Music by Paul McCartney

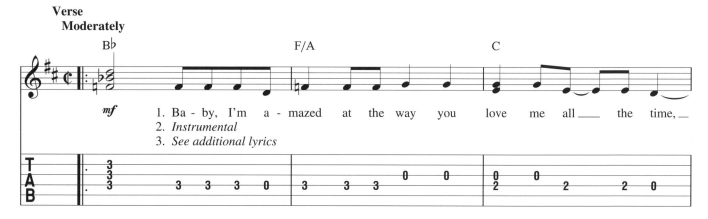

Strum Pattern: 3, 4
Pick Pattern: 3, 4

Verse
Moderately

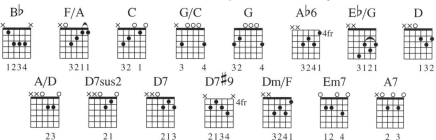

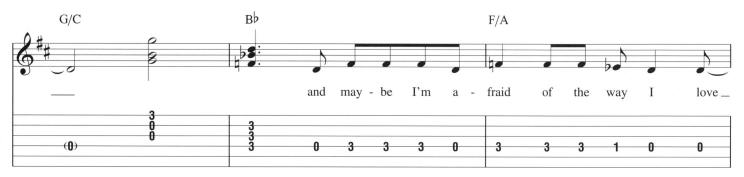

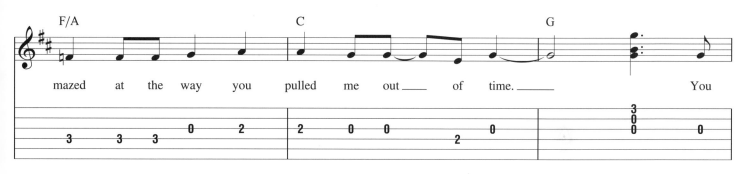

1. Ba - by, I'm a - mazed at the way you love me all ___ the time, ___
2. Instrumental
3. See additional lyrics

and may - be I'm a - fraid of the way I love ___ you.

Ba - by, I'm a - mazed at the way you pulled me out ___ of time. ___ You

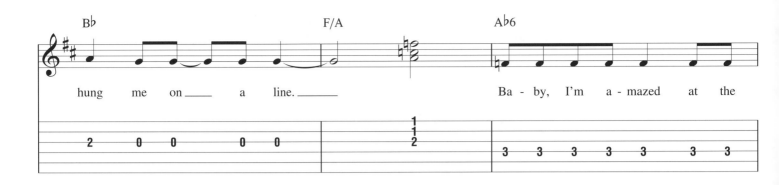

Bb   F/A   Ab6

hung   me   on ___   a   line. ___   Ba - by,   I'm   a - mazed   at   the

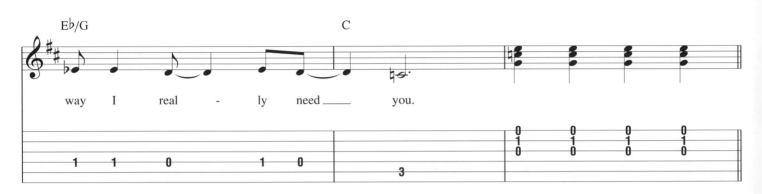

Eb/G   C

way   I   real - ly   need ___   you.

% Chorus

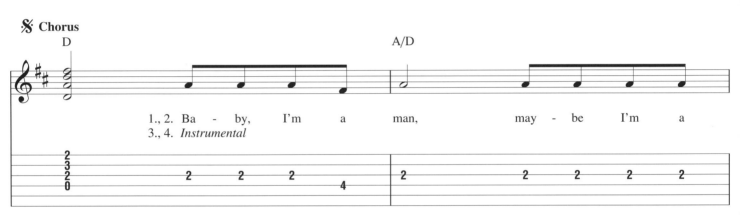

D   A/D

1., 2. Ba - by,   I'm   a   man,   may - be   I'm   a
3., 4. *Instrumental*

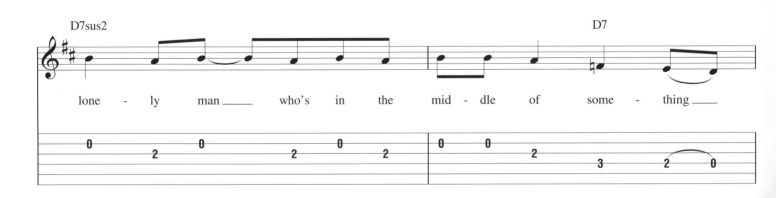

D7sus2   D7

lone - ly   man ___   who's   in   the   mid - dle   of   some - thing ___

G   D7#9

that   he   does - n't   real - ly   un - der - stand. ___

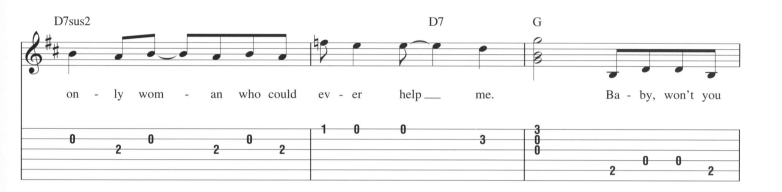

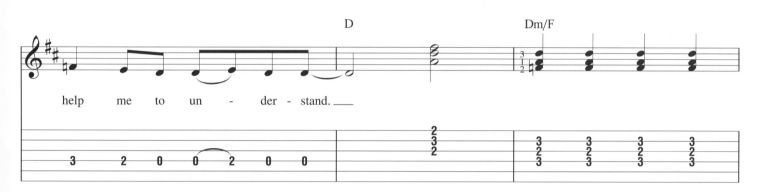

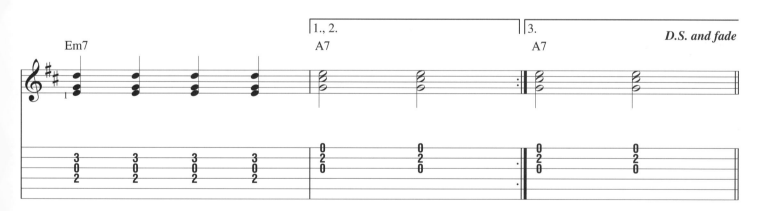

Additional Lyrics

3. Maybe I'm amazed at the way you're with me all the time.
   Maybe I'm afraid of the way I need you.
   Baby, I'm amazed at the way you help me sing my song,
   Right me when I'm wrong.
   Baby, I'm amazed at the way I really need you.

Love Shack

Words and Music by Catherine E. Pierson, Frederick W. Schneider, Keith J. Strickland and Cynthia L. Wilson

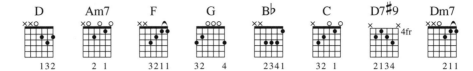

Strum Pattern: 5
Pick Pattern: 4

Intro
Moderate Rock

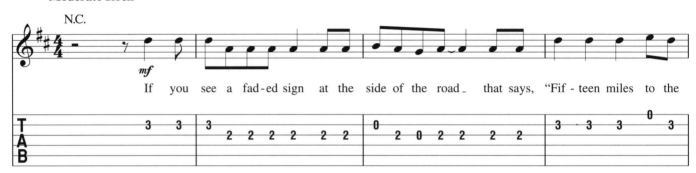

If you see a fad-ed sign at the side of the road that says, "Fif-teen miles to the

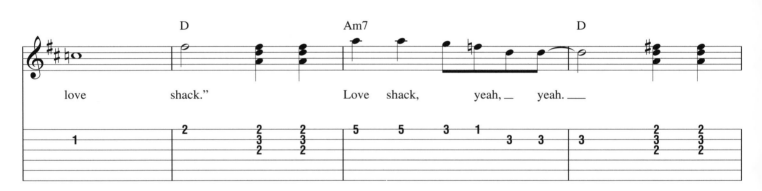

love shack." Love shack, yeah, yeah.

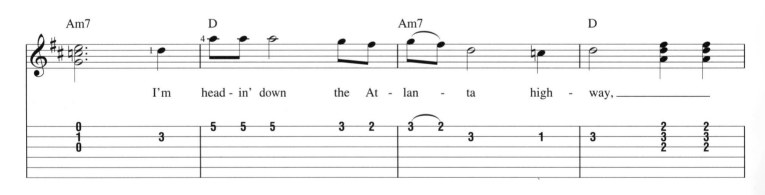

I'm head-in' down the At-lan-ta high - way,

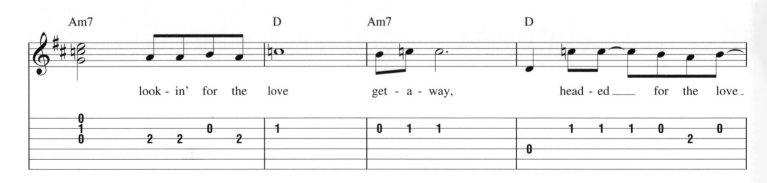

look-in' for the love get-a-way, head-ed for the love

get - a - way. 1. I got me a car, __ it's as big as a whale and we're
3., 6. *See additional lyrics*

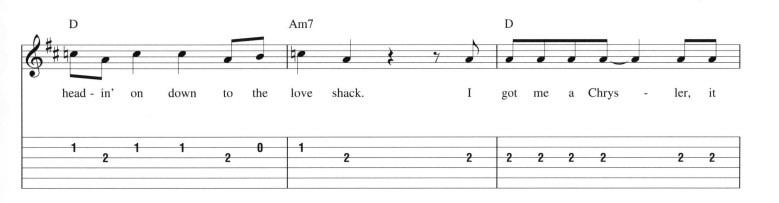

head - in' on down to the love shack. I got me a Chrys - ler, it

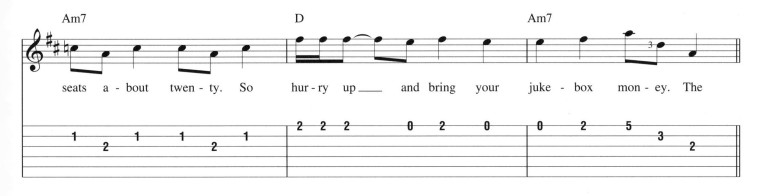

seats a - bout twen - ty. So hur - ry up __ and bring your juke - box mon - ey. The

Chorus

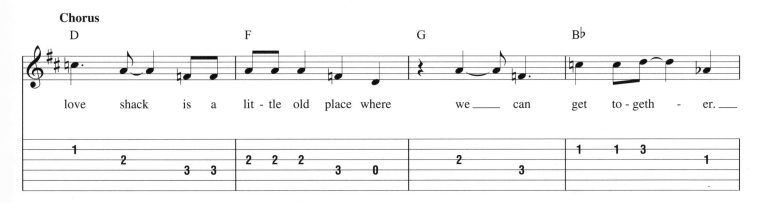

love shack is a lit - tle old place where we __ can get to - geth - er. __

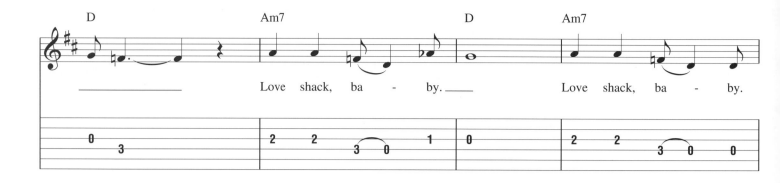

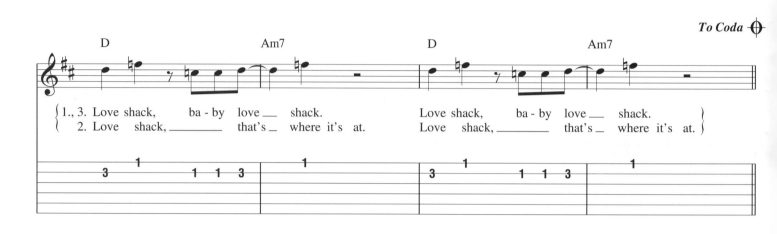

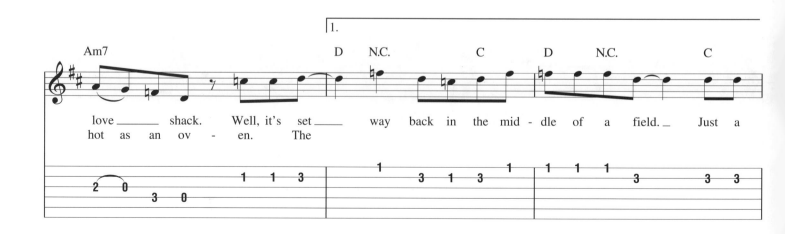

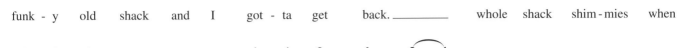

funk - y old shack and I got - ta get back. _____ whole shack shim - mies when

ev - 'ry - bod - y's mov - in' a - round _ and a - round and a - round _ and a - round. _____

Verse

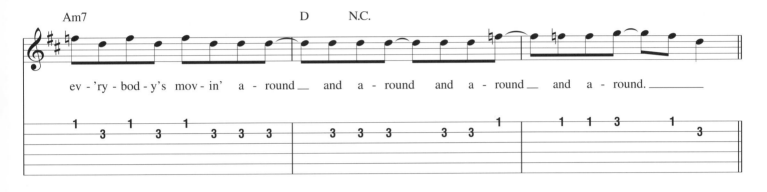

5. Ev - 'ry - bod - y's mov - in', ev - 'ry - bod - y's groov - in', ba - by. Folks lin - in' up out - side

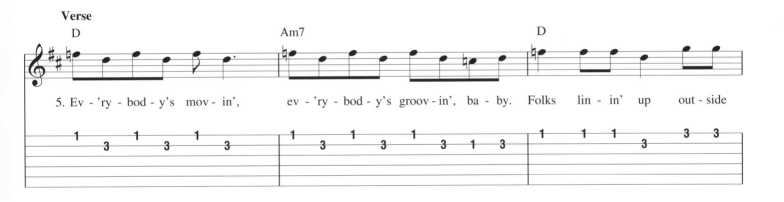

just to get down. _ Ev - 'ry - bod - y's mov - in', ev - 'ry - bod - y's groov - in', ba - by.

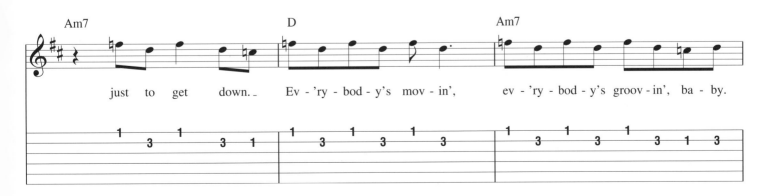

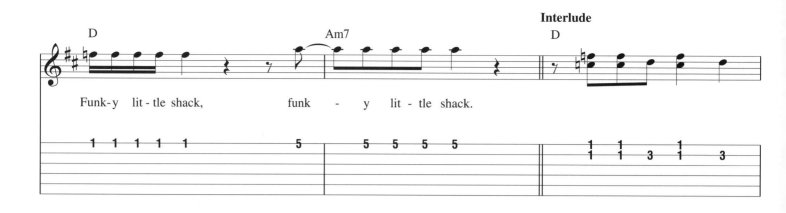

Funk-y lit-tle shack, funk - y lit - tle shack.

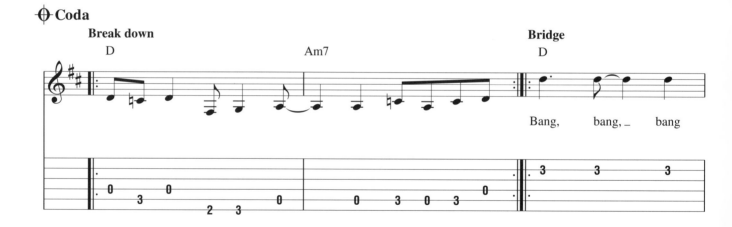

Bang, bang, — bang

on the door, ba - by. Knock a lit - tle loud - er, sug - ar.

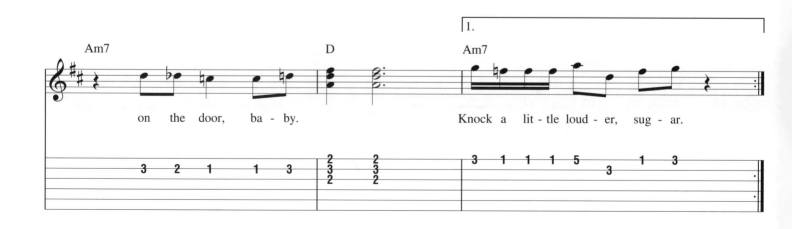

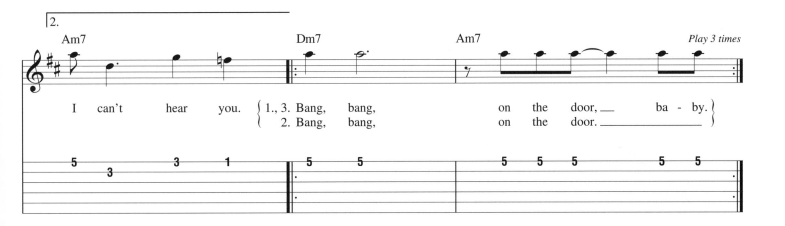

I can't hear you. 1., 3. Bang, bang, on the door, __ ba - by.
2. Bang, bang, on the door. _____

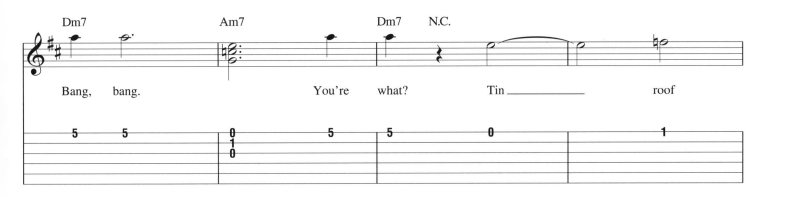

Bang, bang. You're what? Tin _____ roof

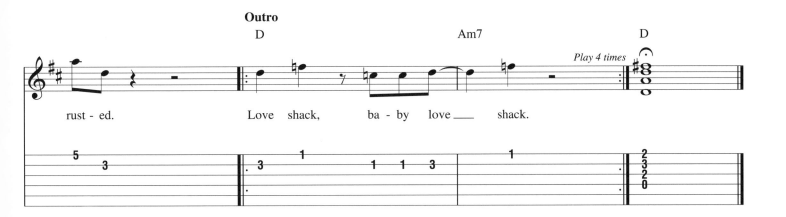

Outro

rust - ed. Love shack, ba - by love __ shack.

Additional Lyrics

3. Glitter on the mattress, glitter on the highway.
Glitter on the front porch, glitter on the hallway.

6. Hop in my Chrysler, it's as big as a whale
And it's about to set sail.
I got me a car, it seats about twenty.
So hurry up and bring your jukebox money.

Miss You

Words and Music by Mick Jagger and Keith Richards

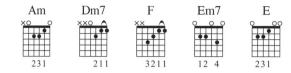

Strum Pattern: 3
Pick Pattern: 4

Intro
Moderately

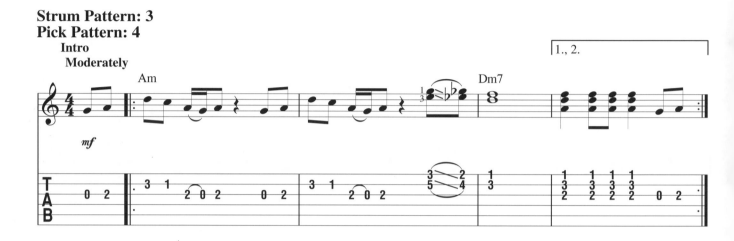

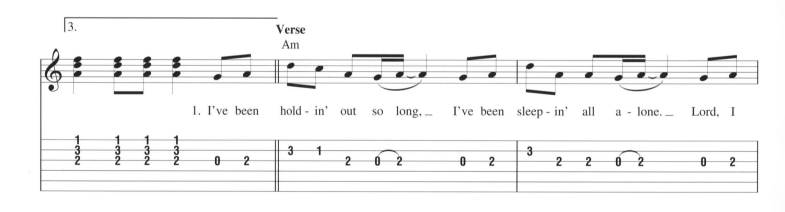

1. I've been hold-in' out so long, ___ I've been sleep-in' all a-lone. ___ Lord, I

miss you. _____

I've been hang-in' on the phone, ___ I've been

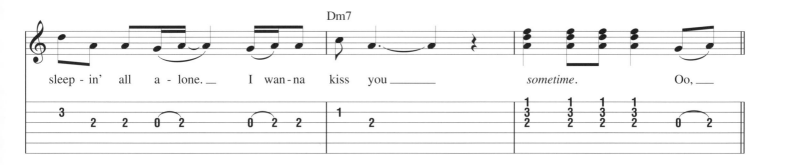

sleep-in' all a-lone. ___ I wan-na kiss you _____ sometime. Oo, ___

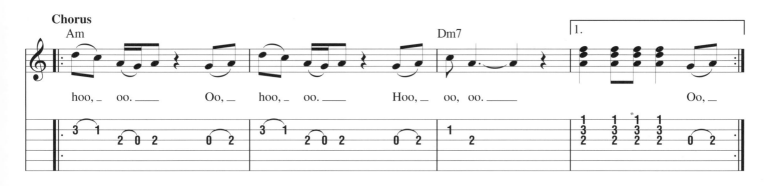

Chorus

hoo, ___ oo. _____ Oo, ___ hoo, ___ oo. _____ Hoo, ___ oo, oo. _____ Oo, ___

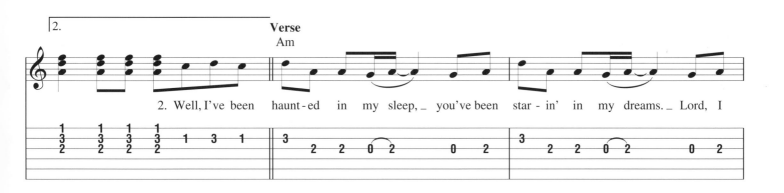

Verse

2. Well, I've been haunt-ed in my sleep, ___ you've been star-in' in my dreams. ___ Lord, I

miss you, child. ___ I've been wait-in' in the hall, ___ been

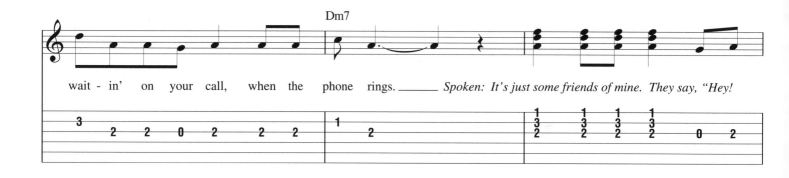

wait - in' on your call, when the phone rings. _____ *Spoken: It's just some friends of mine. They say, "Hey!*

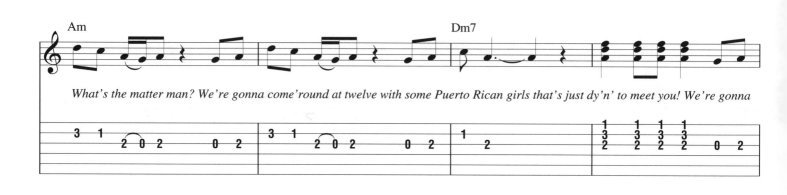

What's the matter man? We're gonna come 'round at twelve with some Puerto Rican girls that's just dy'n' to meet you! We're gonna

bring a case of wine.   Hey, let's go mess and fool around, you know, like we used to!"   Ah, —

Chorus

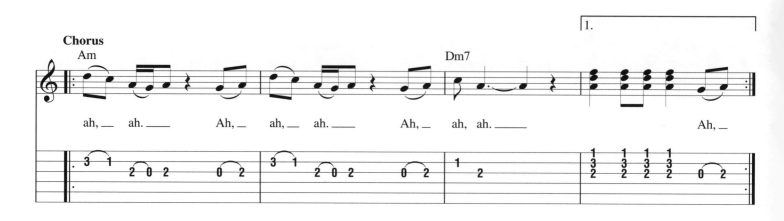

ah, ___ ah. ___   Ah, ___ ah, ___ ah. ___   Ah, ___ ah, ah. ___   Ah, —

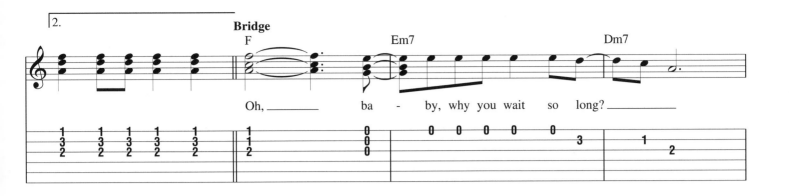

Oh, _____ ba - by, why you wait so long? _____

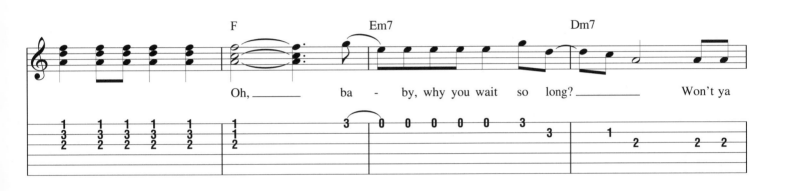

Oh, _____ ba - by, why you wait so long? _____ Won't ya

come home? Come home!

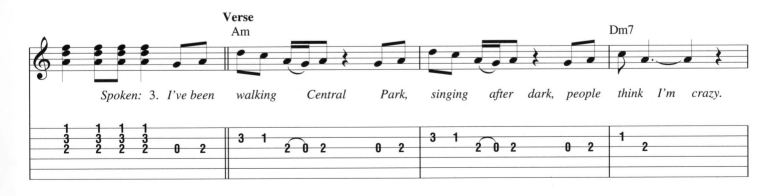

Spoken: 3. I've been walking Central Park, singing after dark, people think I'm crazy.

Stumbling   on   my   feet,   shuffling through   the   street,   asking   me,

"What's the matter with you, boy?"   *Sometimes*   *what   I   wanna   say   to   myself...*

Chorus

Sometimes I say... 1. Oo, __ (2.) hoo, __ oo. __   Oo, __ hoo, __ oo. __   Oo, __ oo. __
3., 4. *Instrumental*

1., 2., 3. |4.   **Verse**

2. Oo, __   4. I guess I'm   ly-ing to my-self, __ it's just   you and no one else, __ Lord, I

wan-na kiss you, child. _____ You've just been blot-tin' out my mind, _____

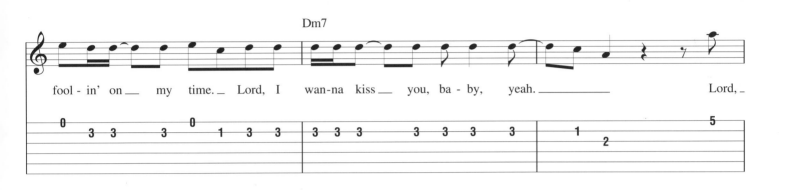

fool-in' on ___ my time. _ Lord, I wan-na kiss ___ you, ba - by, yeah. _____ Lord, _

___ I miss you, child. _____ Oo, ___ hoo. _____ Ah, ___

Outro-Chorus

Repeat and fade

ah, _ ah. _____ Ah, ah, _ ah. _____ Ah, _ ah, ah. Lord, ___ I miss you, child. _ Ah, _

MMM Bop

Words and Music by Isaac Hanson, Taylor Hanson and Zac Hanson

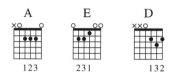

Strum Pattern: 2, 5
Pick Pattern: 1, 6

Intro
Moderately fast

Verse

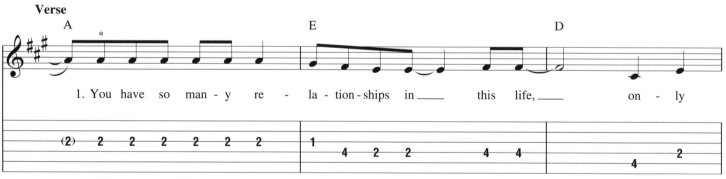

1. You have so man-y re - la-tion-ships in ___ this life, ___ on - ly

*Sung one octave higher throughout.

one or two ___ will last. ___ You're go-ing through all this pain ___ and strife, ___

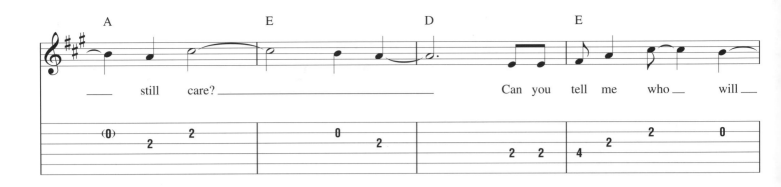

_____ still care? _____ Can you tell me who _____ will

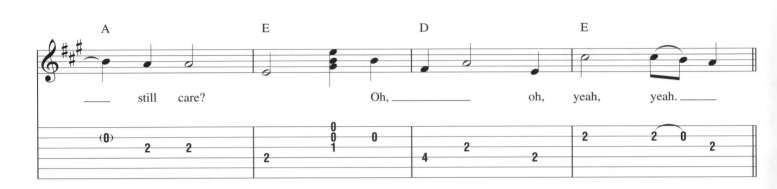

_____ still care? Oh, _____ oh, yeah, yeah. _____

Chorus

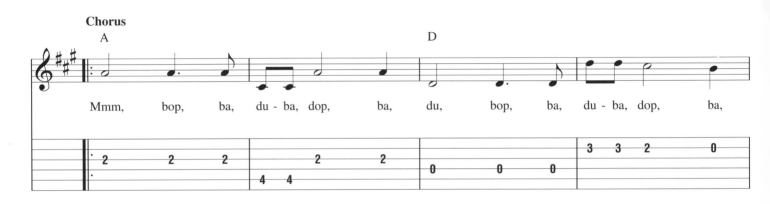

Mmm, bop, ba, du - ba, dop, ba, du, bop, ba, du - ba, dop, ba,

4th time, To Coda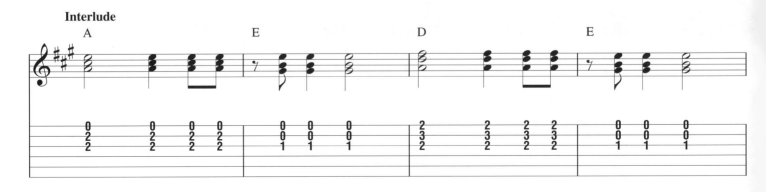

du, bop, ba, du - ba, dop, ba, du, _____ yay - ee, yeah. _____

Interlude

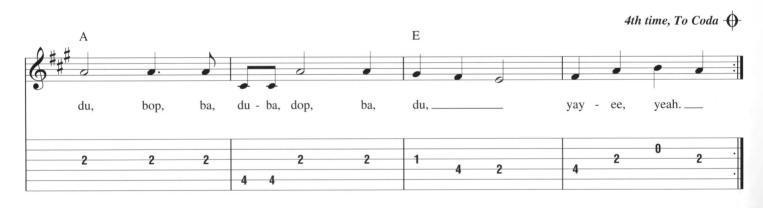

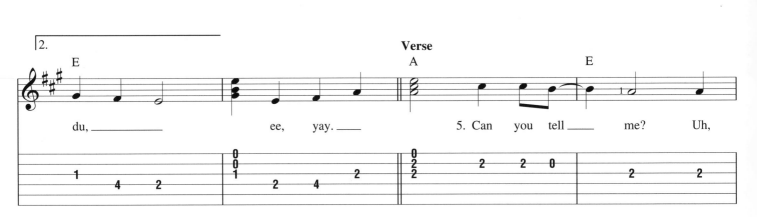

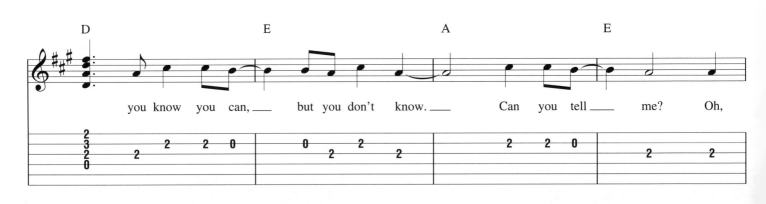

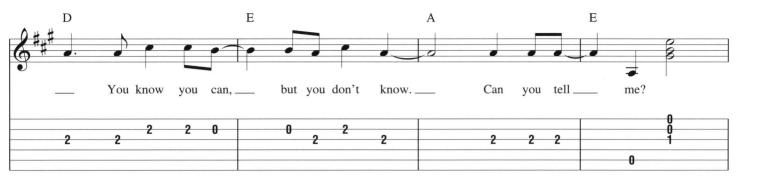

You know you can, ___ but you don't know. ___ Can you tell ___ me?

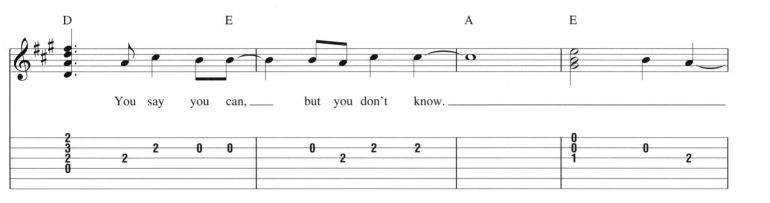

You say you can, ___ but you don't know. _____

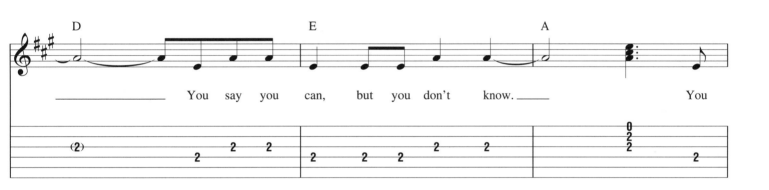

_____ You say you can, but you don't know. ___ You

D.S.S. and fade

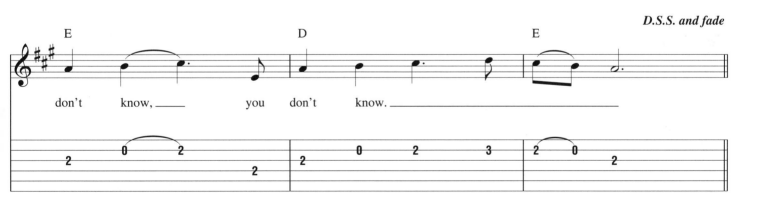

don't know, ___ you don't know. _____

Additional Lyrics

3. Plant a seed; plant a flower; plant a rose.
   You can plant any one of those.
   Keep planting to find out which one grows.
   It's a secret no one knows.
   It's a secret no one knows, no one knows.

My Generation

Words and Music by Peter Townshend

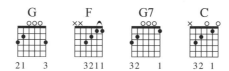

Strum Pattern: 4
Pick Pattern: 5

Verse
Fast Rock

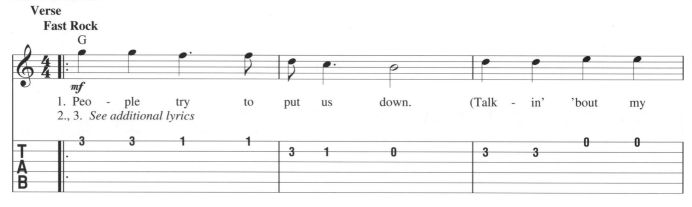

1. Peo - ple try to put us down. (Talk - in' 'bout my
2., 3. *See additional lyrics*

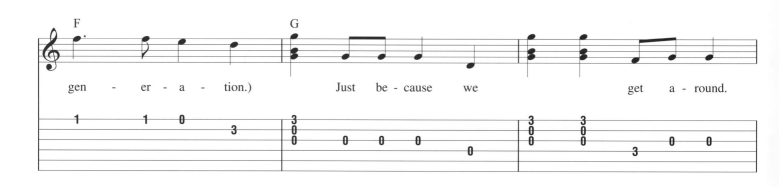

gen - er - a - tion.) Just be - cause we get a - round.

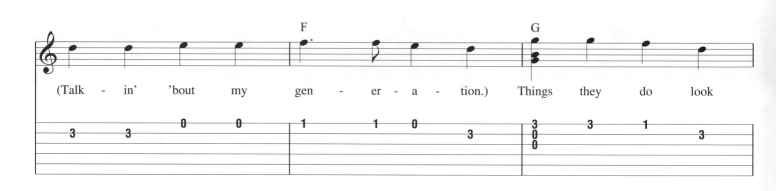

(Talk - in' 'bout my gen - er - a - tion.) Things they do look

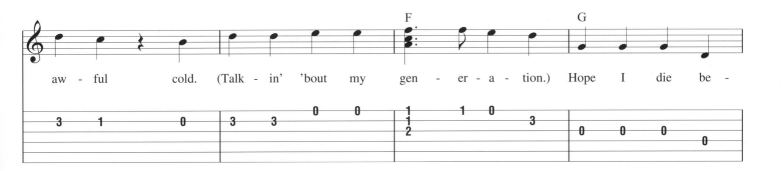

aw - ful   cold.   (Talk - in' 'bout my   gen - er - a - tion.)   Hope   I   die   be -

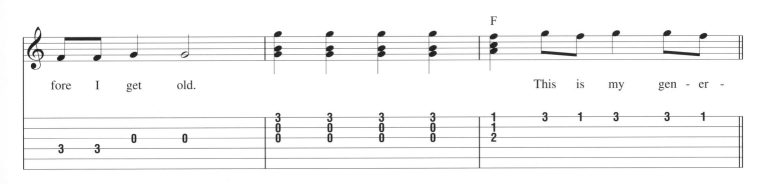

fore   I   get   old.   This   is   my   gen - er -

Chorus

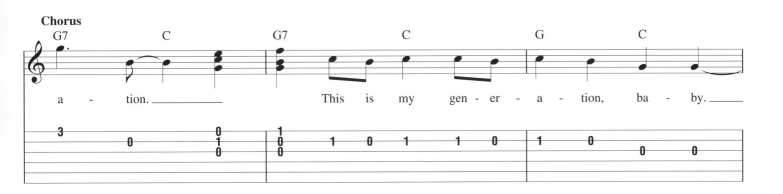

a -   tion. _____   This   is   my   gen - er - a - tion,   ba - by. _____

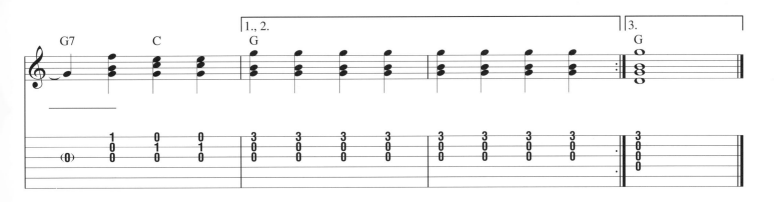

Additional Lyrics

2., 3. Why don't you all fade away? (Talkin' 'bout my generation.)
          Don't try to dig what we all say. (Talkin' 'bout my generation.)
          I'm not tryin' to cause a big sensation. (Talkin' 'bout my generation.)
          I'm just talkin' 'bout my generation. (Talkin' 'bout my generation.)

My Name Is

Words and Music by Labi Siffre

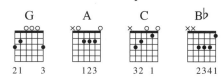

Strum Pattern: 3
Pick Pattern: 5

Chorus
Moderately slow

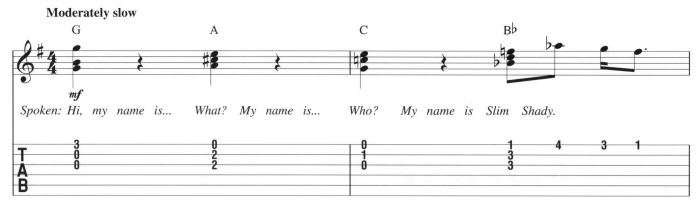

Spoken: Hi, my name is... What? My name is... Who? My name is Slim Shady.

Hi, my name is... Huh? My name is... What? My name is Slim Shady.

Hi, my name is... Huh? My name is...
Ahem... excuse me,

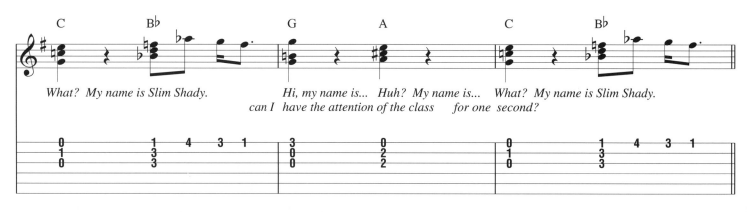

What? My name is Slim Shady.
can I have the attention of the class

Hi, my name is... Huh? My name is... What? My name is Slim Shady.
for one second?

Verse

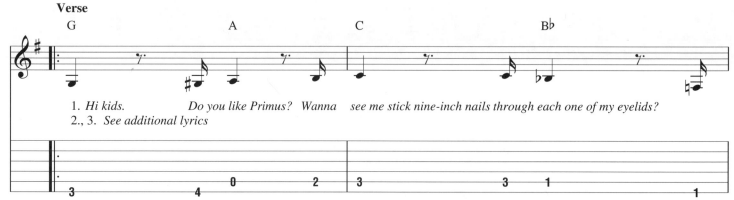

1. Hi kids. Do you like Primus? Wanna see me stick nine-inch nails through each one of my eyelids?
2., 3. See additional lyrics

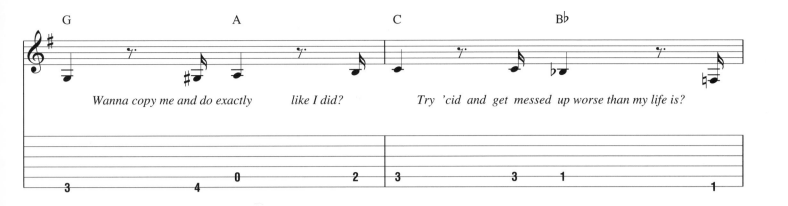

Wanna copy me and do exactly like I did? Try 'cid and get messed up worse than my life is?

My brain's dead weight. From tryin' to get my head straight. I can't figure out which Spice girl I wanna impregnate.

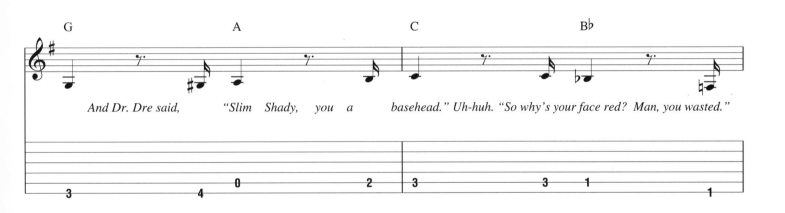

And Dr. Dre said, "Slim Shady, you a basehead." Uh-huh. "So why's your face red? Man, you wasted."

Well, since age twelve, I felt like a caged elf who stayed to himself in one place chasing his tail.

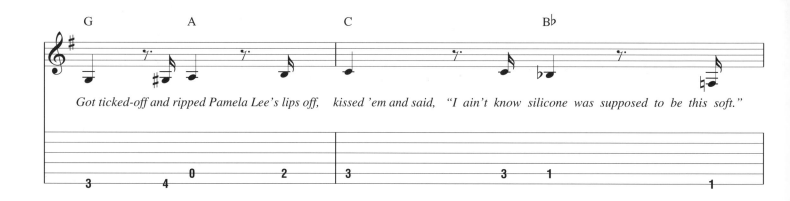

Got ticked-off and ripped Pamela Lee's lips off, kissed 'em and said, "I ain't know silicone was supposed to be this soft."

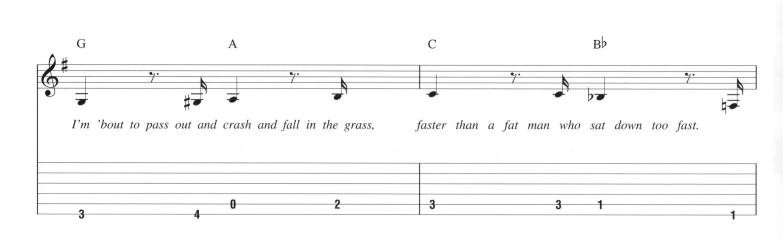

I'm 'bout to pass out and crash and fall in the grass, faster than a fat man who sat down too fast.

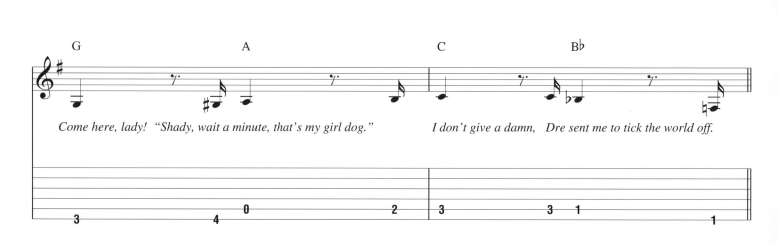

Come here, lady! "Shady, wait a minute, that's my girl dog." I don't give a damn, Dre sent me to tick the world off.

Chorus

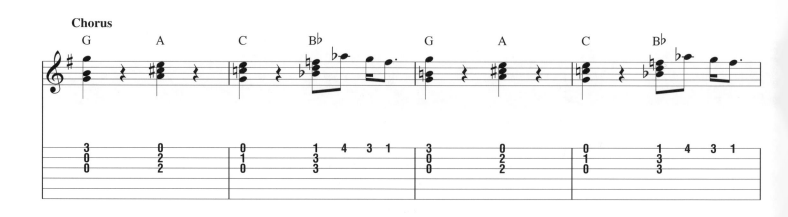

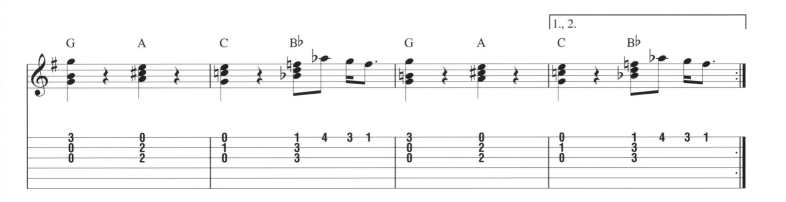

Additional Lyrics

2. *My English teacher wanted to flunk me in junior high,*
   Thanks a lot, next semester I'll be thirty-five.
   I smacked him in his face with an eraser, chased him with a stapler,
   And told him to change the grade on the paper.
   Walked in the strip club, had my jacket zipped up
   Served the bartender, and walked out with the tip cup.
   Extraterrestrial, runnin' over pedestrians in a spaceship
   While they screamin' at me, "Let's just be friends."
   Ninety-nine percent of my life, I was lied to.
   I just found out my mom does more dope than I do.
   I told her I'd grow up to be a famous rapper
   Make a record about doin' drugs and name it after her,
   You know you blew up when the women rush your stands
   And try to touch your hands like some screamin' Usher fans.
   This guy at White Castle asked for my autograph.
   So I signed it, "Dear Dave, thanks for the support, asshole."

3. *Stop the tape. This kid needs to be locked away. Get him!*
   Dr. Dre, don't just stand there... operate!
   I'm not ready to leave, it's too scary to die.
   I'll have to be carried inside the cemetery and buried alive.
   Am I comin' or goin'? I can barely decide.
   I just drank a fifth of Kool-Aid; dare me to drive?
   All my life I was very deprived
   I ain't had a woman in years, and my palms are too hairy to hide.
   Clothes ripped like the Incredible Hulk.
   I spit when I talk, I'll f*** anything that walks.
   When I was little, I used to get so hungry I would throw fits.
   "How you gonna breast-feed me Mom? You ain't got no t*ts!"
   I lay awake and strap myself in bed
   With a bulletproof vest on and tap myself in the head
   Till I'm steamin' mad.
   And by the way, when you see my dad,
   Ask him if he bought a porno mag and see my ad.

Nasty

Words and Music by James Harris III, Terry Lewis and Janet Jackson

*Optional: To match recording, place capo at 1st fret.

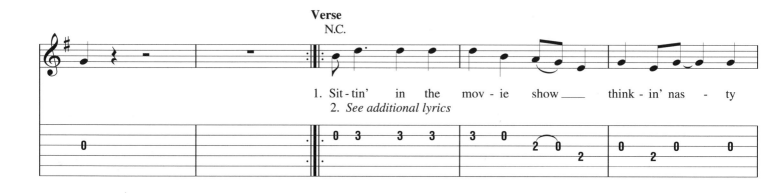

1. Sit-tin' in the mov-ie show ____ think-in' nas - ty
2. *See additional lyrics*

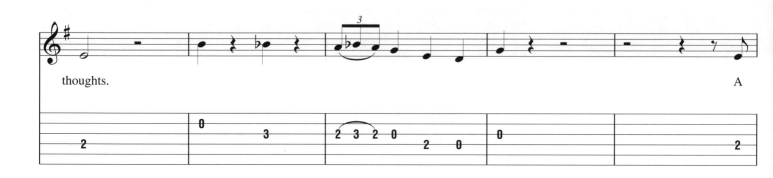

thoughts.

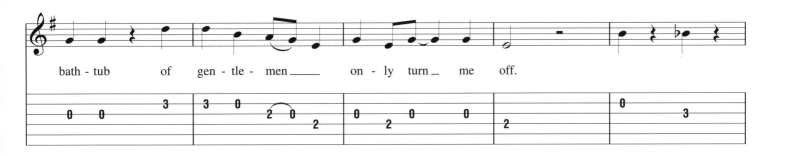

bath-tub of gen-tle-men ____ on-ly turn ____ me off.

%. **Chorus**

Spoken: That's right. *A let me tell ya.* Nas - ty,

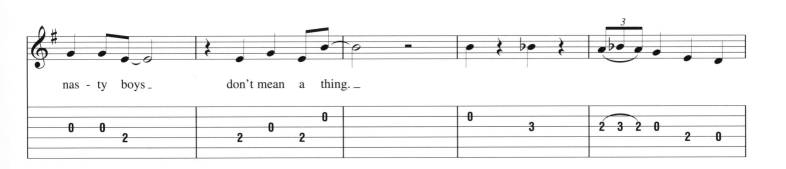

nas - ty boys ___ don't mean a thing. ___

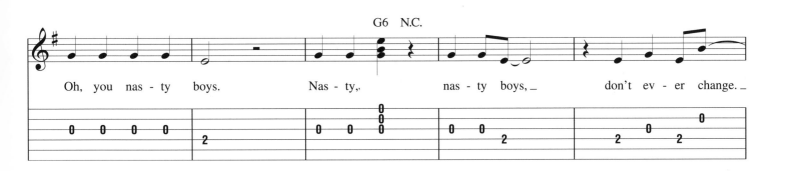

Oh, you nas - ty boys. Nas - ty,, nas - ty boys, ___ don't ev - er change. ___

To Coda ⊕

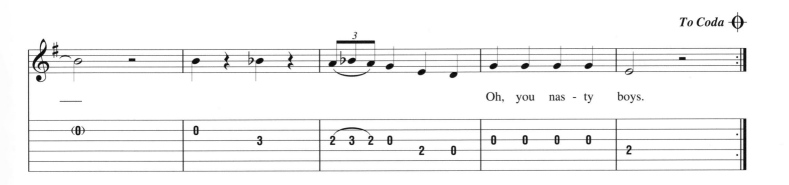

____ Oh, you nas - ty boys.

229

Nas - ty, nas - ty boys, _ give me your nas - ty groove.

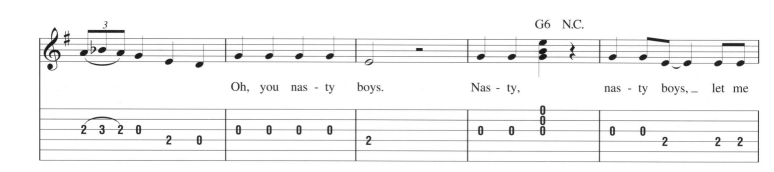

Oh, you nas - ty boys. Nas - ty, nas - ty boys, _ let me

see your nas - ty bod - y move. _

Breakdown

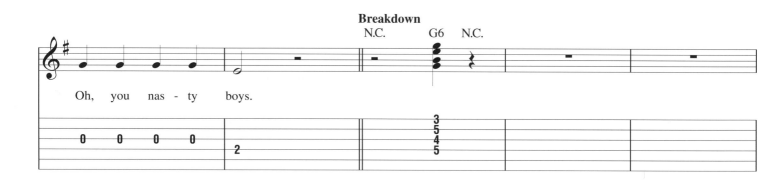

Oh, you nas - ty boys.

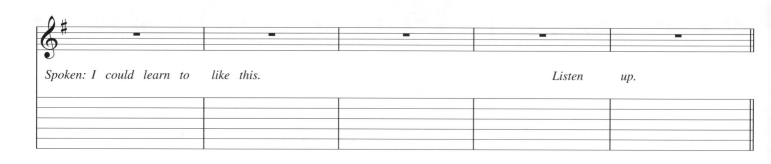

Spoken: I could learn to like this. *Listen up.*

Bridge

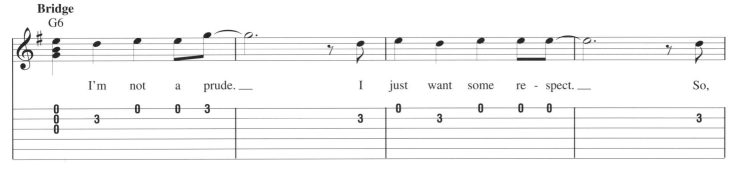

I'm not a prude. ___ I just want some re - spect. ___ So,

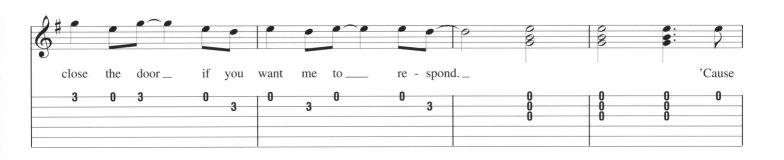

close the door ___ if you want me to ___ re - spond. ___ 'Cause

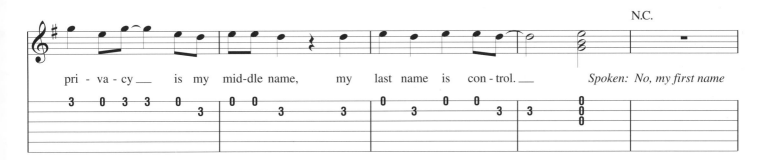

N.C.

pri - va - cy ___ is my mid-dle name, my last name is con - trol. ___ *Spoken: No, my first name*

Coda

D.S. al Coda

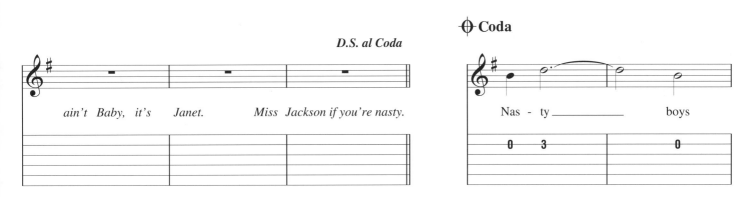

ain't Baby, it's Janet. *Miss Jackson if you're nasty.*

Nas - ty _____ boys

don't mean a thing. ___ Oh, _____ you _____ nas - ty boys *Spoken: don't mean a*

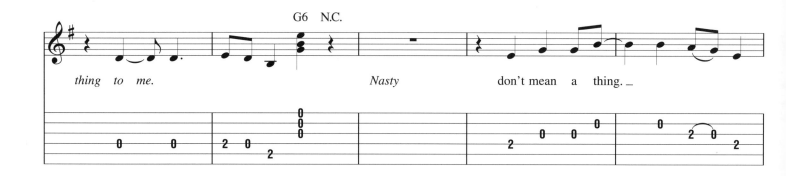

thing to me. Nasty don't mean a thing. _

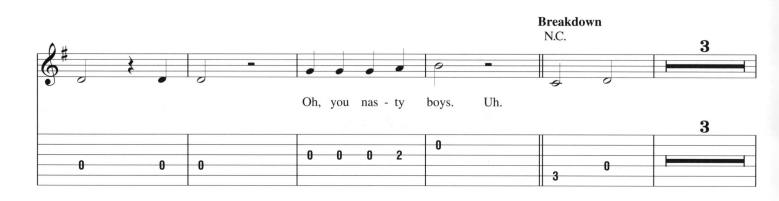

Oh, you nas-ty boys. Uh.

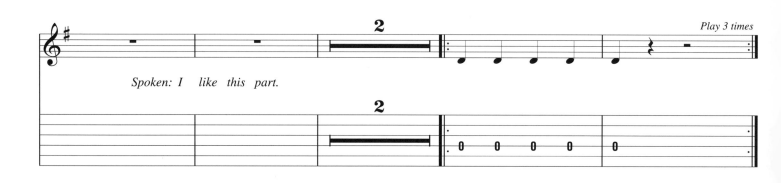

Spoken: I like this part.

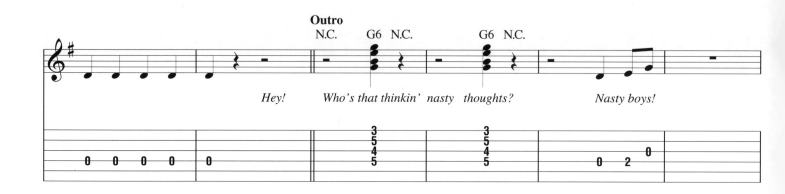

Hey! Who's that thinkin' nasty thoughts? Nasty boys!

Who's that in that nasty car? Nasty boys! Who's that eatin' that

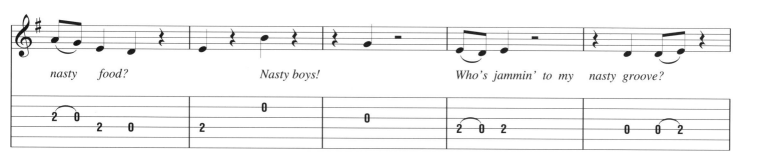

nasty food? Nasty boys! Who's jammin' to my nasty groove?

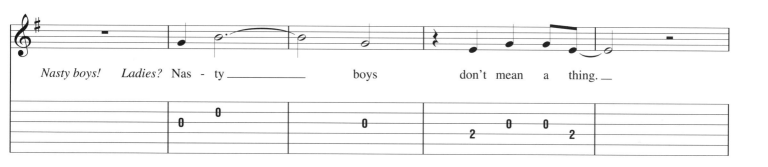

Nasty boys! Ladies? Nas - ty _____ boys don't mean a thing. __

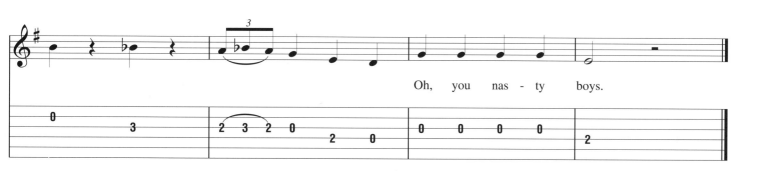

Oh, you nas - ty boys.

Additional Lyrics

2. I don't like no nasty girl,
   I don't like no nasty food.
   The only nasty thing I like
   Is this nasty groove.
Spoken: Will this one do?
   Uh huh, I know.

No Diggity

Words and Music by Chauncey Hannibal, Edward Riley, William Stewart, Richard Vick, Lynise Walters and Bill Withers

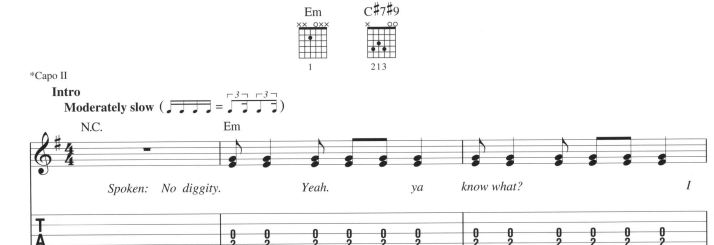

*Capo II

Intro
Moderately slow

Spoken: No diggity.   Yeah.   ya   know what?   I

Optional: To match recording, place capo at 2nd fret.

like the players.   *No diggity,   no doubt.*   *Play on,   playa.*

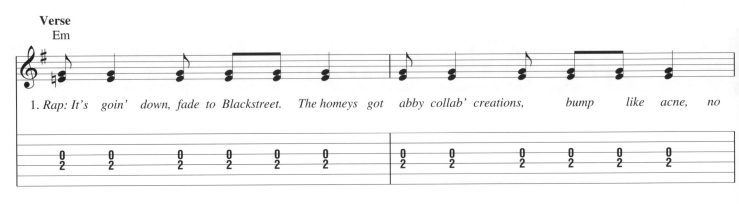

Play on,   playa.   *Yo Dre, drop the verse.*

Verse

1. *Rap:* It's goin' down, fade to Blackstreet.   The homeys got   abby collab' creations,   bump   like   acne,   no

doubt I put it down, never slouch. As long as my credit could vouch a dog couldn't catch me, *ass* out. Tell me

who can stop with Dre makin' moves, attracting honeys like a magnet, giving 'em ear-gasms with my mellow accent.

N.C.

C#7#9

Still moving his flavor with the homeys Blackstreet and Teddy, the original rump shakers.

2. Short - y

Verse

Em

cont. rhy. sim.

get down, ___ good Lord. Ba - by got 'em o - pen all o - ver town. ___

3. See additional lyrics

Strict - ly biz, she don't play a - round, ___ cov - er much grounds, ___ got game by the pound.

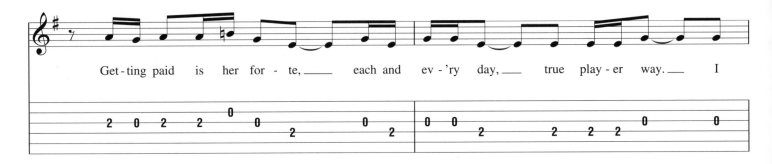

Get-ting paid is her for - te, ____ each and ev -'ry day, ____ true play-er way. ____ I

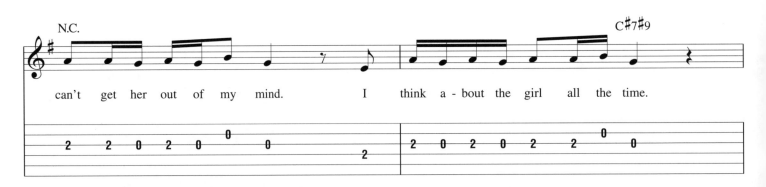

can't get her out of my mind. I think a - bout the girl all the time.

East side to the west side, ____ push your fat rides, it's no sur - prise. ____

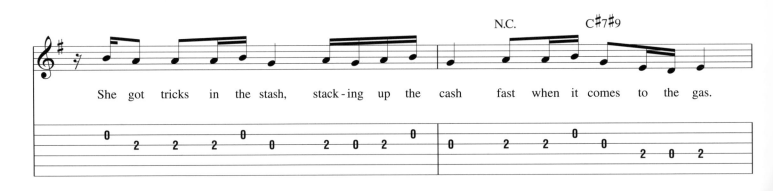

She got tricks in the stash, stack - ing up the cash fast when it comes to the gas.

By no means av' - rage, ____ she's on when she's got to have it.

Ba - by you're a per - fect ten, I wan - na get in. Can I get down so I can __

Chorus

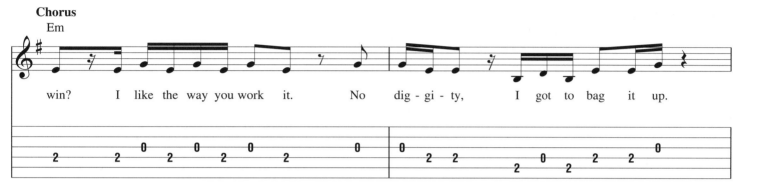

win? I like the way you work it. No dig - gi - ty, I got to bag it up.

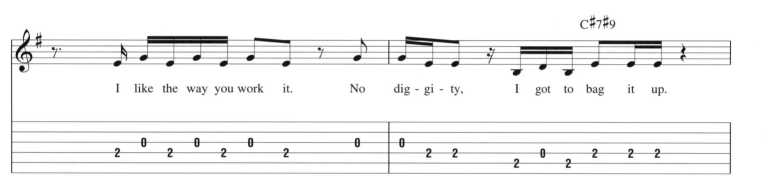

I like the way you work it. No dig - gi - ty, I got to bag it up.

I like the way you work it. No dig - gi - ty, I got to bag it up.

I like the way you work it. No dig - gi - ty, I got to bag it up.

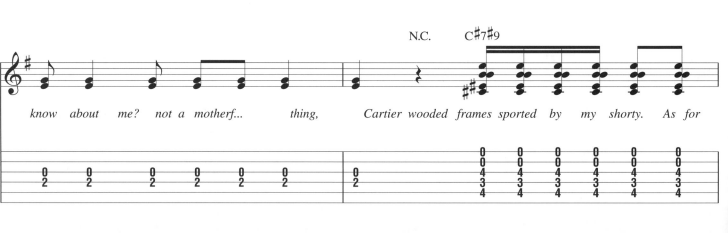

Chorus

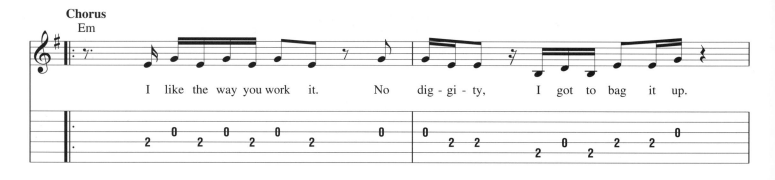

I like the way you work it. No dig-gi-ty, I got to bag it up.

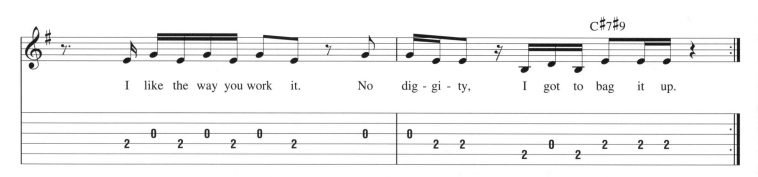

I like the way you work it. No dig-gi-ty, I got to bag it up.

Outro

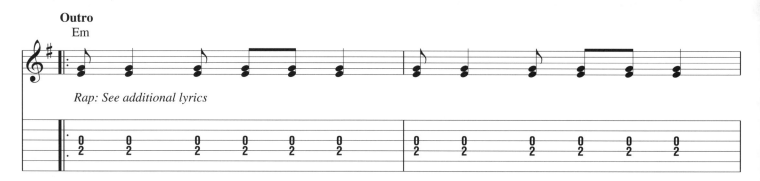

Rap: See additional lyrics

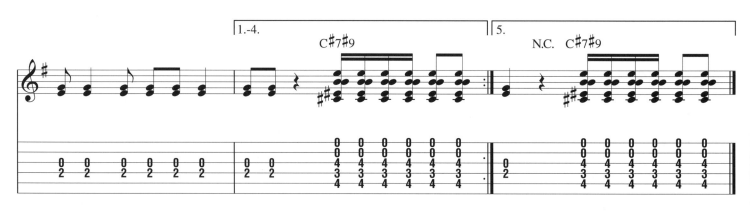

Additional Lyrics

3. She's got class and style,
Street knowledge, by the pound.
Baby never act wild, very low key on the profile.
Catching feelings is a no,
Let me tell you how it goes,
Curve's the word, spin's the verb,
Lovers it curves so freak what you heard.
Rollin' with the fatness,
You don't even know what the half is.
You gotta pay to play,
Just for shorty bang bang to look your way.
I like the way you work it,
Trump tight all day, everyday.
You're blowing my mind, maybe in time,
Baby, I can get you in my ride.

Outro Rap: Yeah, Come on,
Jackie in full effect,
Lisa in full effect,
Nicky in full effect,
Tomeka in full effect,
Ladies in full effect.
Ain't nothing goin' on but the rent.
Yeah, play on play that,
Play on play on
Cuz I like it.
No diggity, no doubt, yeah.
Blackstreet productions,
We out, we out right,
We out, we out.

Oh, Pretty Woman

Words and Music by Roy Orbison and Bill Dees

Strum Pattern: 2
Pick Pattern: 4

Verse

A   F#m   A

wom - an, _____ don't walk on by; ___ pret - ty wom - an, _____ don't

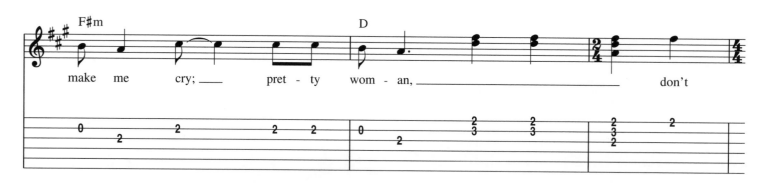

F#m   D

make me cry; ___ pret - ty wom - an, _____ don't

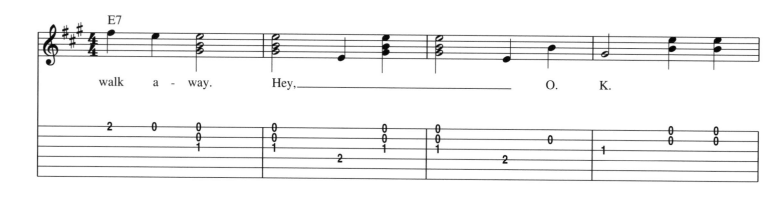

E7

walk a - way. Hey, _____ O. K.

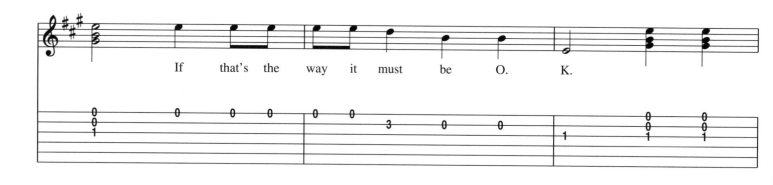

If that's the way it must be O. K.

I guess I'll go on home; it's late. There'll be to -

244

Additional Lyrics

2. Pretty woman, won't you pardon me?
   Pretty woman, I couldn't help but see;
   Pretty woman, that you look lovely as can be.
   Are you lonely just like me?

O.P.P.

**Words and Music by Alphonso Mizell, Freddie Perren, Dennis Lussier,
Berry Gordy, Anthony Criss, Keir Gist and Vincent Brown**

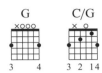

*Capo II

Strum Pattern: 3
Pick Pattern: 3

Intro
Moderate Rap

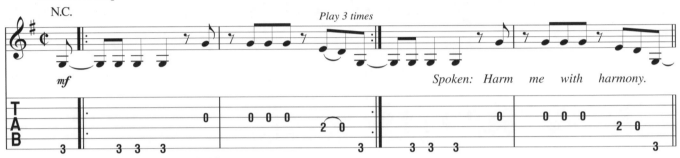

*Optional: To match recording, place capo at 2nd fret.

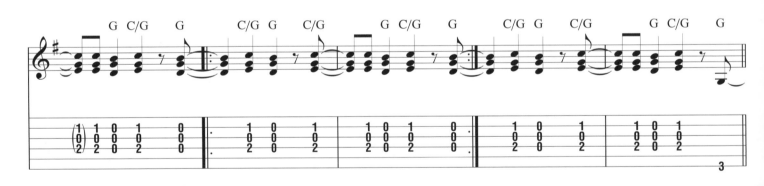

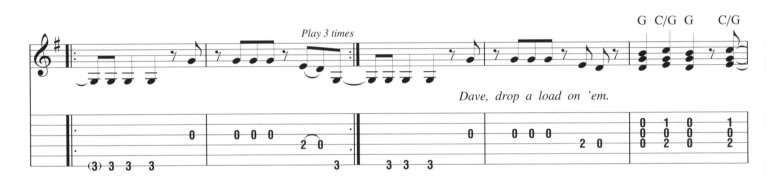

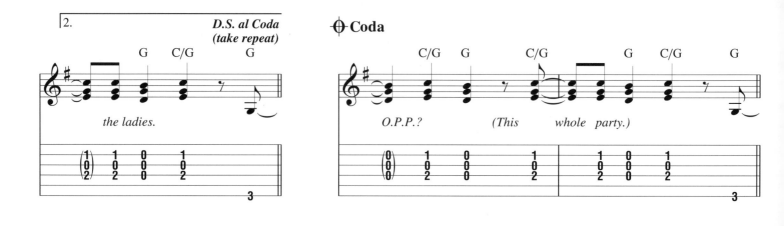

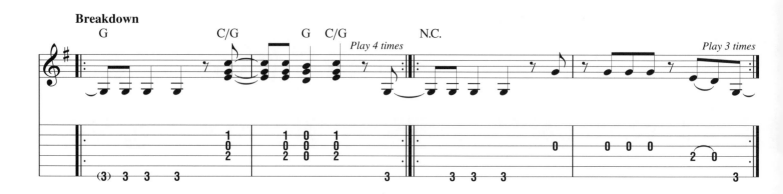

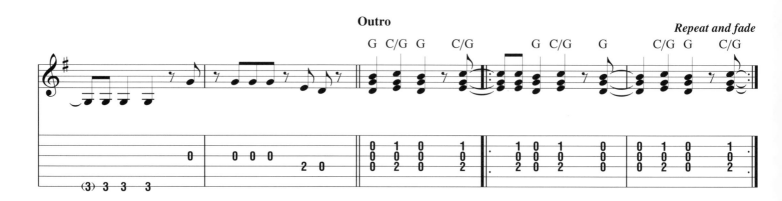

Additional Lyrics

Rap 1. O.P.P.: how can I explain it?
I'll take you frame by frame it.
To have y'all jumpin', shall we singin' it.
O is for "other," P is for "people," scratchin' temple.
The last P, well, that's not that simple, huh.
It's sorta like a, well, another way to call a cat a kitten.
It's five letters that are missin' here.
You get it on occasion at the other party as a game,
An' it seems I gotta start the explainin'. Bust it.
You ever had a girl and met her on a nice hello?
You get her name and number, then you feelin' real mellow.
You get home, wait a day; she's what you wanna know about.
Then you call up and it's her girlfriend's or her cousin's house.
It's not a fronter, F to the R to the O to the N to the T.
It's just her boyfriend's at her house. (Oh, that's what is scary.)
It's O.P.P. time, other people's what you get it.
There's no room for relationship, there's just room to hit it.
How many brothers out there know just what I'm gettin' at?
Who thinks it's wrong 'cause I was splittin' and co-hittin' at?
Well, if you do, that's O.P.P., and you're not down with it,
But if you don't, here's your membership.

Rap 2. As for the ladies, O.P.P. means something gifted.
        The first two letters are same, but the last is something different.
        It's the longest, loveliest, lean – I call it the leanest.
        It's another five letter word rhymin' with cleanest and meanest.
        I won't get into that; I'll do it, uh, sorta properly.
        I say the last P...hmm...stands for "property."
        Now, lady, here comes a kiss, blow a kiss back to me.
        Now, tell me, exactly.
        Have you ever known a brother who had another, like a girl or wife?
        And you just had to stop and just 'cause he look just as nice.
        You looked at him, he looked at you, and you knew right away
        That he had someone, but he was gonna be yours anyway.
        You couldn't be seen with him, and honestly, you didn't care
        'Cause in a room behind a door, no one but y'all are there.
        When y'all are finished, y'all can leave, and only y'all would know,
        And y'all could throw that skeleton bone right in the closet door.
        Now, don't be shocked, 'cause if you're down, I want your hands up high.
        Say, "O.P.P." (O.P.P.), I like to say with pride.
        Now when you do it, do it well, and make sure that it counts.
        You're now down with a discount.

Rap 3. This girl tried to O.P.P. me.
        I had a girl, and she knew that, matter-of-fact, uh, my girl was partners
        That had a fallout, disagreement, yeah, an argument.
        She tried to do me so we did it in my apartment, bust it.
        That wasn't the thing, it must have been the way she hit the ceiling,
        'Cause after that, she kept on comin' back and catchin' feelings.
        I said, "Let's go, my girl is comin', so you gotta leave."
        She said, "Oh no, I love you, Treach."
        I said, "Now, child, please,
        You gots to leave, come grab your coat right now, you gotta go."
        I said, "Now, look you to the stairs and to the stair window.
        This was a thing, a little thing – you shouldn't have put your heart,
        'Cause you know I was O.P.P., hell, from the very start."
        Come on, come on, now let me tell you what it's all about.
        When you get down, you can't go 'round runnin' off at the mouth.
        That's rule number one in this O.P.P. establishment.
        You keep your mouth shut and it won't get back to her or him.
        Exciting, isn't it? A special kinda business.
        Many of you will catch the same sorta O.P.P. visit with
        Him or her, for sure, are goin' to admit it.
        When O.P.P. comes, damn, skippy, I'm with it.

One

Lyrics by Bono and The Edge
Music by U2

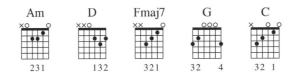

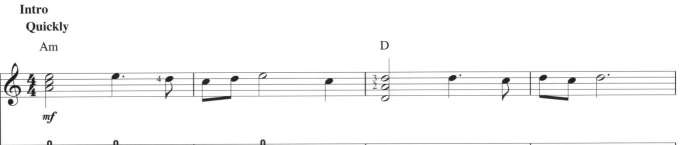

Strum Pattern: 4
Pick Pattern: 4

Intro
Quickly

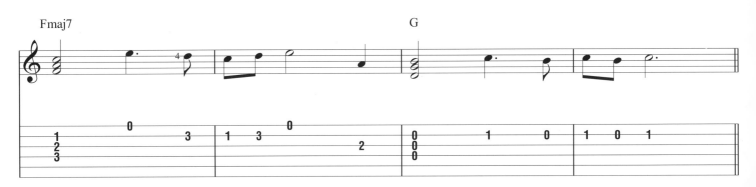

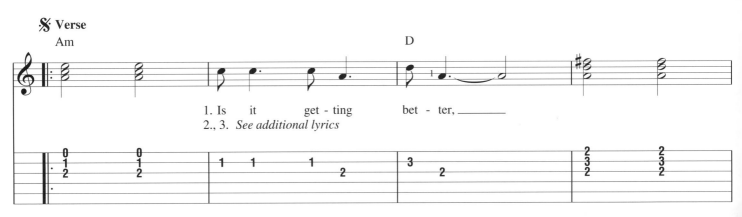

1. Is it get-ting bet-ter, _____
2., 3. *See additional lyrics*

or do you feel the same? ___

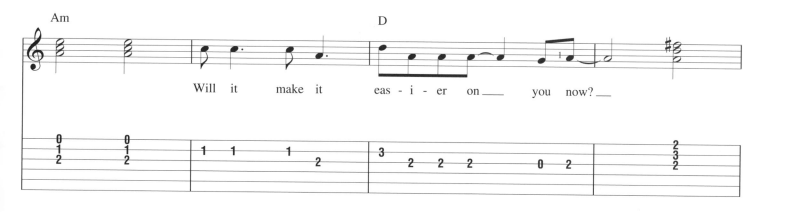

Will it make it eas - i - er on ___ you now? ___

You got some - one ___ to blame. ___   1. You said

Chorus

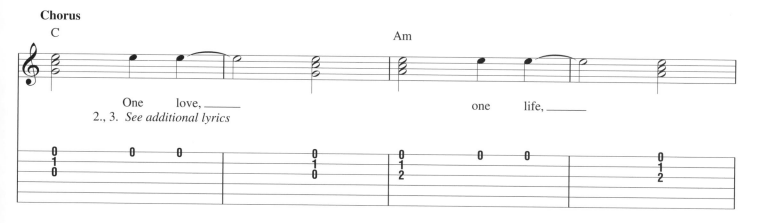

One love, ___   one life, ___
2., 3. *See additional lyrics*

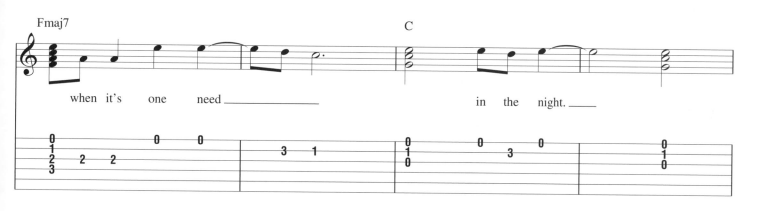

when it's one need ___   in the night. ___

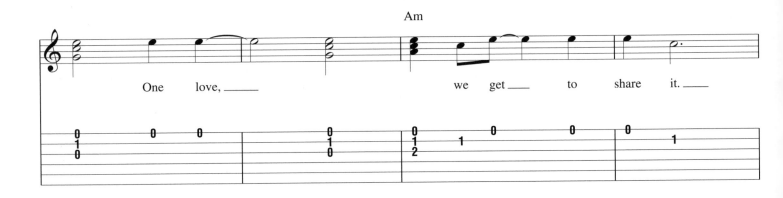

One love, _____ we get _____ to share it. _____

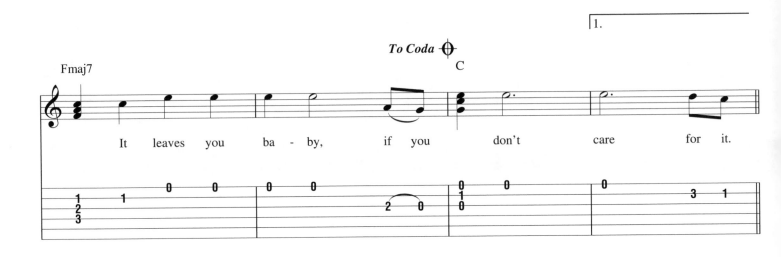

It leaves you ba - by, if you don't care for it. _____

Interlude

Interlude

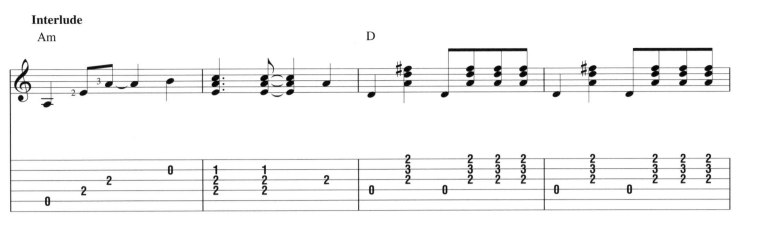

D.S. al Coda

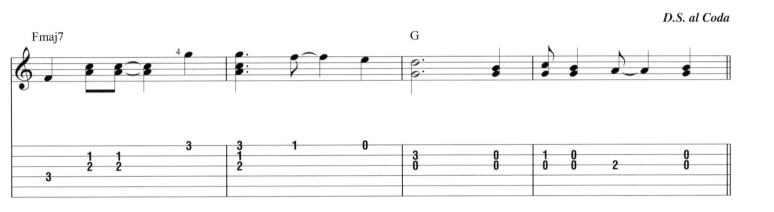

⊕ Coda

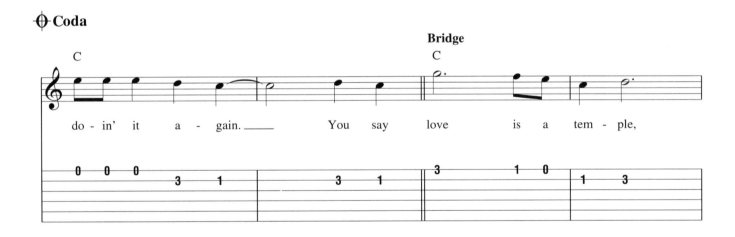

do - in' it a - gain. _____ You say love is a tem - ple,

Bridge

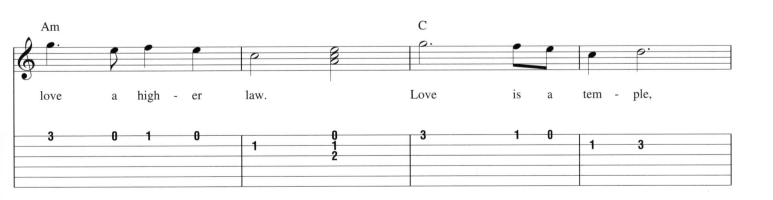

love a high - er law. Love is a tem - ple,

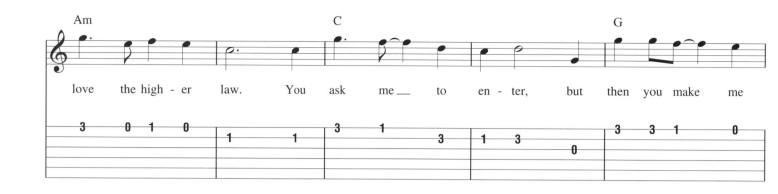

love the high - er law. You ask me _ to en - ter, but then you make me

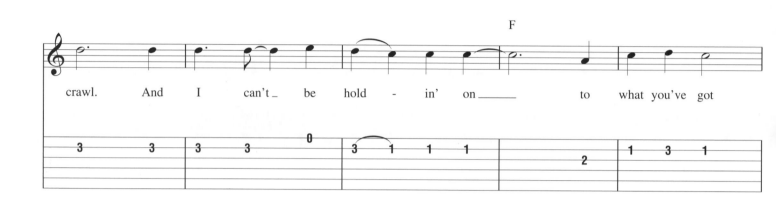

crawl. And I can't _ be hold - in' on _____ to what you've got

Outro-Chorus

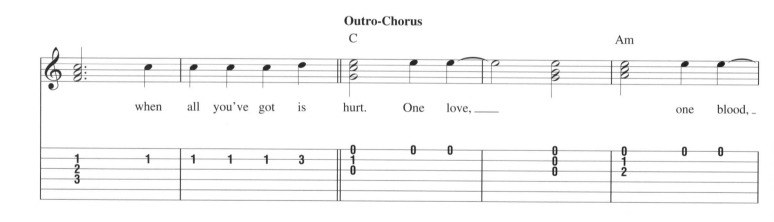

when all you've got is hurt. One love, ____ one blood, _

____ one life ____ you've got to do what you should. ___

One life, _____ but we're _____ not the same. We got to

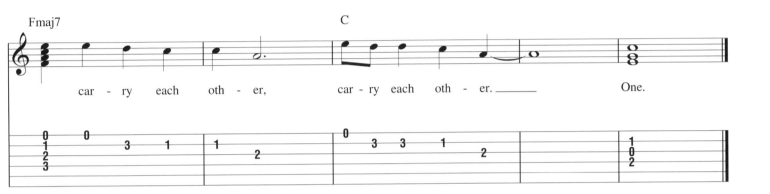

car - ry each oth - er, car - ry each oth - er. _____ One.

Additional Lyrics

2. Did I disappoint you
   Or leave a bad taste in your mouth?
   You act like you've never had love
   And you want me to go without.

Chorus 2. Well, it's too late tonight
   To drag the past out into the light.
   We're one, but we're not the same.
   We got to carry each other, carry each other. One.

3. Have you come here for forgiveness?
   Have you come to raise the dead?
   Have you come here to play Jesus
   To the lepers in your head?

Chorus 3. Did I ask too much, more than a lot?
   You gave me nothin', now it's all I got.
   We're one, but we are not the same.
   Where we hurt each other, and we're doin' it again.

One Headlight

Words and Music by Jakob Dylan

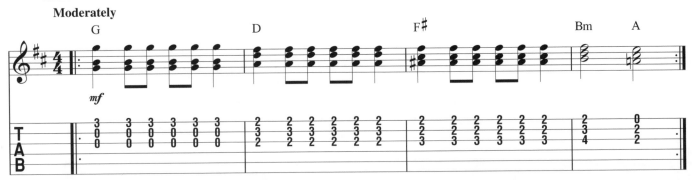

Strum Pattern: 2, 3
Pick Pattern: 3, 4

Intro
Moderately

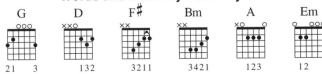

1. So long a - go, I don't re - mem - ber when, that's when they say I lost my on - ly
2. *See additional lyrics*

friend. ___ Well, they said she died eas - y of a bro - ken - heart dis - ease, as I

lis - tened through the cem - e - ter - y trees. ___

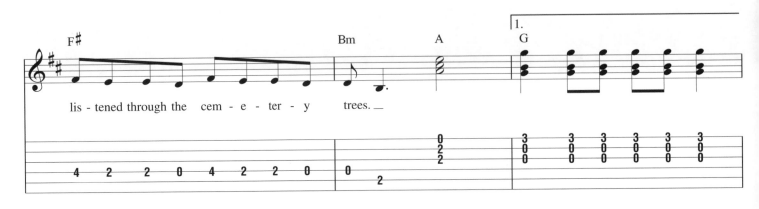

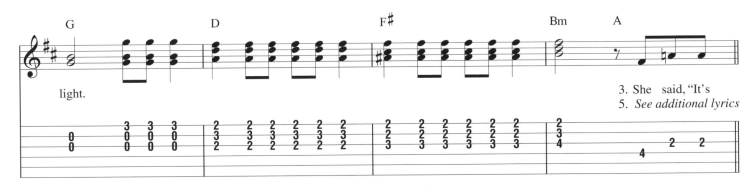

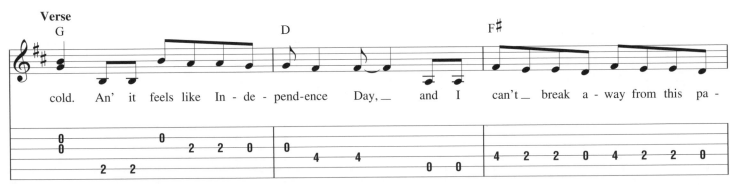

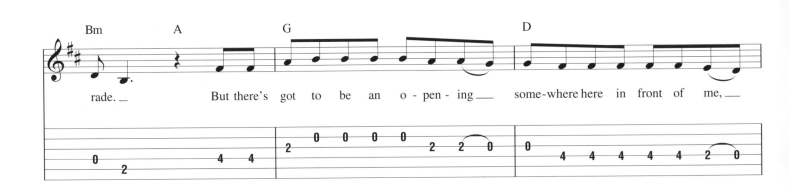

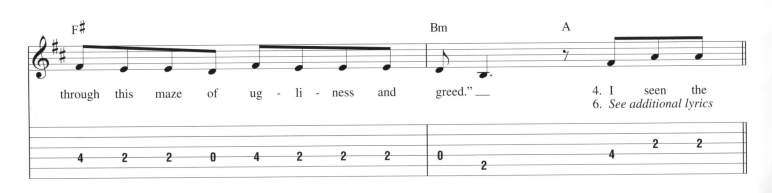

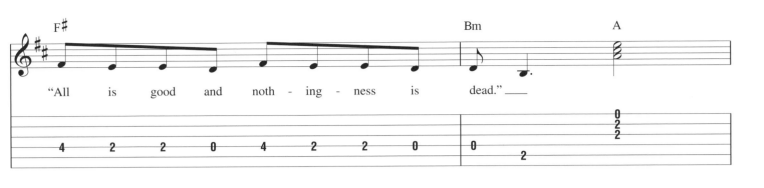

"All is good and noth - ing - ness is dead." ___

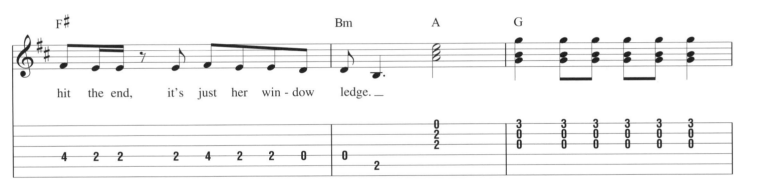

Run - ning till she's out of breath, she ran un - til there's noth - ing left. She

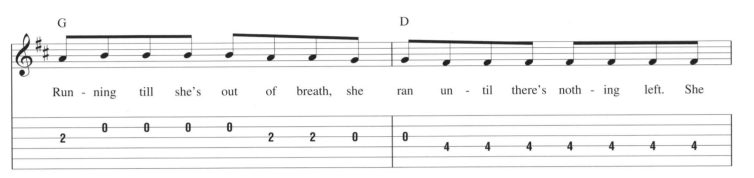

hit the end, it's just her win - dow ledge. __

1.

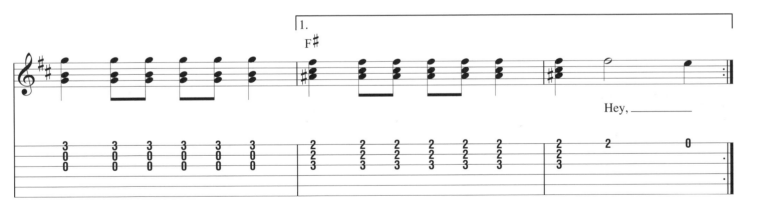

Hey, _____

2.

D.S. al Coda

Hey, hey, ___ hey, _____

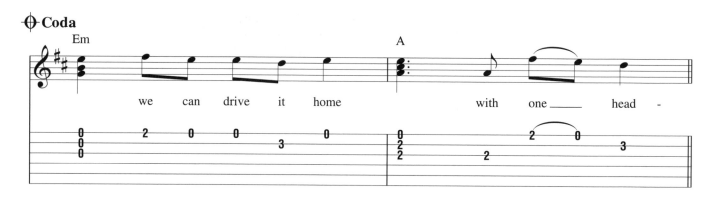

Coda

we can drive it home with one ___ head -

Outro

light. ___

Repeat and fade

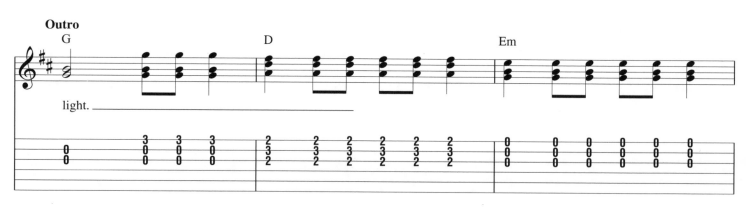

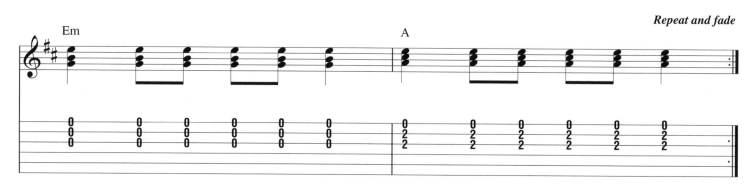

Additional Lyrics

2. I seen the sun comin' up at the funeral at dawn,
   Of the long broken arm of human law.
   Now, it always seemed such a waste,
   She always had a pretty face;
   I wondered why she hung around this place.

5. This place is old, and it feels just like a beat-up truck.
   I turn the engine, but the engine doesn't turn.
   It smells of cheap wine and cigarettes,
   This place is always such a mess;
   Sometimes I think I'd like to watch it burn.

6. Now I sit alone, and I feel just like somebody else.
   Man, I ain't changed, but I know I ain't the same.
   But somewhere here, in between these city walls of dying dreams,
   I think her death, it must be killing me.

The One I Love

Words and Music by Bill Berry, Peter Buck, Mike Mills, Michael Stipe

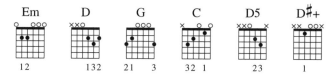

Strum Pattern: 1, 2
Pick Pattern: 2, 4

Intro
Moderately

Verse

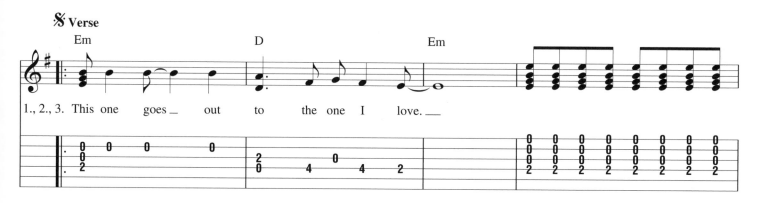

1., 2., 3. This one goes _ out to the one I love. _

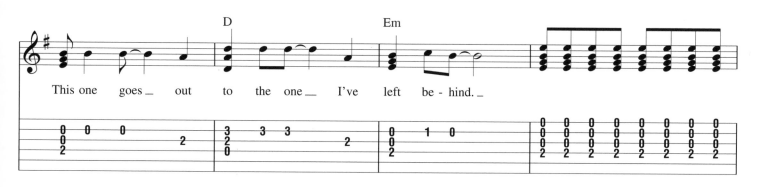

This one goes _ out to the one _ I've left be - hind. _

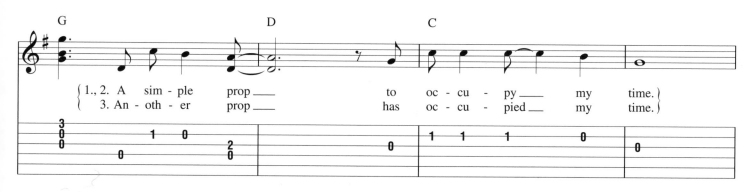

1., 2. A sim - ple prop ____ to oc - cu - py ____ my time.
3. An - oth - er prop ____ has oc - cu - pied ____ my time.

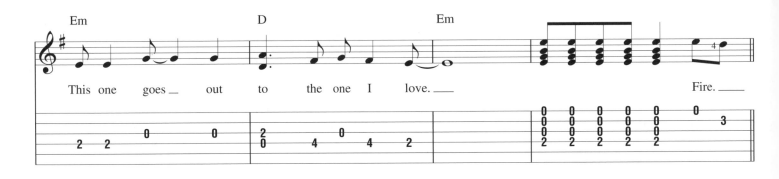

This one goes ___ out to the one I love. ___ Fire. ___

Chorus

Fire. ___

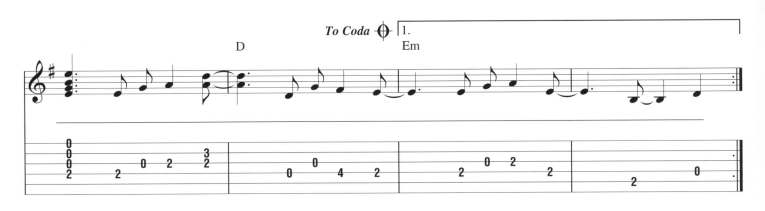

To Coda ⊕ | 1.

2.

Interlude

Coda

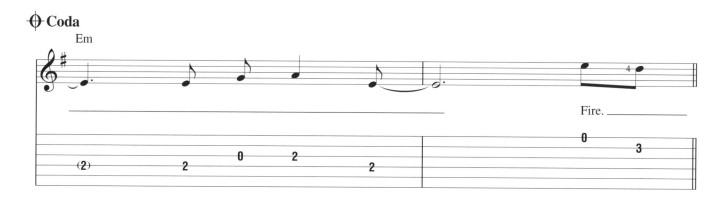

Outro-Chorus

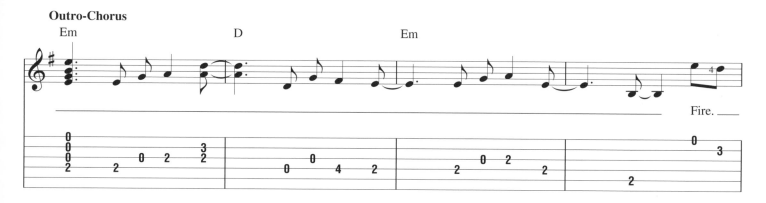

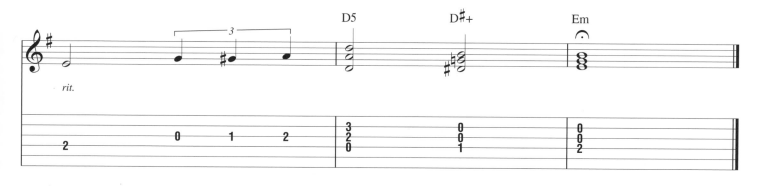

Only Happy When It Rains

Words and Music by Duke Erikson, Shirley Ann Manson, Steve Marker and Butch Vig

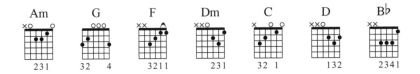

*Tune down 1/2 step:
(low to high) E♭–A♭–D♭–G♭–B♭–E♭

Strum Pattern: 2, 5
Pick Pattern: 3, 4

*Optional: To match recording, tune down 1/2 step.

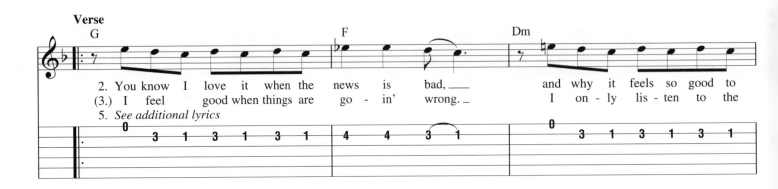

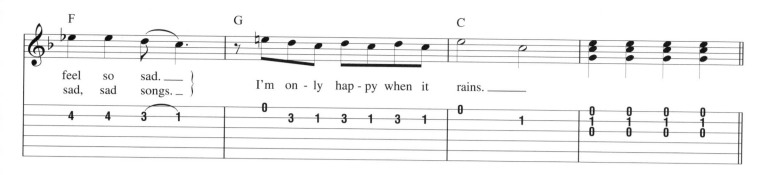

feel   so   sad. ___
sad,   sad   songs. _

I'm on - ly hap - py when it   rains. _____

Chorus

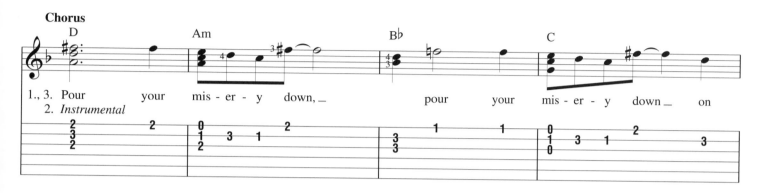

1., 3. Pour   your   mis - er - y   down, _   pour   your   mis - er - y   down _   on
2. *Instrumental*

To Coda

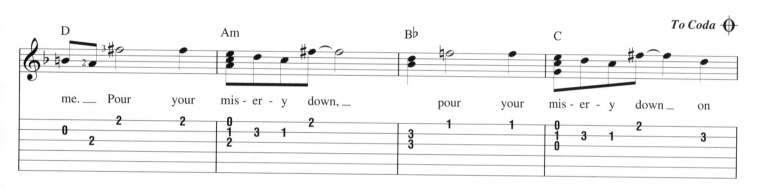

me. _   Pour   your   mis - er - y   down, _   pour   your   mis - er - y   down _   on

1.   **Verse**   2.   *D.S. al Coda*

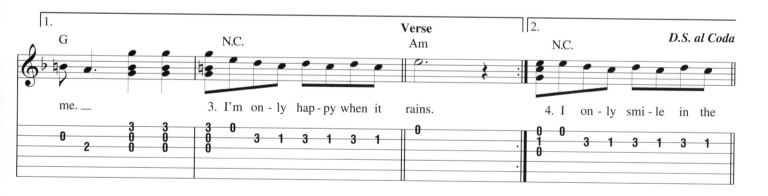

me. _   3. I'm on - ly hap - py when it   rains.   4. I   on - ly smi - le in the

 Coda

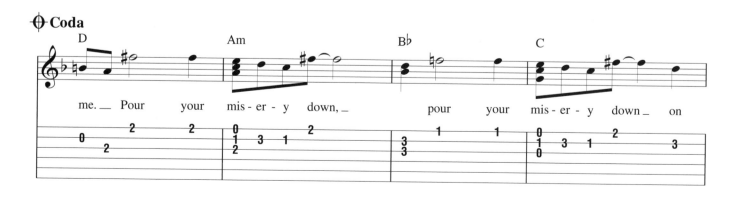

me. _   Pour   your   mis - er - y   down, _   pour   your   mis - er - y   down _   on

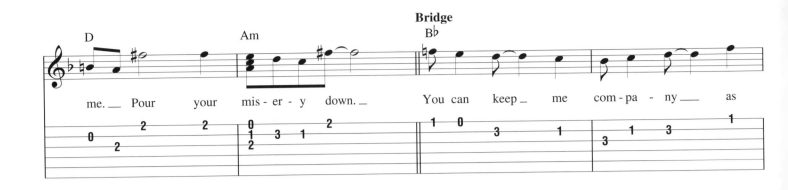

Bridge

me. __ Pour your mis - er - y down. __ You can keep __ me com - pa - ny __ as

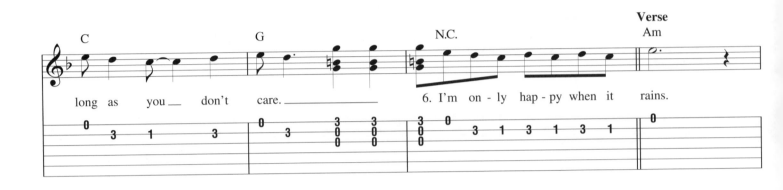

Verse

long as you __ don't care. _____ 6. I'm on - ly hap - py when it rains.

You wan - na hear a - bout my new ob - ses - sion? I'm rid - ing high up - on a deep de - pres - sion.

Outro-Chorus

Repeat and fade

I'm on - ly hap - py when it rains. __ Pour some mis - er - y down __ on me. I'm on - ly hap - py when it

Additional Lyrics

4. I only smile in the dark.
   My only comfort is the night gone black.
   I didn't accidentally tell you that.
   I'm only happy when it rains.

5. You'll get the message by the time I'm through.
   When I complain about me and you.
   I'm only happy when it rains.

Our Lips Are Sealed

Words and Music by Jane Wiedlin and Terry Hall

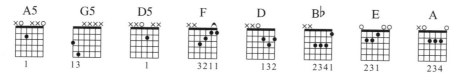

*Tune down 1/2 step:
(low to high) Eb–Ab–Db–Gb–Bb–Eb

Strum Pattern: 1
Pick Pattern: 2

Intro
Moderately fast

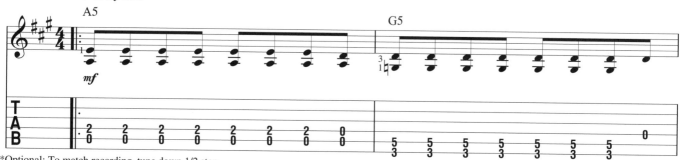

*Optional: To match recording, tune down 1/2 step.

1. Can you hear___

**Sung one octave higher throughout.

% Verse

(3.)___ them?___ They talk a-bout us.___ Tell-ing lies, well, that's no sur-prise.—Can you see___

2. *See additional lyrics*

___ them? See right through___ them?___ They have no shields, no se-crets to re-veal.

Pre-Chorus

Does-n't mat-ter   what they say   in the jeal-ous games   peo-ple play. __   Hey. _____

*Strum chords once and let ring in Pre-Chorus sections.

Chorus

To Coda ⊕ ⌐1.

__   Our lips are   sealed. __   2. There's a weap-

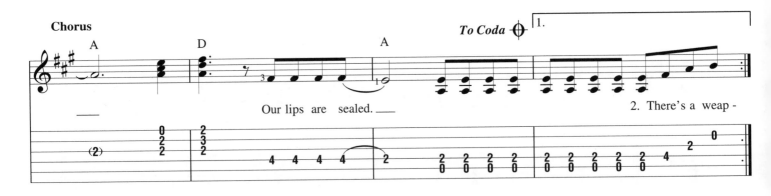

⌐2.

Pre-Chorus

Pay no mind   to   what they say.   Does-n't mat-ter   an - y   way. __   Hey. _____

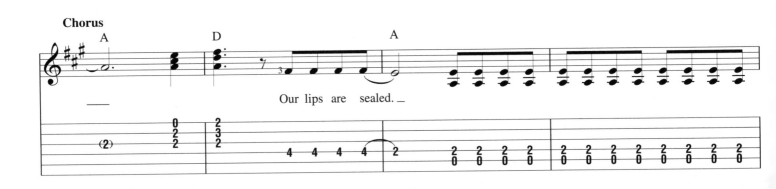

Chorus

__   Our lips are   sealed. __

Interlude

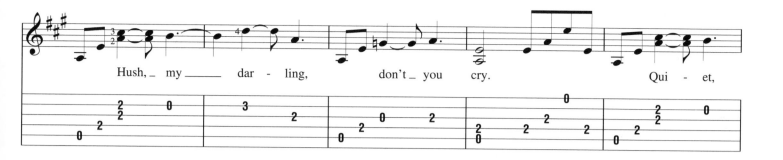

Hush, _ my _____ dar - ling, don't _ you cry. Qui - et,

D.S. al Coda

*A

an - gel, _ for-get their lies. _ 3. Can you hear _

*Let chord ring.

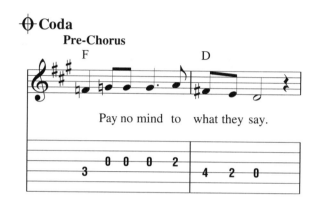

Coda

Pre-Chorus

F   D

Pay no mind to what they say.

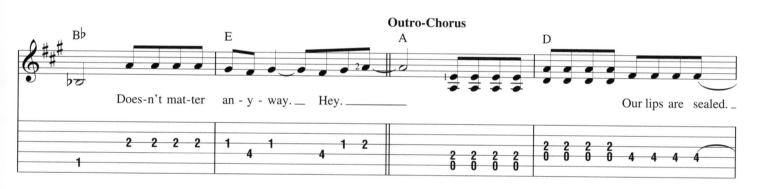

Outro-Chorus

Bb   E   A   D

Does-n't mat-ter an - y - way. _ Hey. _____ Our lips are sealed. _

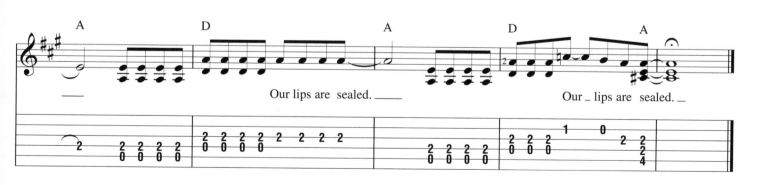

A   D   A   D   A

_ Our lips are sealed. _____ Our _ lips are sealed. _

Additional Lyrics

2. There's a weapon that we must use in our defense.
   Silence when you look at them, look right through them.
   That's when they'll disappear, that's when we'll be feared.

Papa Don't Preach

Words and Music by Brian Elliot

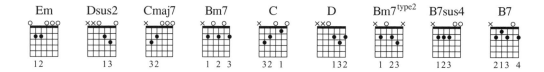

*Capo I

Strum Pattern: 3, 6
Pick Pattern: 2, 4

Verse
Moderately

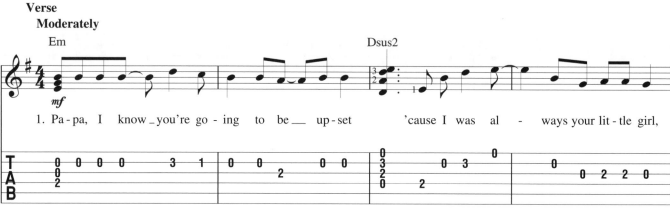

*Optional: To match recording, place capo at 1st fret.

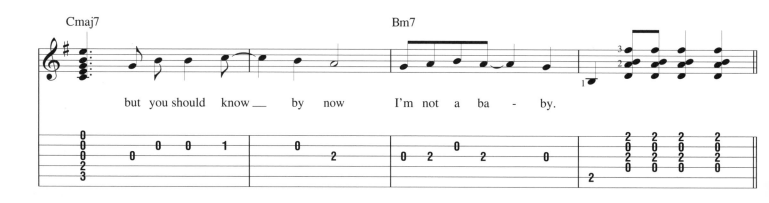

% Verse

I may be young_ at heart,_ but I know what I'm say - ing.

Pre-Chorus

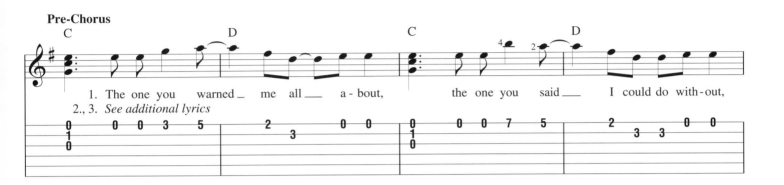

1. The one you warned_ me all_ a - bout, the one you said_ I could do with-out,
2., 3. *See additional lyrics*

To Coda 1

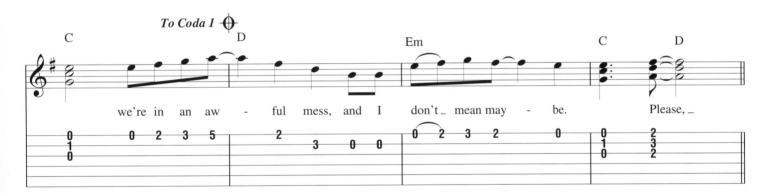

we're in an aw - ful mess, and I don't_ mean may - be. Please,_

Chorus

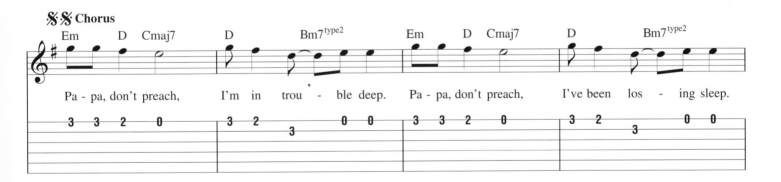

Pa-pa, don't preach, I'm in trou - ble deep. Pa-pa, don't preach, I've been los - ing sleep.

To Coda 2

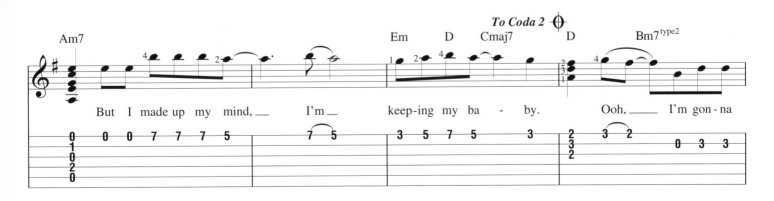

But I made up my mind,_ I'm_ keep-ing my ba - by. Ooh,_ I'm gon - na

Additional Lyrics

3. He says that he's going to marry me.
We can raise a little family.
Maybe we'll be alright, it's a sacrifice.

Pre-Chorus 2. But my friends keep tellin' me to give it up,
Saying I'm too young, I ought a live it up.
What I need right now is some good advice.
Please...

Pre-Chorus 3. Daddy, Daddy, if you could only see
Just how good he's been treating me,
You'd give us your blessing right now,
'Cause we are in love, we are in love.
So please...

Proud Mary

Words and Music by John Fogerty

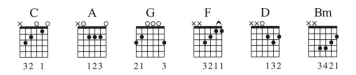

Strum Pattern: 1
Pick Pattern: 2

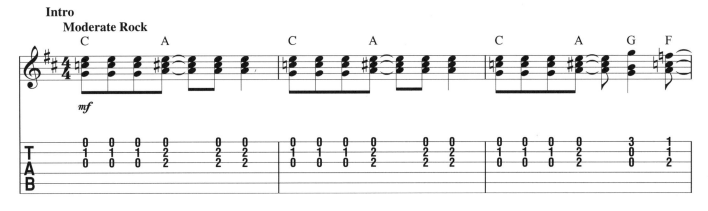

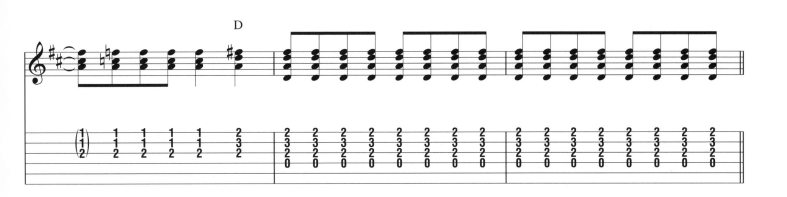

1. Left a good job in the ci-ty, work-in' for the man ev-'ry
2., 4. *See additional lyrics*
3. *Instrumental*

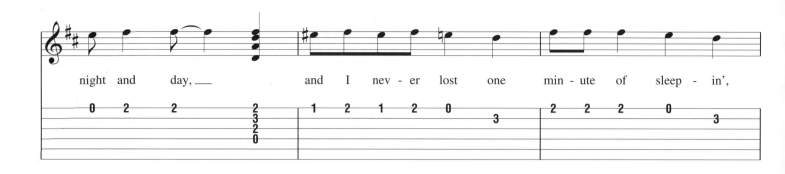

night and day, _____ and I nev-er lost one min-ute of sleep-in',

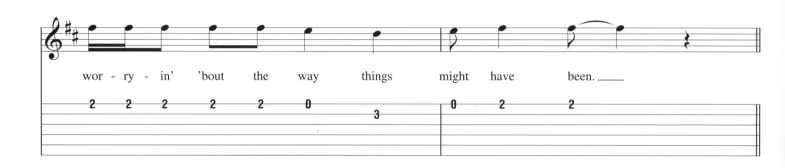

wor - ry - in' 'bout the way things might have been. ____

Chorus

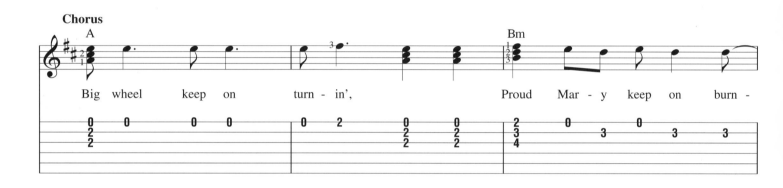

Big wheel keep on turn - in', Proud Mar - y keep on burn-

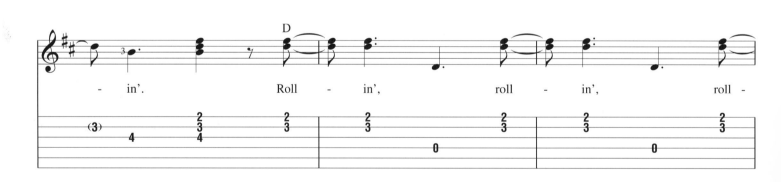

- in'. Roll - in', roll - in', roll-

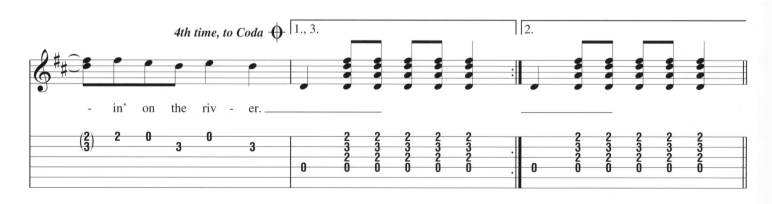

- in' on the riv - er. _____

4th time, to Coda

Interlude

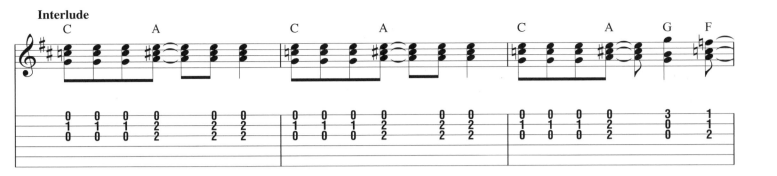

D.S. al Coda
(take repeat)

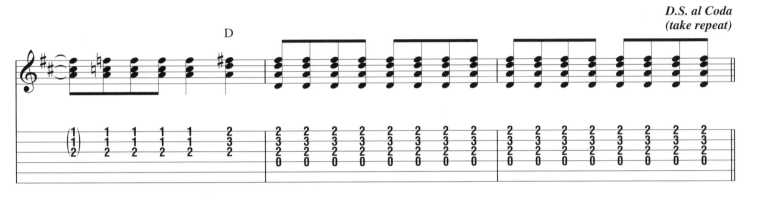

Coda

Outro

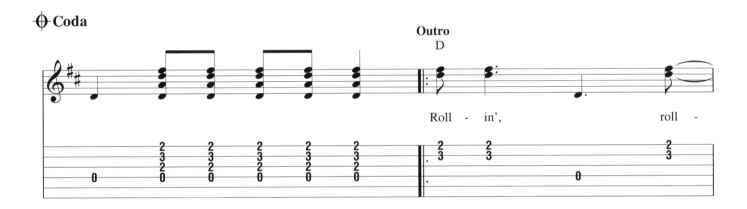

Roll - in', roll -

Repeat and fade

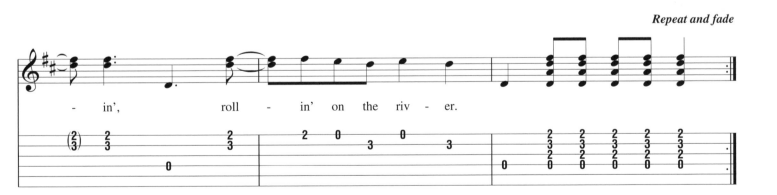

- in', roll - in' on the riv - er.

Additional Lyrics

2. Cleaned a lot of plates in Memphis,
   Pumped a lot of pain in New Orleans,
   But I never saw the good side of the city,
   Until I hitched a ride on a river boat queen.

4. If you come down to the river,
   Bet you gonna find some people who live.
   You don't have to worry 'cause you have no money,
   People on the river are happy to give.

Photograph

Words and Music by Robert Lange, Lawrence Elliott, Stephen Clark, Peter Willis and Richard Savage

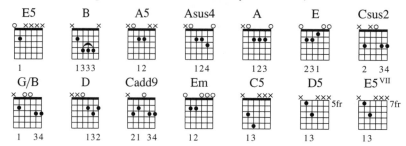

Strum Pattern: 1, 2
Pick Pattern: 2, 4

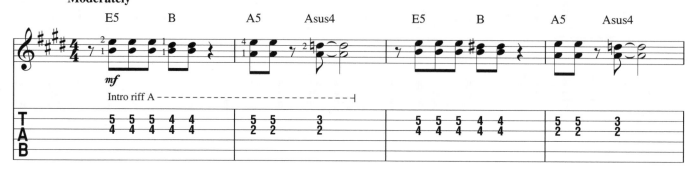

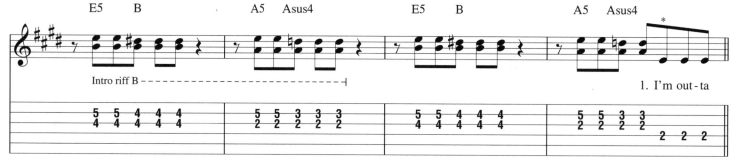

*Sung one octave higher throughout.

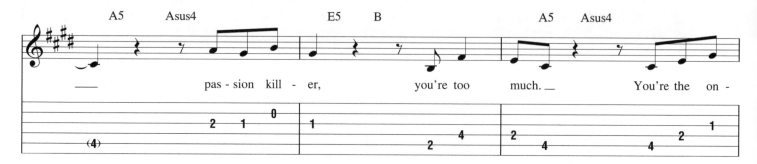

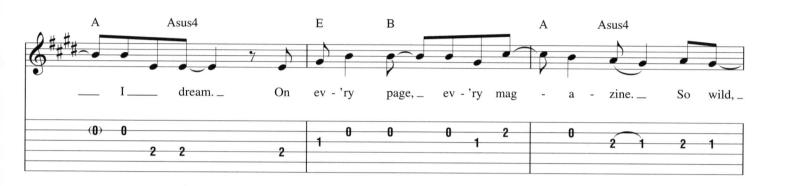

𝄋 Pre-Chorus

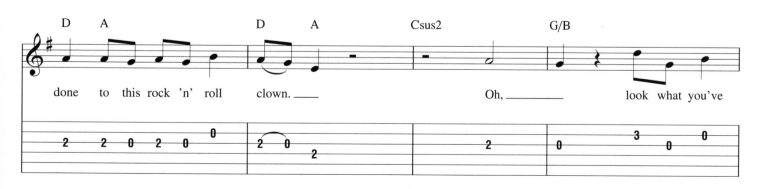

Chorus

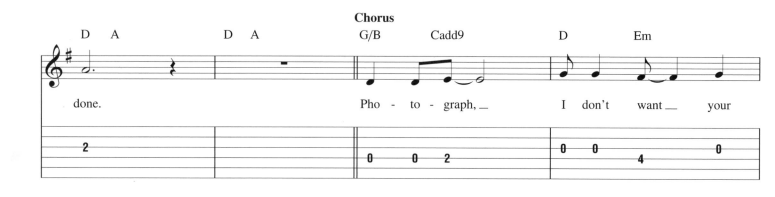

done.

Pho - to - graph, __ I don't want __ your

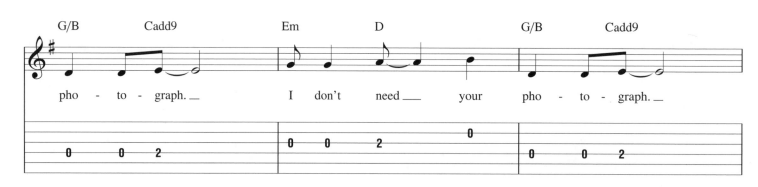

pho - to - graph. __ I don't need __ your pho - to - graph. __

To Coda ⊕ | 1.

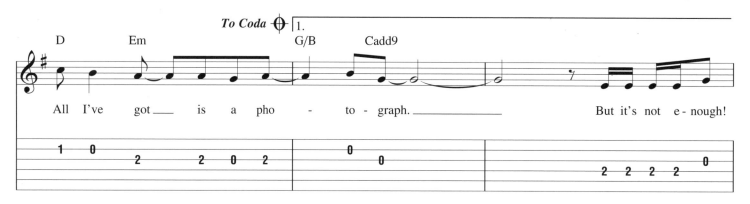

All I've got __ is a pho - to - graph. _____ But it's not e - nough!

| 2.

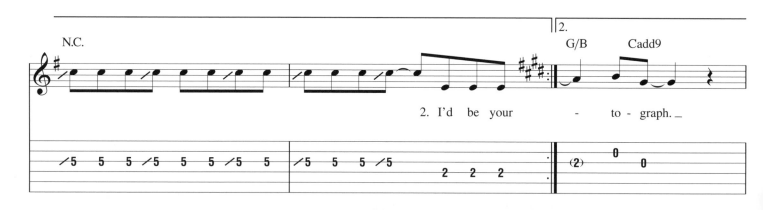

2. I'd be your - to - graph. __

Interlude

w/ Intro riff A (2 times)

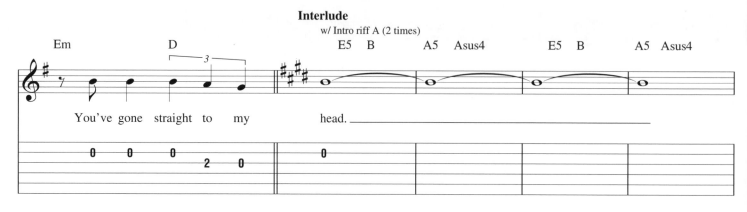

You've gone straight to my head. _____

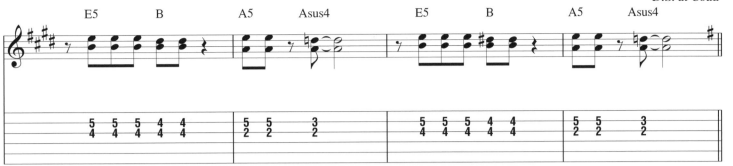

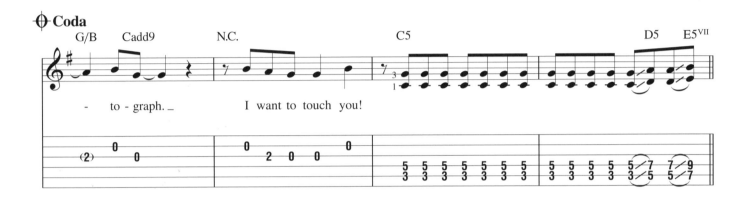

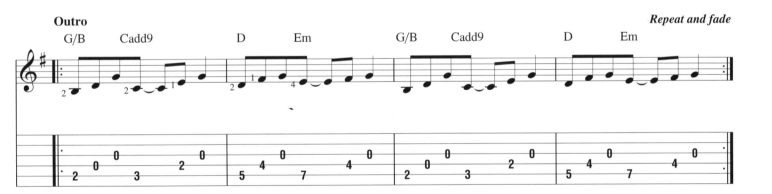

Additional Lyrics

2. I'd be your lover, if you were there.
   Put your hurt on me, if you dare.
   Such a woman, you got style.
   You make ev'ry man feel like a child.
   You got some kind a hold on me.
   You're all wrapped up in mystery.
   So wild, so free, so far from me.
   You're all I want, my fantasy.

Respect

Words and Music by Otis Redding

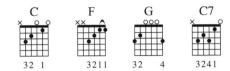

Strum Pattern: 5
Pick Pattern: 1

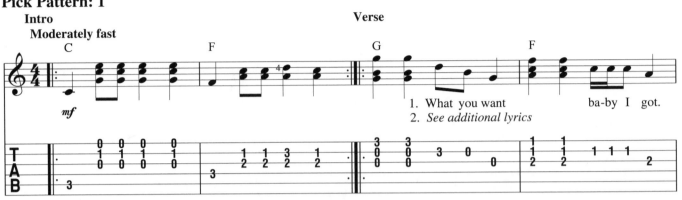

in re - turn, hon - ey, is to give me my pro-per re - spect when you get

home. __ Yeah, ba - by, when you get home.

Chorus

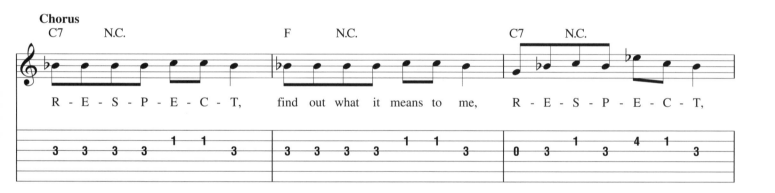

R - E - S - P - E - C - T, find out what it means to me, R - E - S - P - E - C - T,

Outro

Repeat and fade

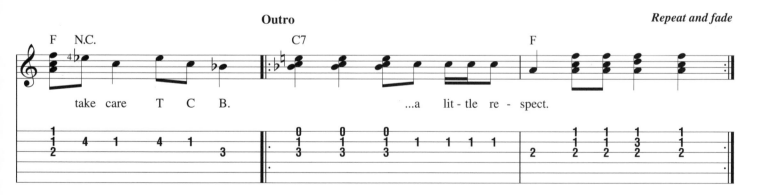

take care T C B. ...a lit - tle re - spect.

Additional Lyrics

2. I ain't gonna do you wrong
While you gone.
I ain't gonna do you wrong
'Cause I don't wanna.
All I'm askin' is for a little respect,
When you come home.
Baby, when you come home,
Respect.

4. Ooh, your kisses,
Sweeter than honey,
But guess what,
So here's my money.
All I want you to do for me
Is give me some here when you get home.
Yeah, baby, when you get home.

Rock with You

Words and Music by Rod Temperton

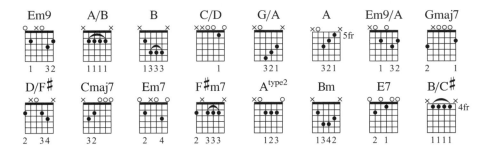

*Tune down 1/2 step:
(low to high) E♭–A♭–D♭–G♭–B♭–E♭

Strum Pattern: 6
Pick Pattern: 4

Intro
Moderately fast

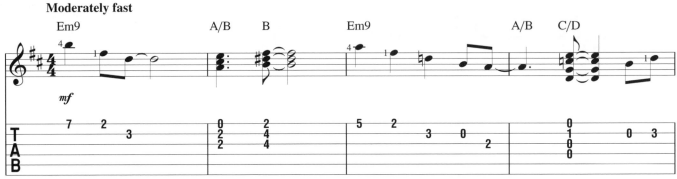

*Optional: To match recording, tune down 1/2 step.

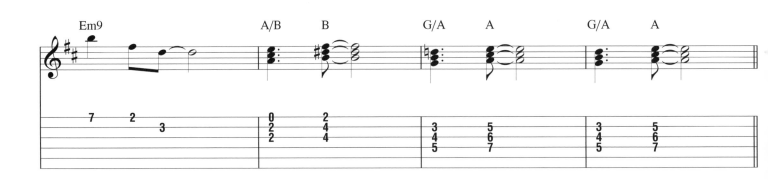

Verse

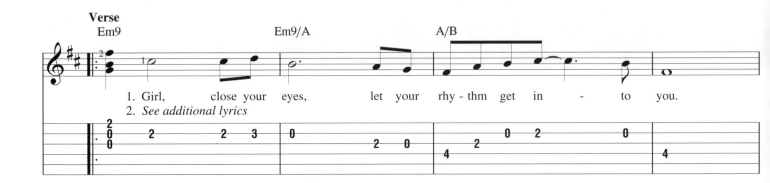

1. Girl, close your eyes, let your rhy-thm get in-to you.
2. *See additional lyrics*

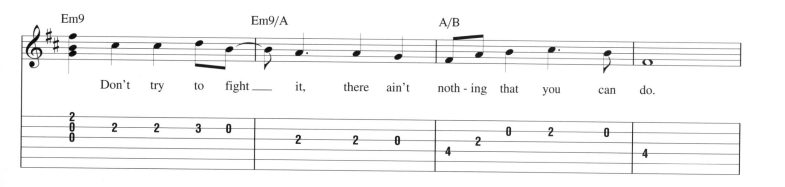

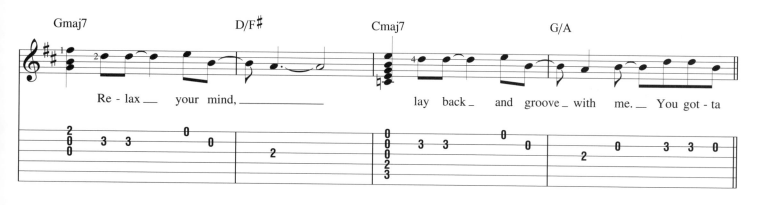

Pre-Chorus

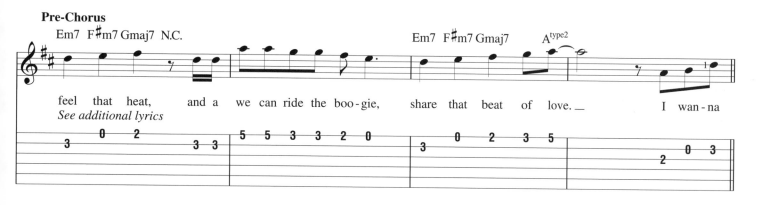

Chorus

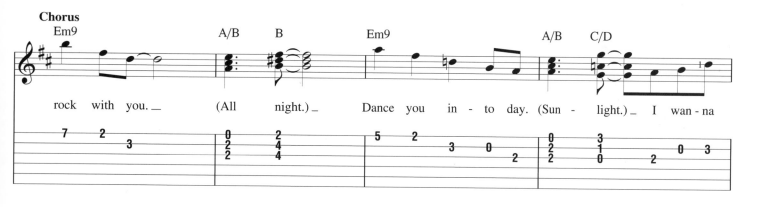

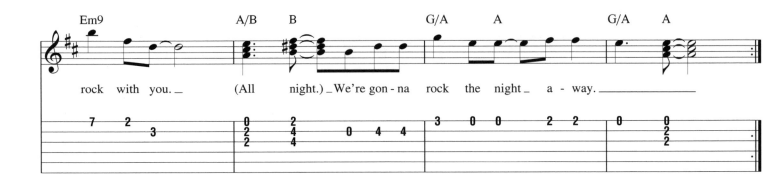

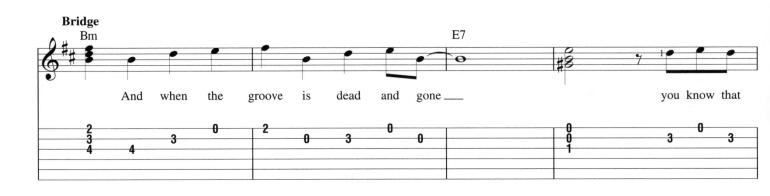

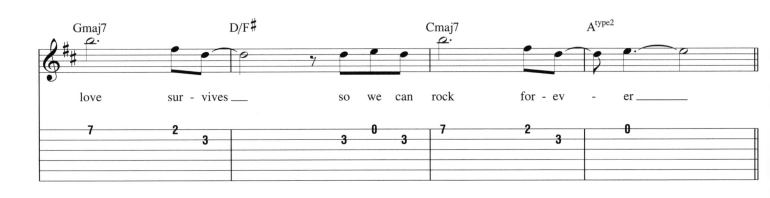

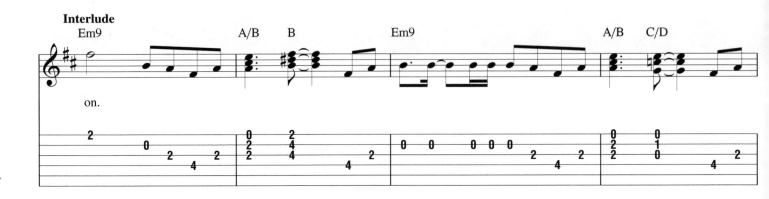

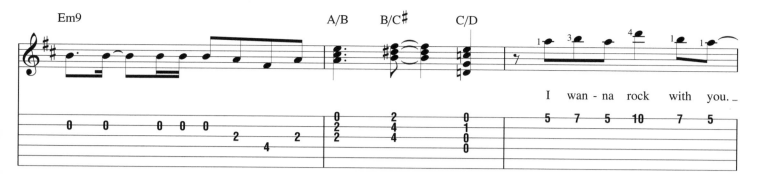

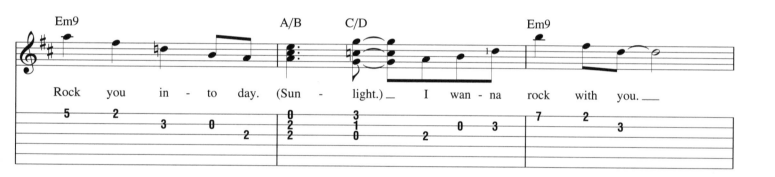

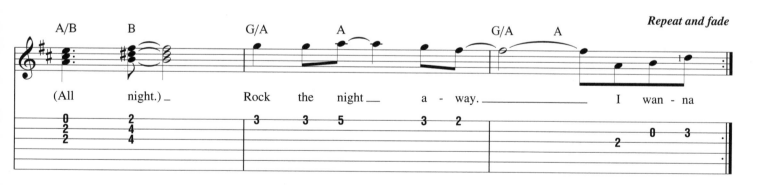

Additional Lyrics

2. Out on the floor
   There ain't there nobody but us.
   Girl, when you dance
   There's a magic that must be love.
   Just take it slow,
   'Cause we've got so far to go.

Pre-Chorus When you feel that heat,
   And a we're gonna ride the boogie,
   Share that beat of love.

She Drives Me Crazy

Words and Music by David Steele and Roland Gift

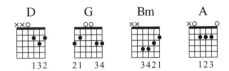

Strum Pattern: 6, 4
Pick Pattern: 5

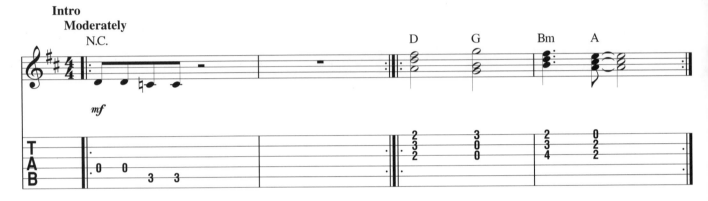

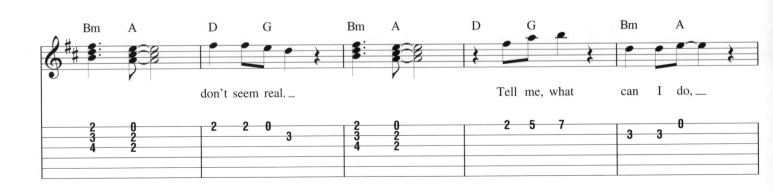

'cause we're run - ning   out of time? _   Won't you ev - er   set me free? _____

Chorus

This wait-ing 'round's   kill-ing me. _   She drives me cra-zy   like no one else. _

She drives me cra-zy   and   I can't help _ my-self. _____

Interlude

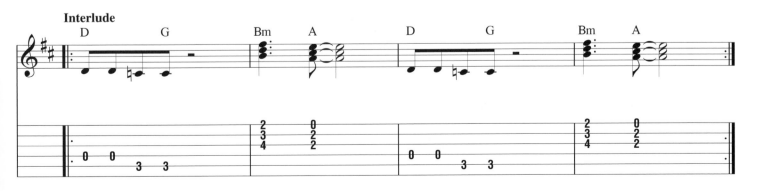

Verse

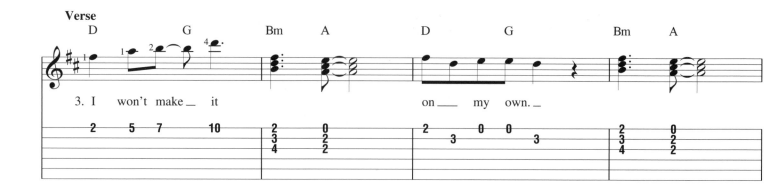

3. I won't make __ it on __ my own. __

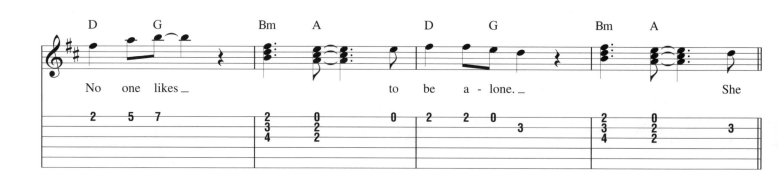

No one likes __ to be a - lone. __ She

Outro-Chorus

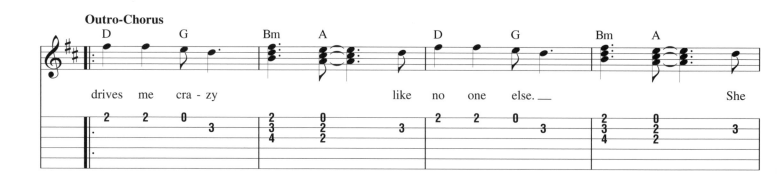

drives me cra - zy like no one else. __ She

Repeat and fade

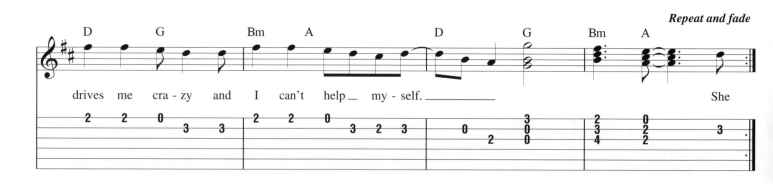

drives me cra - zy and I can't help __ my - self. _____ She

Additional Lyrics

2. I can't get any rest.
   People say I'm obsessed.
   Ev'rything that's serious lasts,
   But to me there's no surprise.
   What I had for you was true.
   Things go wrong, they always do.

Smells Like Teen Spirit

Words and Music by Kurt Cobain, Krist Novoselic and Dave Grohl

Additional Lyrics

2. I'm worse at what I do best,
   And for this gift I feel blessed.
   Our little group has always been
   And always will until the end.

3. And I forget just why I taste.
   Oh yeah, I guess it makes me smile.
   I found it hard, it was hard to find.
   Oh, well, whatever, nevermind.

Smooth

Words by Rob Thomas
Music by Rob Thomas and Itaal Shur

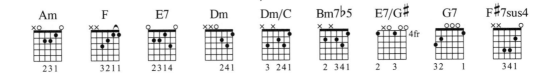

Strum Pattern: 2, 3
Pick Pattern: 3, 4

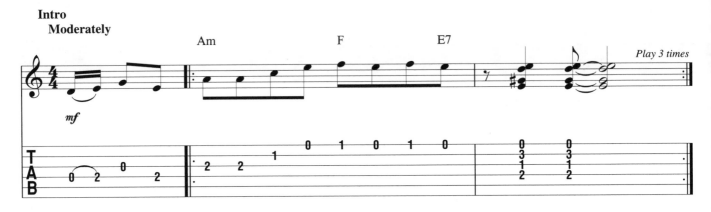

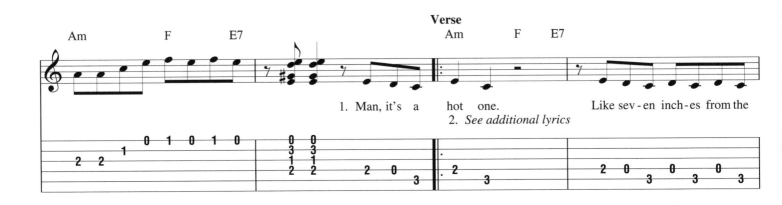

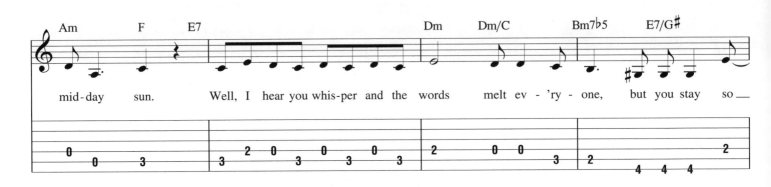

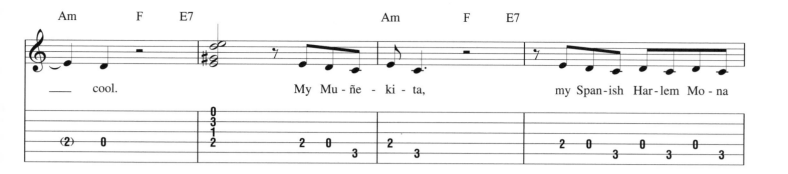

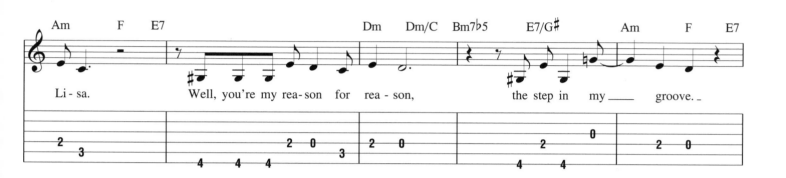

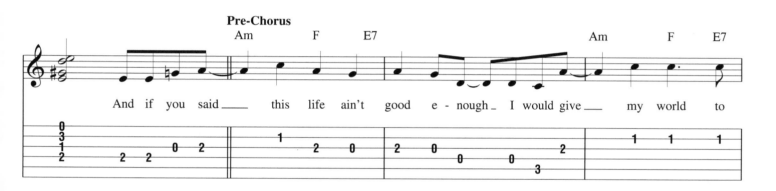

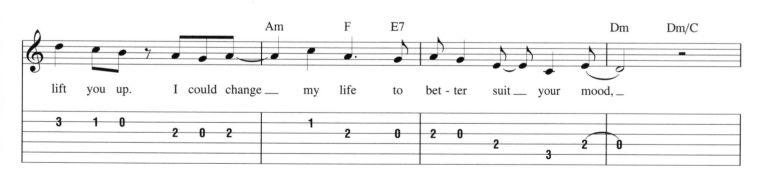

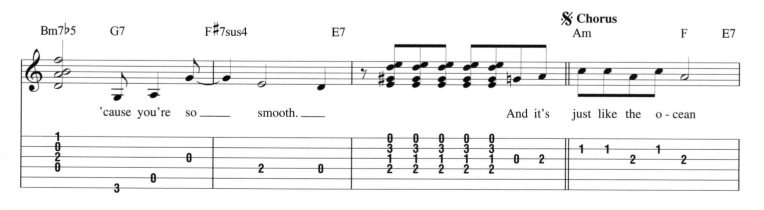

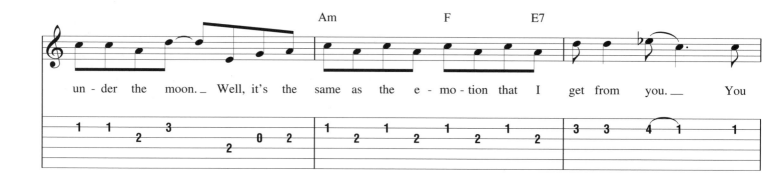

un - der the moon. __ Well, it's the same as the e - mo - tion that I get from you. __ You

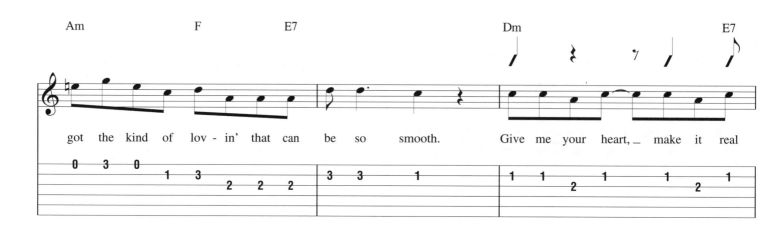

got the kind of lov - in' that can be so smooth. Give me your heart, __ make it real

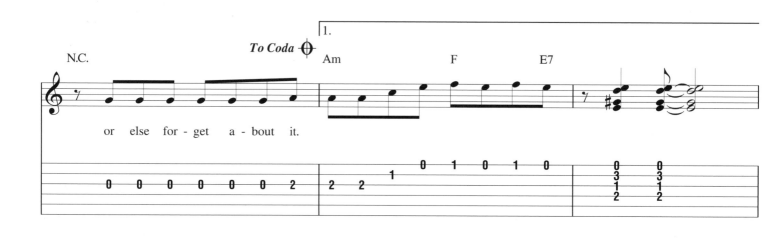

or else for - get a - bout it.

2. Well, I'll tell you

Guitar Solo

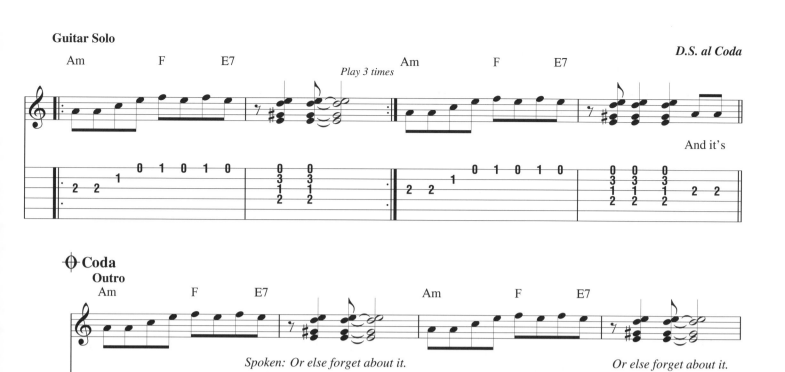

$\oint$ Coda
Outro

Additional Lyrics

2. Well, I'll tell you one thing,
   If you would leave it'd be a crying shame.
   In ev'ry breath and ev'ry word,
   I hear your name calling me out.
   Out from the barrio,
   You hear my rhythm on your radio.
   You feel the turning of the world so soft and slow,
   Turning me 'round and 'round.

Stayin' Alive

from the Motion Picture SATURDAY NIGHT FEVER

Words and Music by Robin Gibb, Maurice Gibb and Barry Gibb

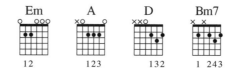

Strum Pattern: 2
Pick Pattern: 4

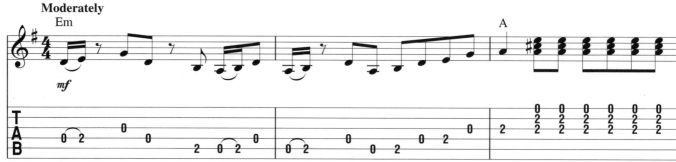

1. Well, you can

1. tell by the way I use my walk, I'm a wom-an's man, no time to talk.
2. *See additional lyrics*

Mu-sic loud and wom-en warm. I've been kicked a-round since I was born. And now it's

Pre-Chorus

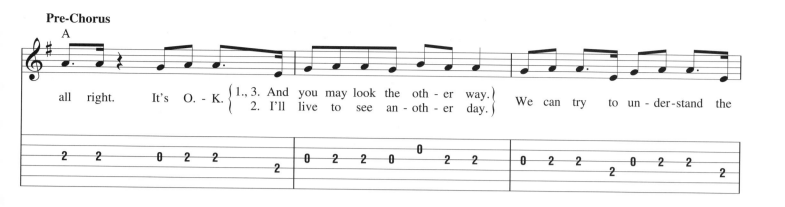

all right. It's O. - K. { 1., 3. And you may look the oth - er way.
{ 2. I'll live to see an - oth - er day. } We can try to un - der-stand the

Chorus

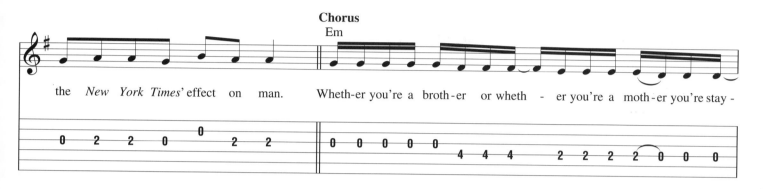

the *New York Times'* effect on man. Wheth-er you're a broth-er or wheth - er you're a moth-er you're stay -

- in' a - live, stay-in' a - live. Feel the cit - y break in' and ev - 'ry-bod-y shak-in' and we're

stay - in' a - live, stay - in' a - live. Ah, ha, ha, ha,

stay - in' a - live, stay - in' a - live. Ah, ha, ha, ha,

stay - in' a - live.

1.

Bm7   Em

Oh, when you   walk.   2. Well now,   I

2.

Bm7   Em

Bridge

A

Life go - in' no - where. _____   Some - bod - y help   me. _____

Em

Some - bod - y help __ me, yeah. _____

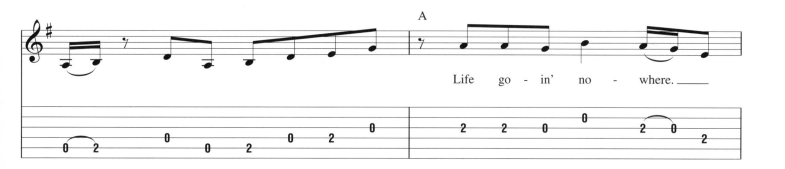

Life go - in' no - where. ____

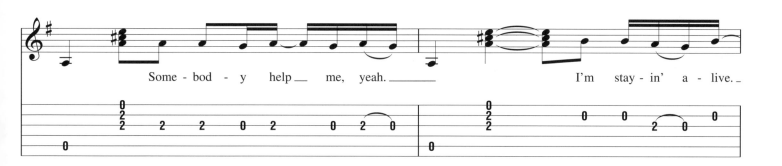

Some - bod - y help ___ me, yeah. _____ I'm stay - in' a - live. _

D.S. al Coda

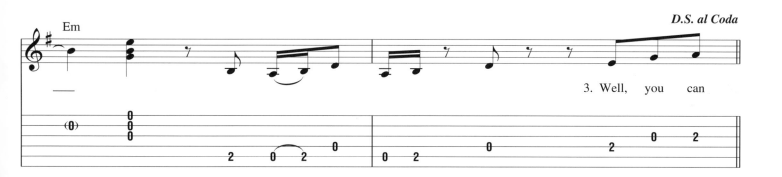

Em

____ 3. Well, you can

✛ **Coda**

Bm7   Em

_____ Oh, yeah. _

Outro

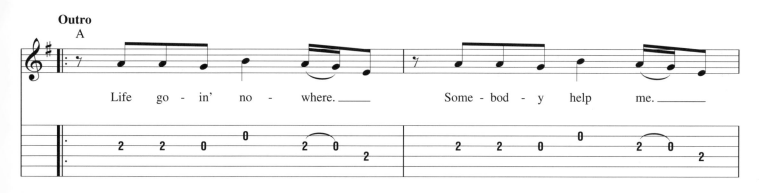

A

Life go - in' no - where. _____ Some - bod - y help me. _____

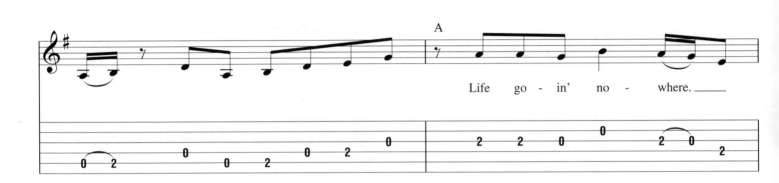

Play 4 times and fade

Additional Lyrics

2. Well now, I get low, and I get high,
And if I can't get either, I really try.
Got the wings of heaven on my shoes.
I'm a dancin' man, and I just can't lose.

Surrender

Words and Music by Rick Nielsen

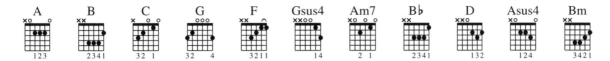

Strum Pattern: 2
Pick Pattern: 1

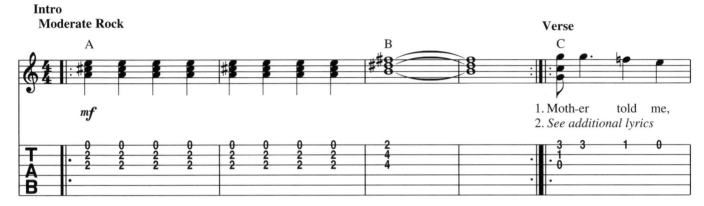

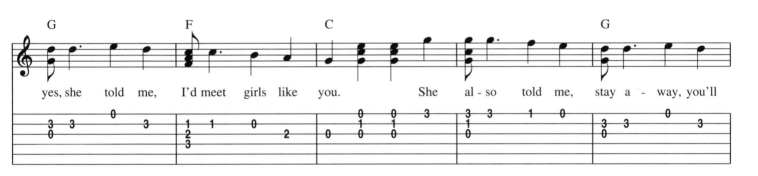

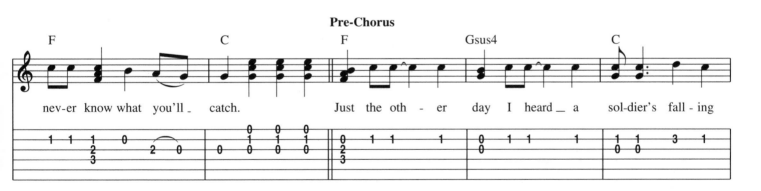

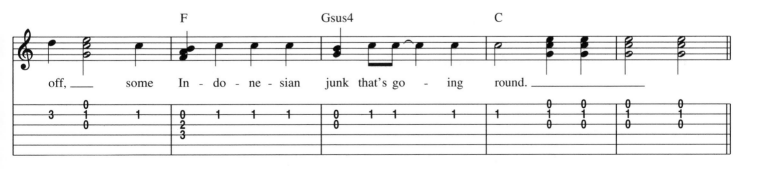

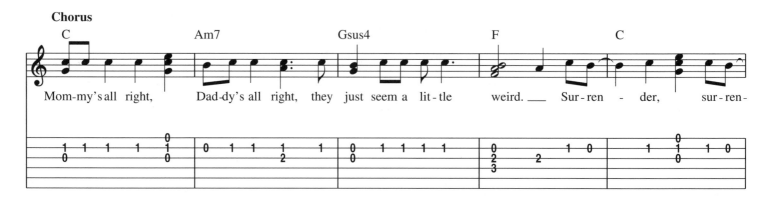

Chorus

Mom-my's all right, Dad-dy's all right, they just seem a lit-tle weird. ___ Sur-ren - der, sur-ren-

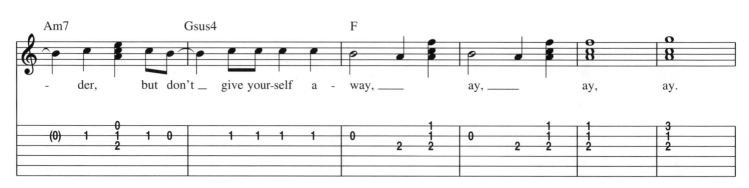

- der, but don't __ give your-self a - way, ___ ay, ___ ay, ay.

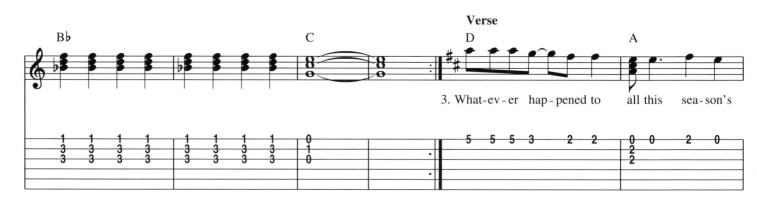

Verse

3. What-ev - er hap - pened to all this sea-son's

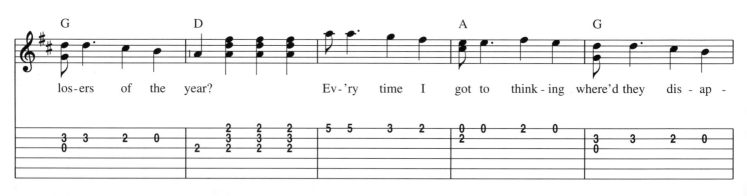

los-ers of the year? Ev-'ry time I got to think-ing where'd they dis-ap-

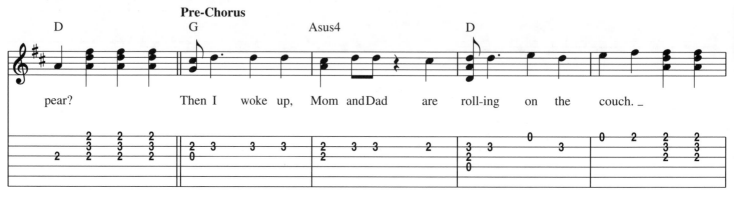

Pre-Chorus

pear? Then I woke up, Mom and Dad are roll-ing on the couch. _

Additional Lyrics

2. Father says, "Your mother's right, she's really up on things.
   Before we married, Mommy served in the WACS in the Philippines.
   Now I had heard the WACS recruited old maids for the war.
   But Mommy isn't one of those, I've known her all these years."

Superstition

Words and Music by Stevie Wonder

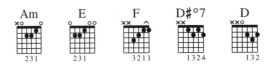

Am   E   F   D#°7   D

Strum Pattern: 5
Pick Pattern: 1

Intro
Moderately

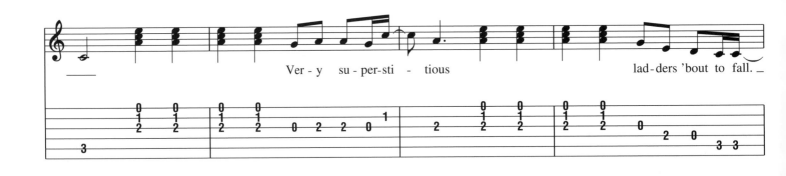

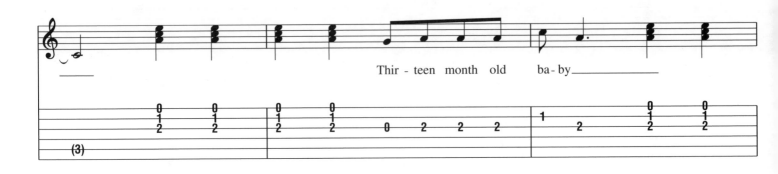

broke the look - ing glass. _____ Sev - en years of bad _

_____ luck, _____ the good things in your past. _

Chorus

E   F   E   D#°7

When you be - lieve ___ in things that you don't un - der - stand ___ then you suf - fer. _

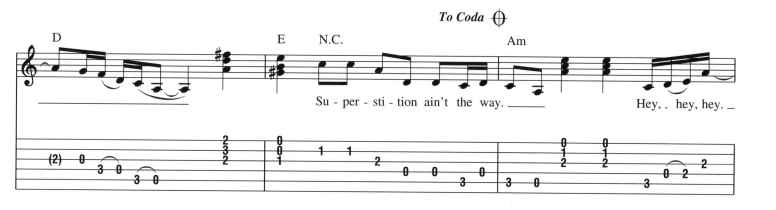

To Coda ⊕

D   E   N.C.   Am

_____ Su - per - sti - tion ain't the way. _____ Hey, _ hey, hey. _

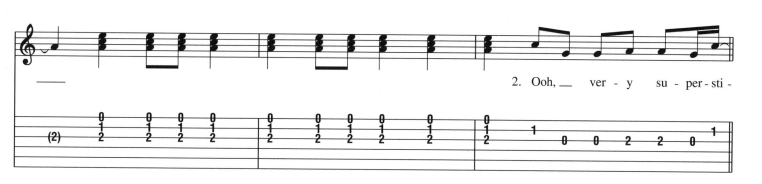

_____ 2. Ooh, ___ ver - y su - per - sti -

305

Verse

Am

- tious, _____ wash your face and hands. _

Rid me of the pro - blem, do all _ that you

can. Keep me in a day - dream _____

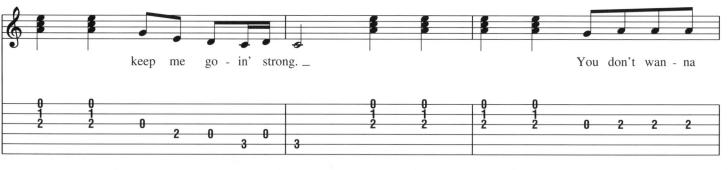

keep me go - in' strong. _ You don't wan - na

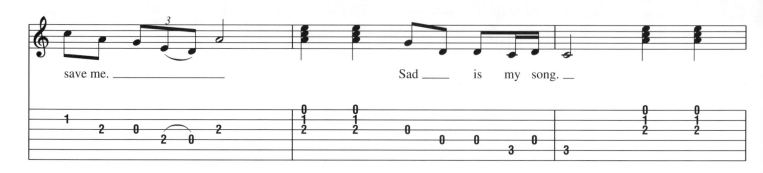

save me. _____ Sad __ is my song. _

Additional Lyrics

3. Very superstitious, nothing more to say.
Very superstitious, the devil's on his way.
Thirteen month old baby broke the looking glass.
Seven years of bad luck, the good things in your past.

Sweet Child o' Mine

Words and Music by W. Axl Rose, Slash, Izzy Stradlin', Duff McKagan and Steven Adler

Strum Pattern: 6
Pick Pattern: 4, 5

Intro
Moderate Rock

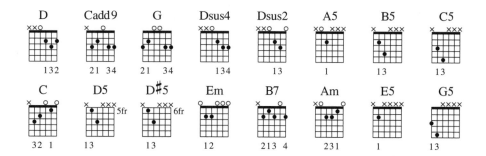

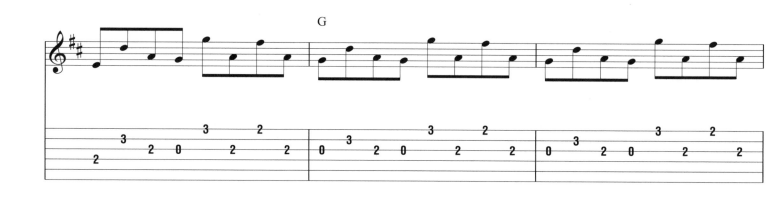

Verse

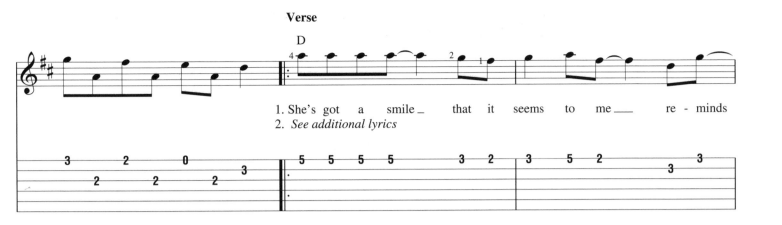

1. She's got a smile _ that it seems to me _ re - minds
2. *See additional lyrics*

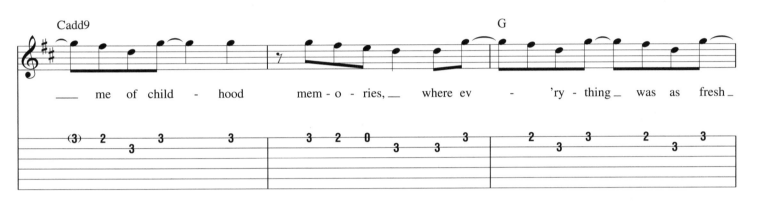

_ me of child - hood mem - o - ries, _ where ev - 'ry - thing _ was as fresh _

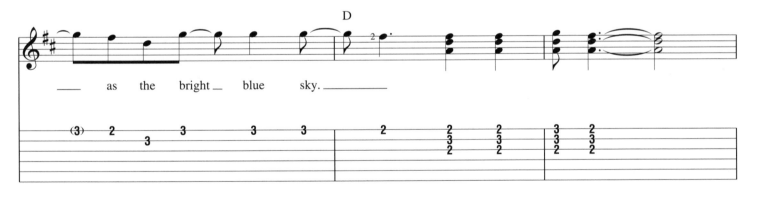

_ as the bright _ blue sky. _____

Now and then _ when I see her face _ she takes me a - way _ to that

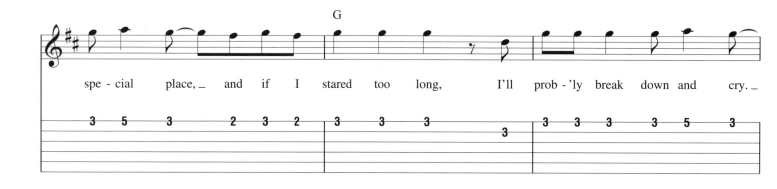

spe - cial place, _ and if I stared too long, I'll prob - 'ly break down and cry. _

%. **Chorus**

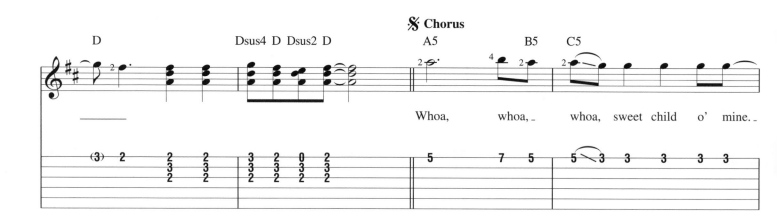

_____ Whoa, whoa, _ whoa, sweet child o' mine. _

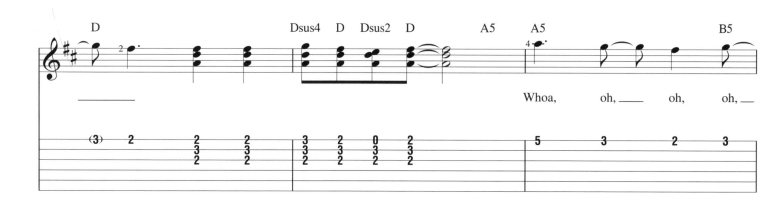

_____ Whoa, oh, ___ oh, oh, _

To Coda ⊕

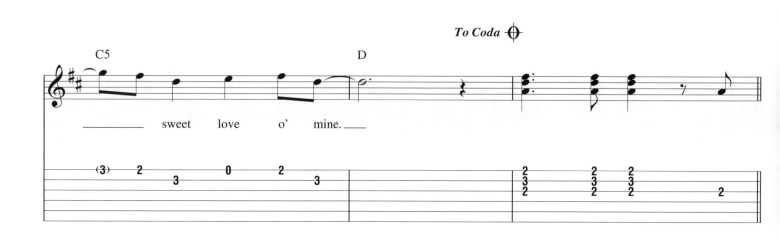

_____ sweet love o' mine. ___

Interlude

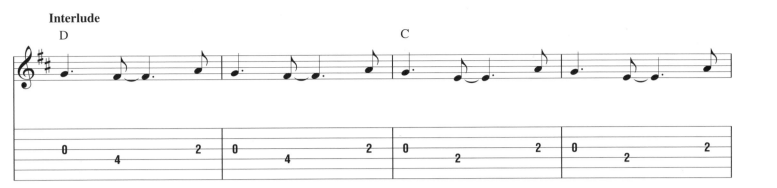

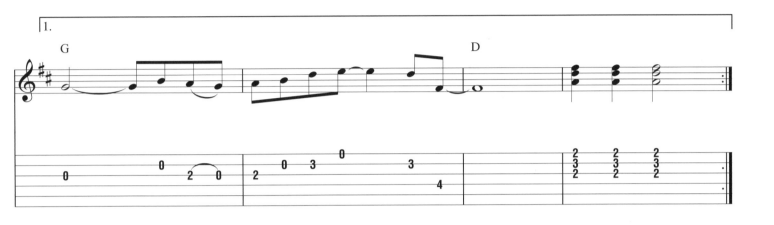

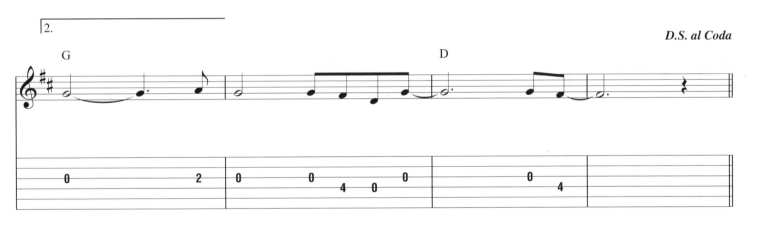

D.S. al Coda

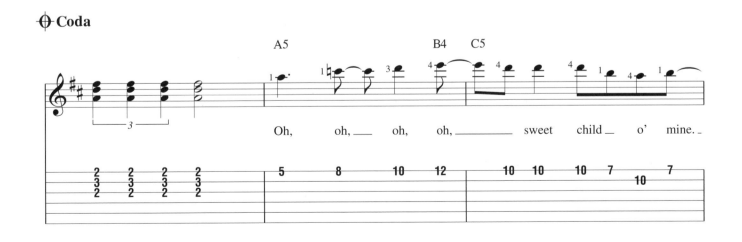

Coda

Oh, oh,___ oh, oh,_____ sweet child__ o' mine.__

Woo, _____ yeah, __ yeah! Ooh, _____

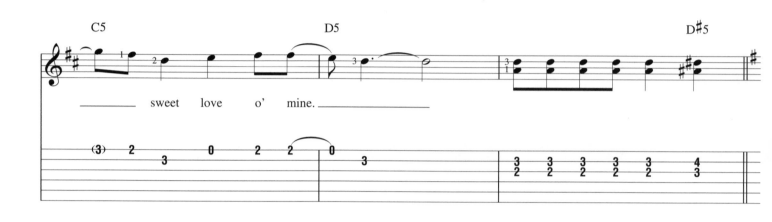

_____ sweet love o' mine. _____

Guitar Solo

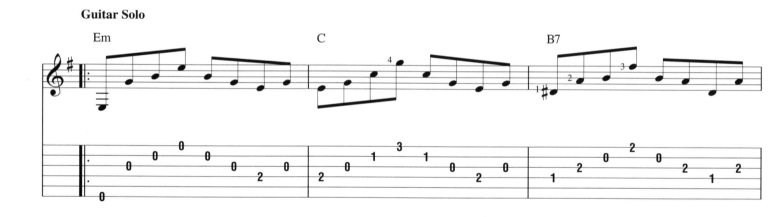

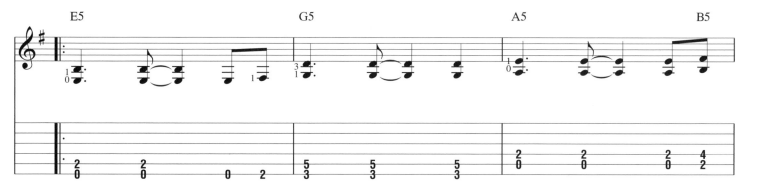

Outro

w/ Voc. ad lib. on repeats

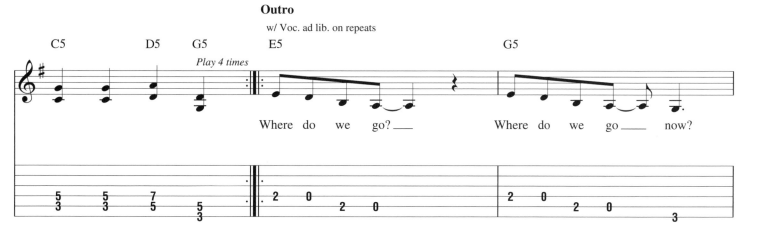

Where do we go? ___ Where do we go ___ now?

Repeat and fade

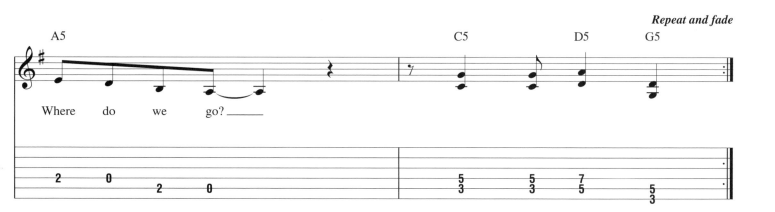

Where do we go? _____

Additional Lyrics

2. She's got eyes of the bluest skies,
   As if they thought of rain.
   I'd hate to look into those eyes
   And see an ounce of pain.
   Her hair reminds me of a warm safe place
   Where as a child I'd hide,
   And pray for the thunder and the rain
   To quietly pass me by.

Tainted Love

Words and Music by Ed Cobb

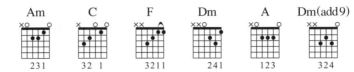

Am   C   F   Dm   A   Dm(add9)

*Tune down 1 step:
(low to high) D–G–C–F–A–D

Strum Pattern: 3, 4
Pick Pattern: 4, 5

Intro
Moderately

*Optional: To match recording, tune down 1 step.

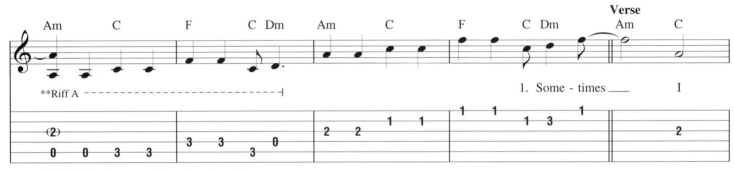

**Riff A is basic accompaniment throughout Verse,
Chorus, and Bridge. Chord symbols are implied.

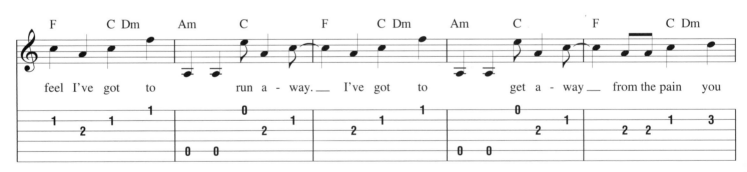

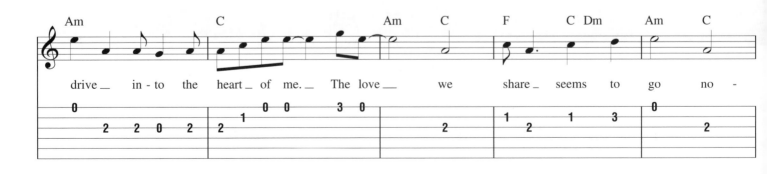

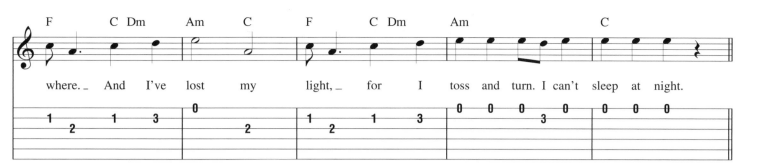

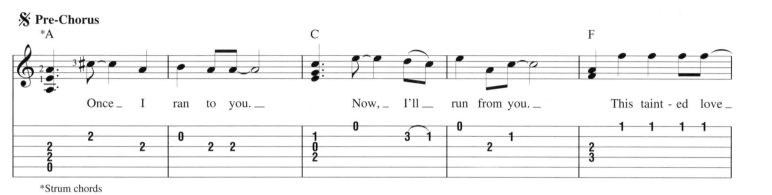

To Coda

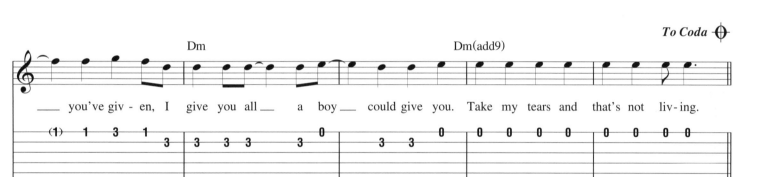

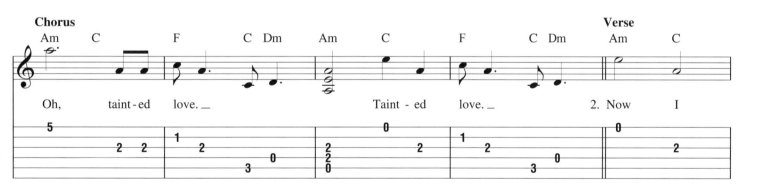

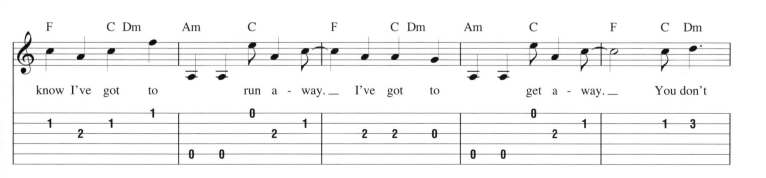

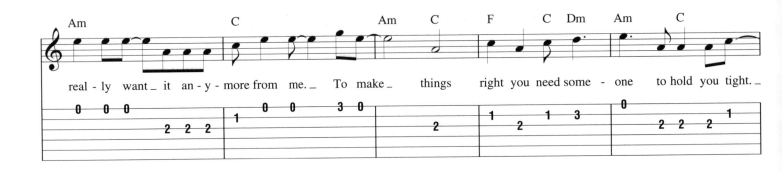

real - ly want _ it an - y - more from me. _ To make _ things right you need some - one to hold you tight. _

D.S. al Coda

_ And you'll think love is to pray. _____ But I'm sor - ry, I don't pray that way.

⊕ Coda
Chorus

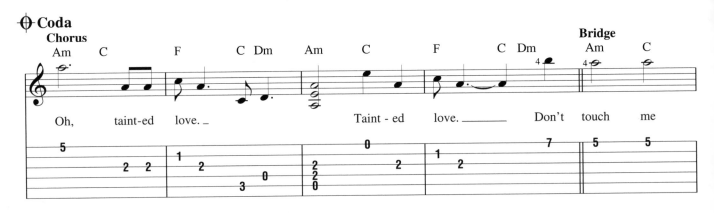

Oh, taint-ed love. _ Taint - ed love. _____ Don't touch me

Bridge

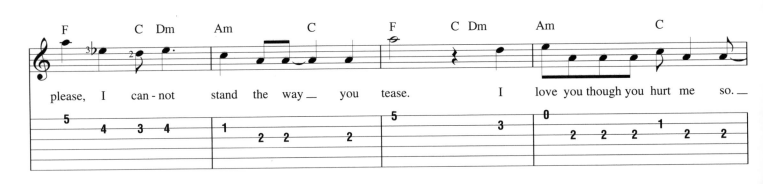

please, I can - not stand the way _ you tease. I love you though you hurt me so. _

Outro-Chorus

Repeat and fade

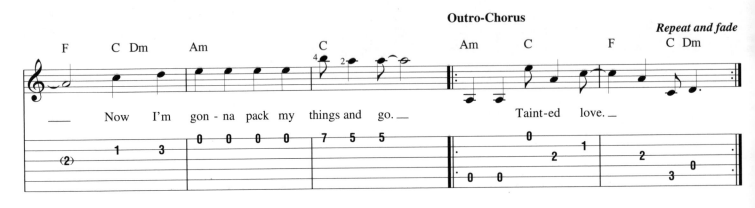

_ Now I'm gon - na pack my things and go. _ Taint-ed love. _

Tangled Up in Blue

Words and Music by Bob Dylan

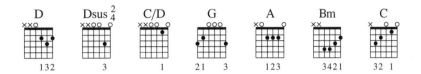

Strum Pattern: 2, 3
Pick Pattern: 2, 4

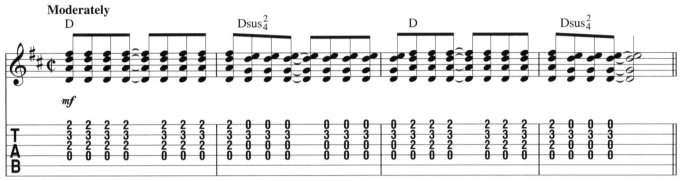

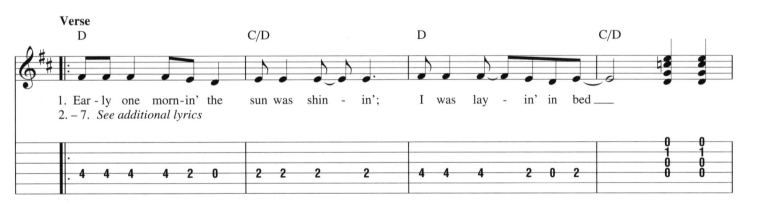

1. Ear - ly one morn - in' the sun was shin - in'; I was lay - in' in bed __
2. – 7. *See additional lyrics*

won - d'rin' if __ she'd changed at all, __ if her hair __ was __ still red.

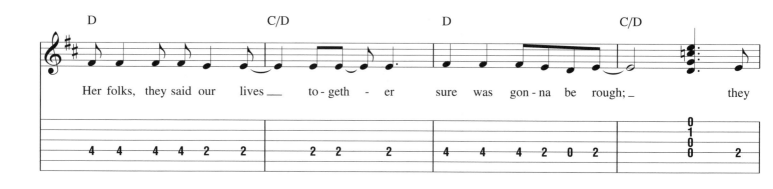

Her folks, they said our lives ___ to-geth - er sure was gon-na be rough; ___ they

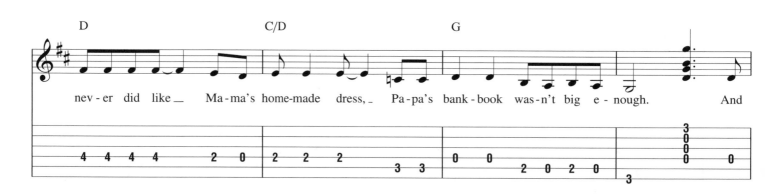

nev - er did like ___ Ma-ma's home-made dress, ___ Pa-pa's bank-book was-n't big e - nough. And

I was stand - in' on the side of the road, rain fall-in' on my shoes, ___

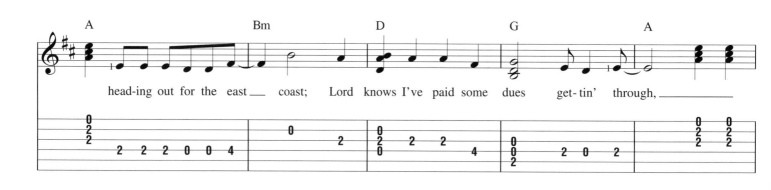

head-ing out for the east ___ coast; Lord knows I've paid some dues get-tin' through, _____

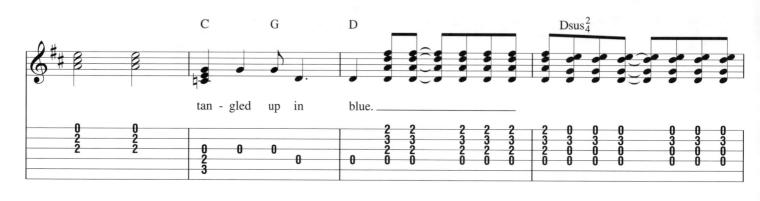

tan - gled up in blue. _____

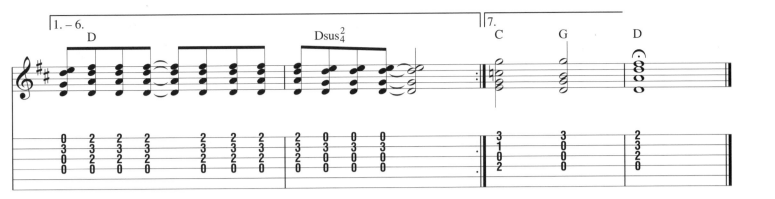

Additional Lyrics

2. She was married when we first met
   Soon to be divorced.
   I helped her out of a jam, I guess
   But I used a little too much force.
   We drove that car as far as we could,
   Abandoned it out west.
   Split up on a dark sad night,
   Both agreeing it was best.
   She turned around to look at me
   As I was walkin' away,
   I heard her say over my shoulder,
   "We'll meet again some day
   On the avenue,"
   Tangled up in blue.

3. I had a job in the great north woods
   Working as a cook for a spell,
   But I never did like it all that much,
   And one day the axe just fell.
   So I drifted down to New Orleans
   Where I happened to be employed
   Workin' for a while on a fishin' boat
   Right outside of Delacroix.
   But all the while I was alone
   The past was close behind,
   I seen a lot of women
   But she never escaped my mind,
   And I just grew,
   Tangled up in blue.

4. She was workin' in a topless place
   And I stopped in for a beer.
   I just kept lookin' at the side of her face
   In the spotlight so clear.
   And later on as the crowd thinned out,
   I's just about to do the same,
   She was standing there in back of my chair,
   Said to me, "Don't I know your name?"
   I muttered somethin' underneath my breath,
   She studied the lines on my face.
   I must admit I felt a little uneasy
   When she bent down to tie the laces
   Of my shoe,
   Tangled up in blue.

5. She lit a burner on the stove
   And offered me a pipe,
   "I thought you'd never say hello," she said,
   "You look like the silent type."
   Then she opened up a book of poems
   And handed it to me,
   Written by an Italian poet
   From the thirteenth century.
   And every one of them words rang true
   And glowed like burnin' coal
   Pourin' off of every page
   Like it was written in my soul
   From me to you,
   Tangled up in blue.

6. I lived with them on Montague Street
   In a basement down the stairs,
   There was music in the cafes at night
   And revolution in the air.
   Then he started into dealing with slaves
   And something inside of him died,
   She had to sell everything she owned
   And froze up inside.
   And when finally the bottom fell out
   I became withdrawn.
   The only thing I knew how to do
   Was to keep on keepin' on
   Like a bird that flew,
   Tangled up in blue.

7. So now I'm goin' back again,
   I got to get her somehow,
   All the people we used to know,
   They're an illusion to me now.
   Some are mathematicians,
   Some are carpenters' wives.
   Don't know how it all got started,
   I don't know what they're doin' with their lives.
   But me, I'm still on the road
   Headin' for another joint,
   We always did feel the same,
   We just saw it from a different point
   Of view,
   Tangled up in blue.

Tears in Heaven

Words and Music by Eric Clapton and Will Jennings

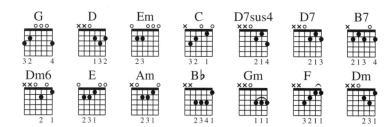

Strum Pattern: 6
Pick Pattern: 4

Intro
Moderately

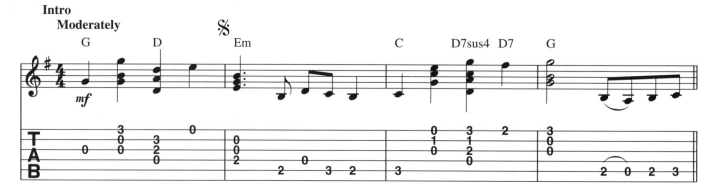

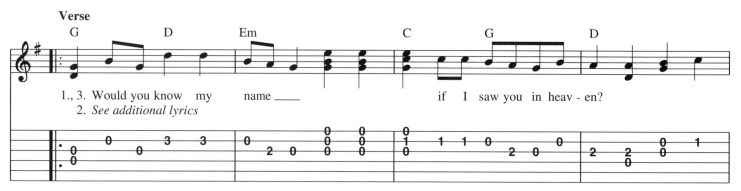

1., 3. Would you know my name ____ if I saw you in heav-en?
2. *See additional lyrics*

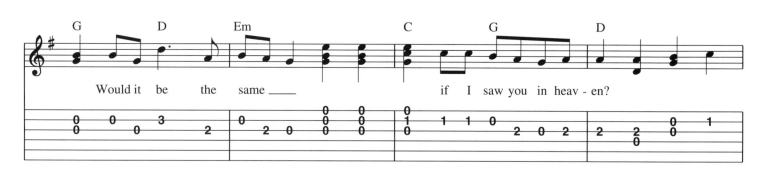

Would it be the same ____ if I saw you in heav-en?

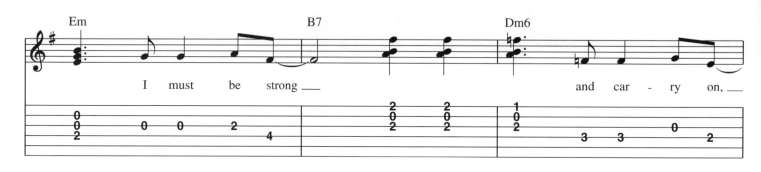

I must be strong ____ and car-ry on, ____

'cause I know I don't be - long _____ here in heav -

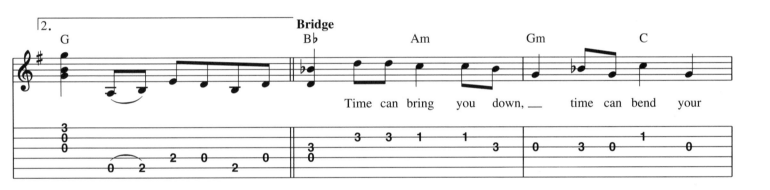

en.

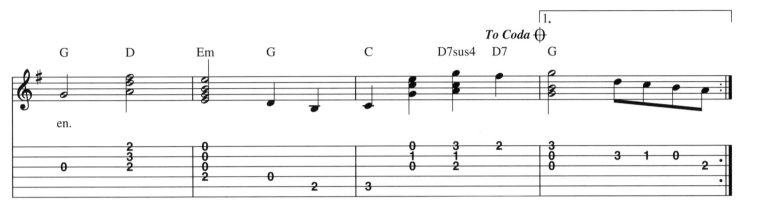

Time can bring you down, __ time can bend your

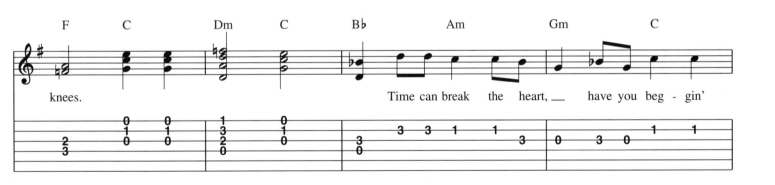

knees. Time can break the heart, __ have you beg - gin'

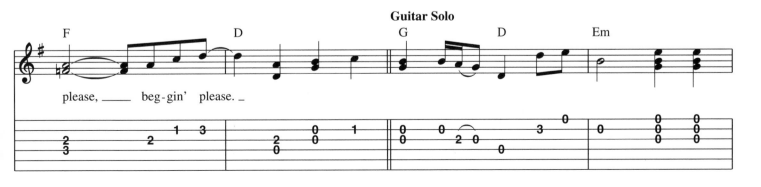

please, _____ beg - gin' please. __

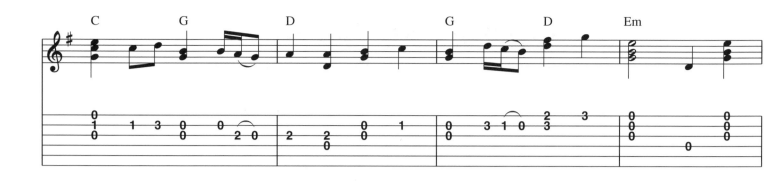

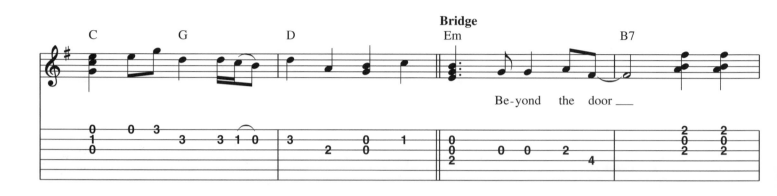

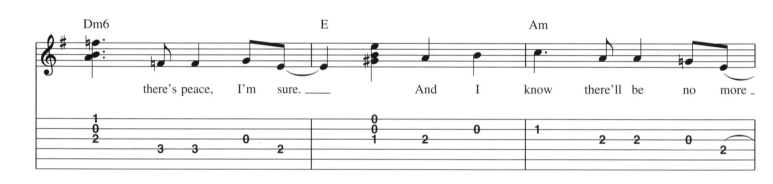

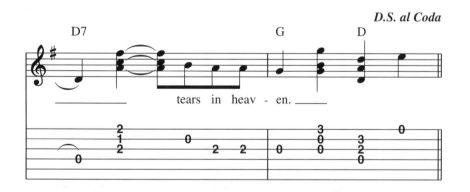

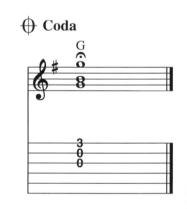

Additional Lyrics

2. Would you hold my hand
   If I saw you in heaven?
   Would you help me stand
   If I saw you in heaven?
   I'll find my way through night and day,
   'Cause I know I just can't stay here in heaven.

Under the Bridge

Words and Music by Anthony Kiedis, Flea, John Frusciante and Chad Smith

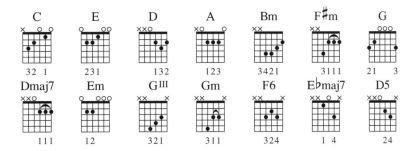

*Capo II

Strum Pattern: 6
Pick Pattern: 6

Intro

Slow Rock

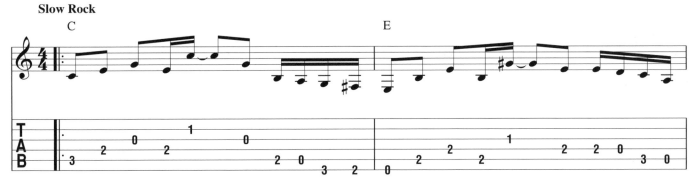

*Optional: To match recording, place capo on 2nd fret.

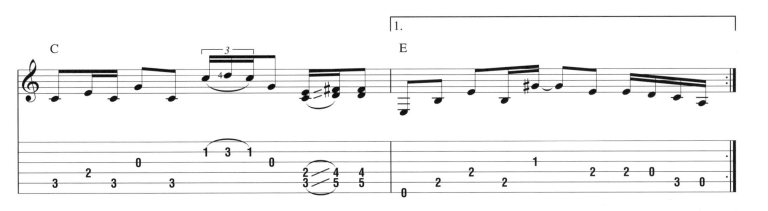

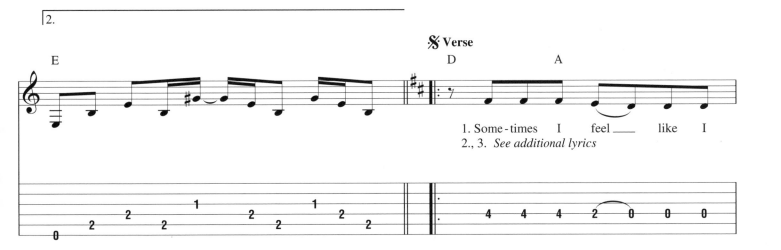

1. Some-times I feel ___ like I
2., 3. *See additional lyrics*

don't have a part - ner. Some - times I feel ___ like my on - ly friend ___ is the

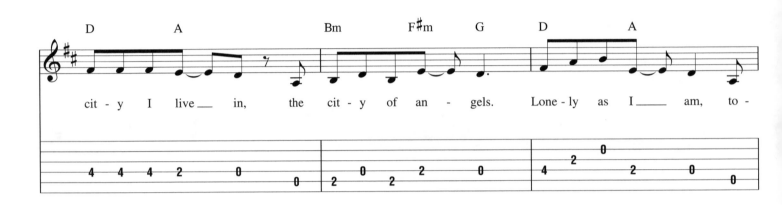

cit - y I live ___ in, the cit - y of an - gels. Lone - ly as I ___ am, to -

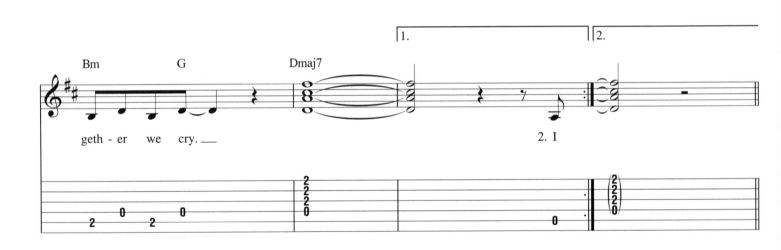

geth - er we cry. ___

2. I

Chorus

I don't ev - er want to feel ___ like I did that day. Take me to the place I love, ___

take me all the way. _ I don't ev - er want to feel _____ like I did that day.

To Coda ⊕

Take me to the place I love, _____ take me all the way, _____ yeah, _

D.S. al Coda
(take 2nd ending)

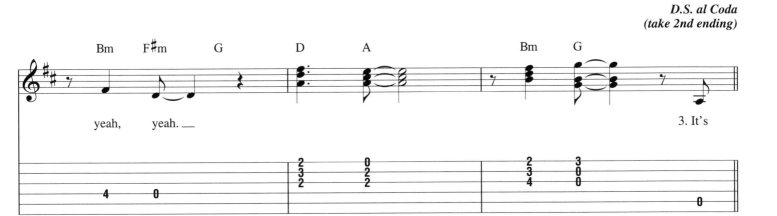

yeah, yeah. _

3. It's

⊕ **Coda**

Outro

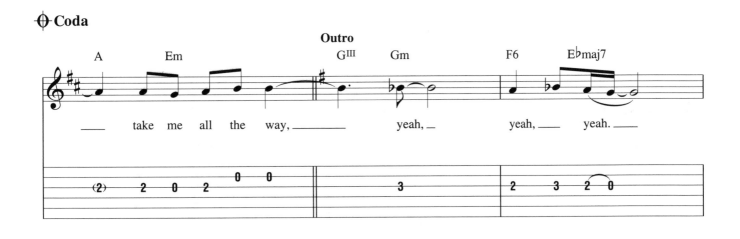

_ take me all the way, _____ yeah, _ yeah, ___ yeah. ___

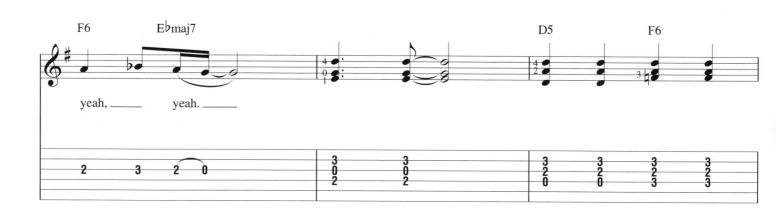

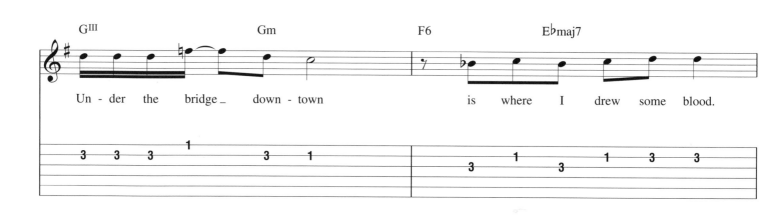

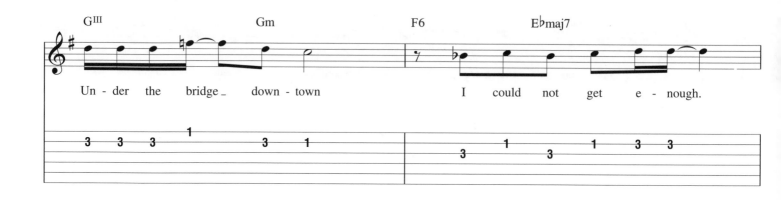

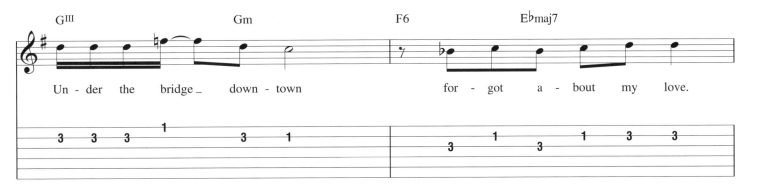

Under the bridge down-town   for-got a-bout my love.

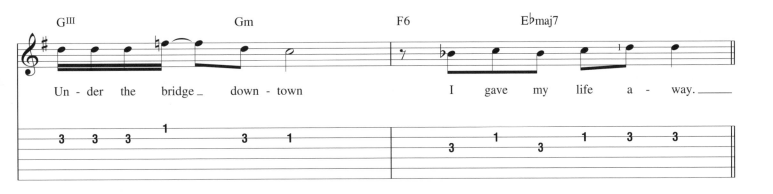

Under the bridge down-town   I gave my life a-way.

w/ Voc. ad lib. on repeats

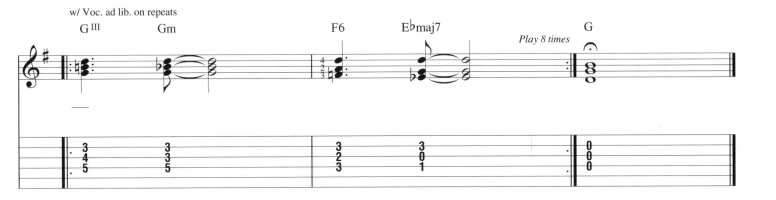

Additional Lyrics

2. I drive on her streets
   'Cause she's my companion.
   I walk through her hills
   'Cause she knows who I am.
   She sees my good deeds
   And she kisses me windy.
   I never worry.
   Now that is a lie.

3. It's hard to believe
   That there's nobody out there.
   It's hard to believe
   That I'm all alone.
   At least I have her love,
   The city, she loves me.
   Lonely as I am,
   Together we cry.

Time After Time

Words and Music by Cyndi Lauper and Rob Hyman

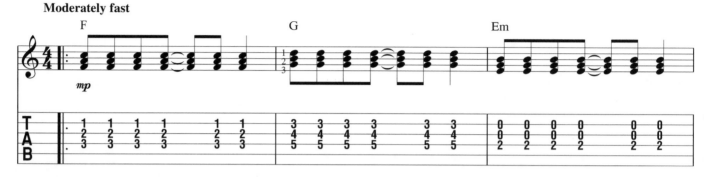

Strum Pattern: 6
Pick Pattern: 4

Intro
Moderately fast

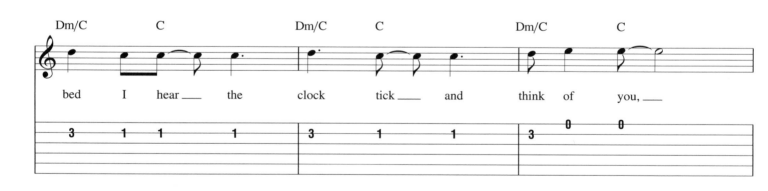

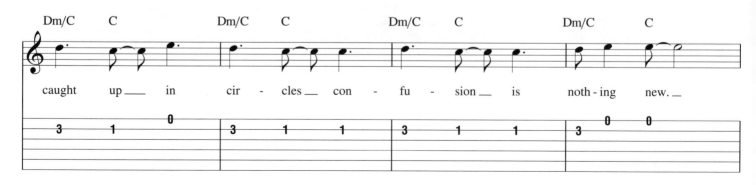

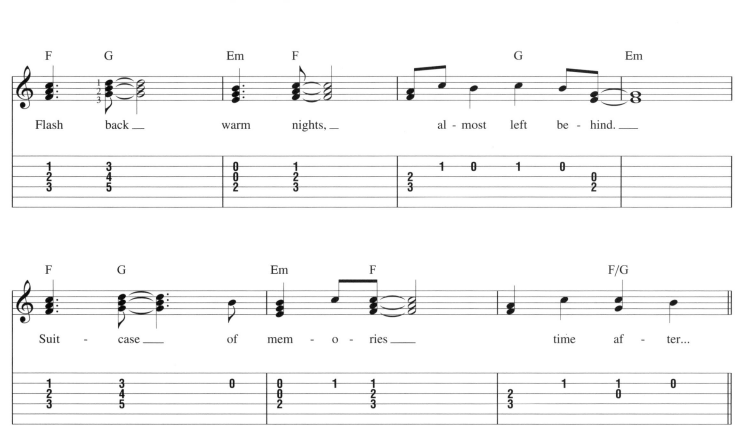

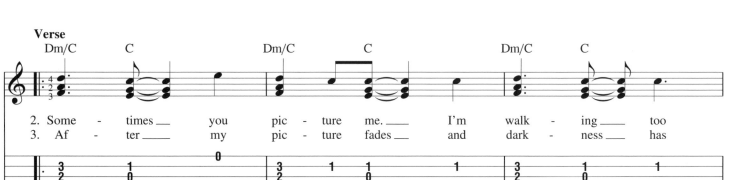

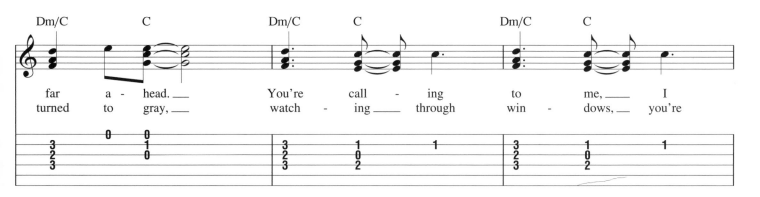

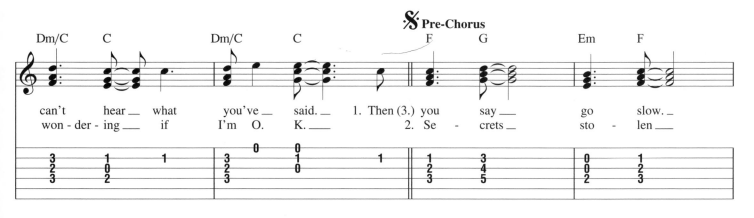

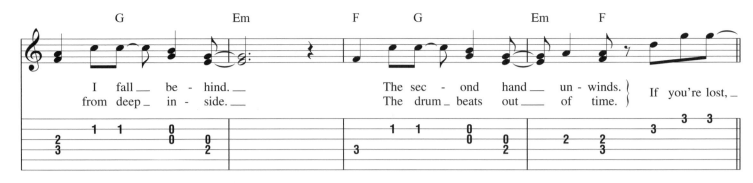

Chorus

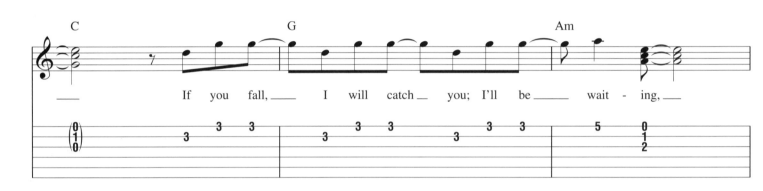

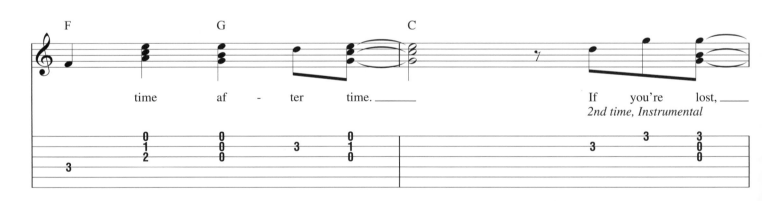

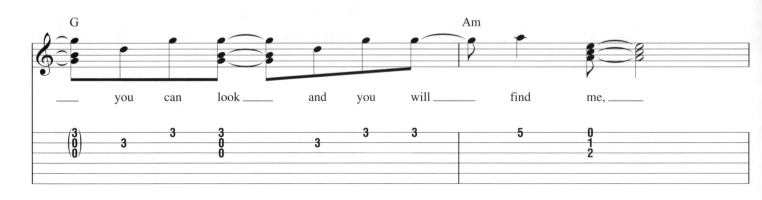

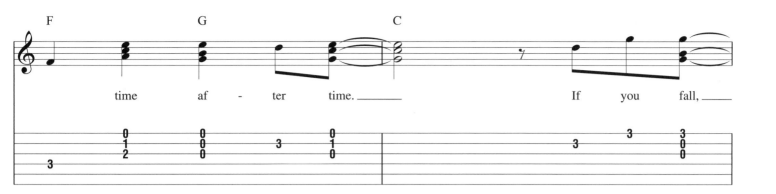

time af - ter time. _____ If you fall, _____

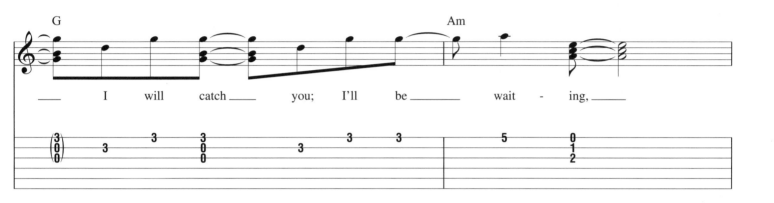

_____ I will catch _____ you; I'll be _____ wait - ing, _____

To Coda ⊕ | 1. | 2. | *D.S. al Coda*

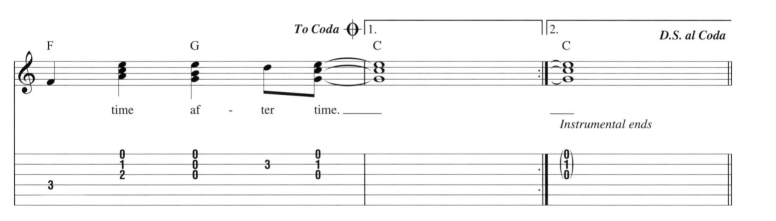

time af - ter time. _____

Instrumental ends

⊕ **Coda**

Outro

Repeat and fade

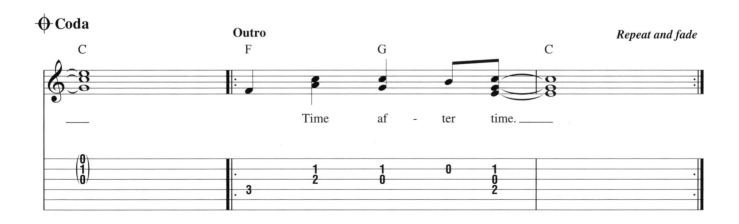

_____ Time af - ter time. _____

Tiny Dancer

Words and Music by Elton John and Bernie Taupin

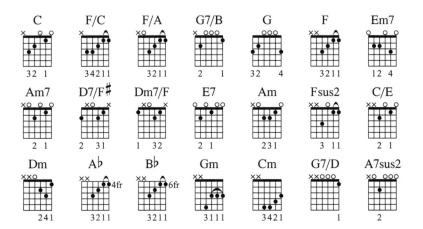

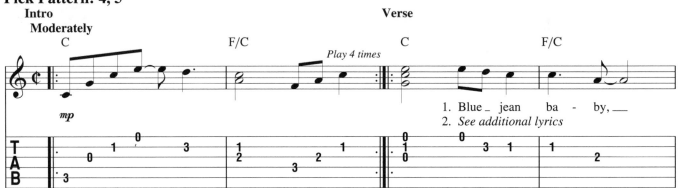

Strum Pattern: 3, 4
Pick Pattern: 4, 5

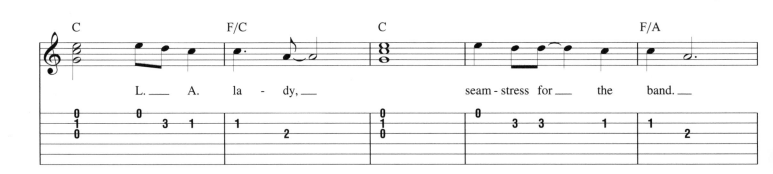

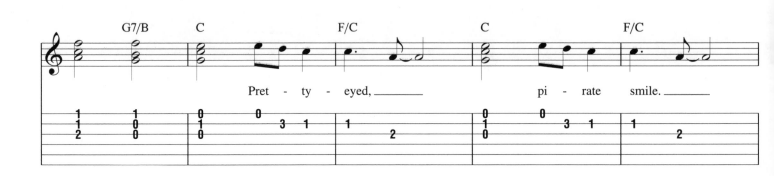

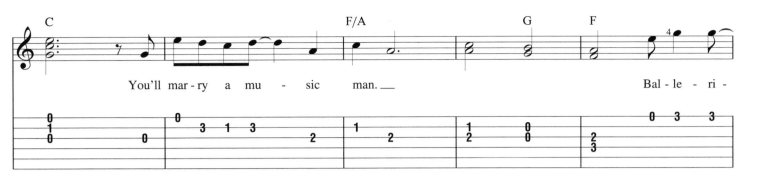

You'll mar-ry a mu - sic man. ___ Bal - le - ri -

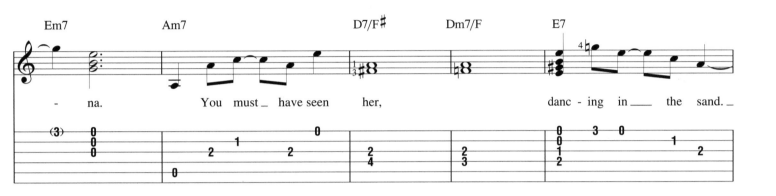

- na. You must ___ have seen her, danc - ing in ___ the sand. ___

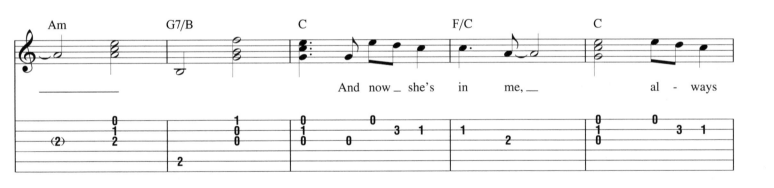

___ And now ___ she's in me, ___ al - ways

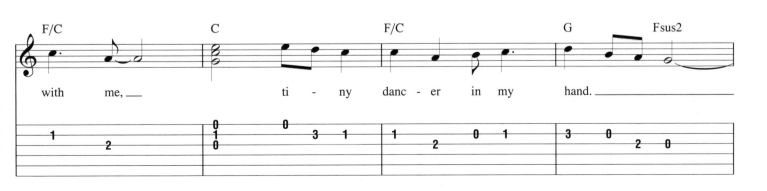

with me, ___ ti - ny danc - er in my hand. ___

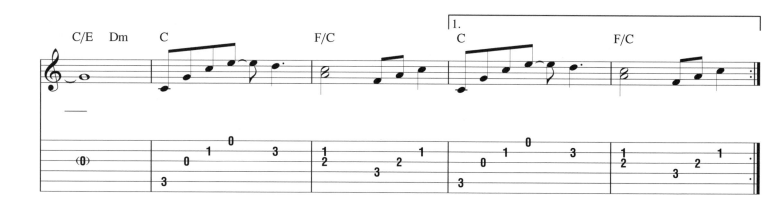

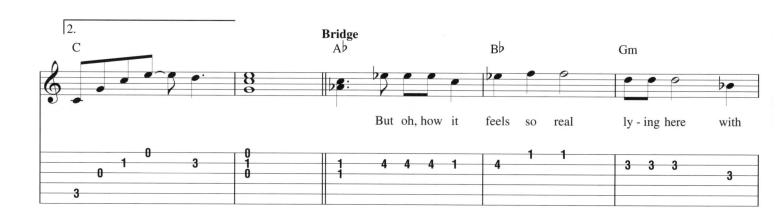

But oh, how it feels so real ly - ing here with

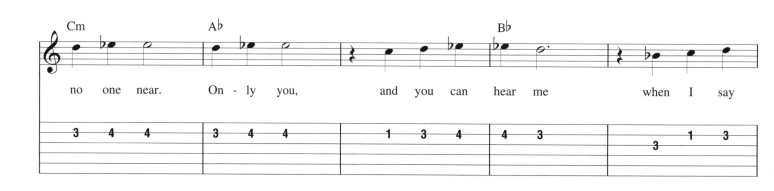

no one near. On - ly you, and you can hear me when I say

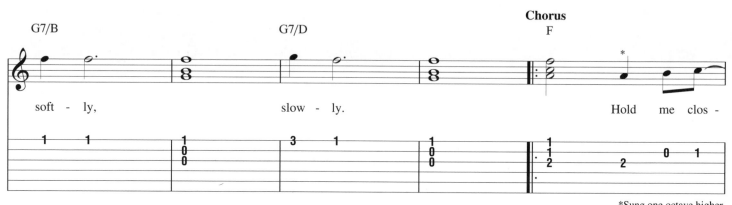

soft - ly, slow - ly. Hold me clos-

*Sung one octave higher
throughout Chorus.

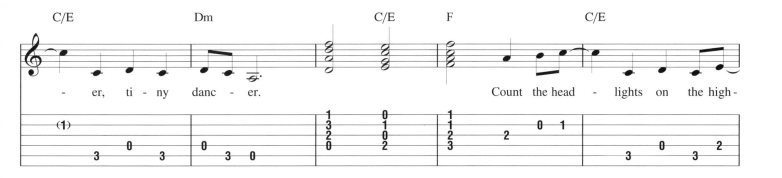

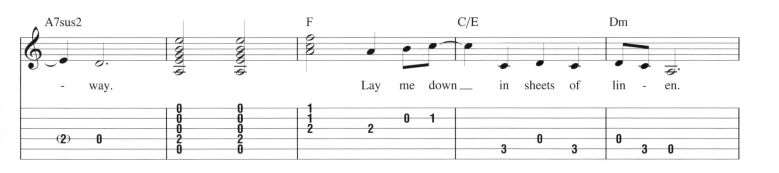

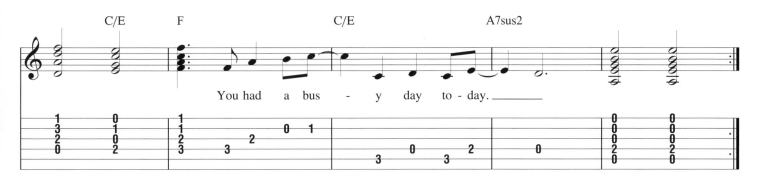

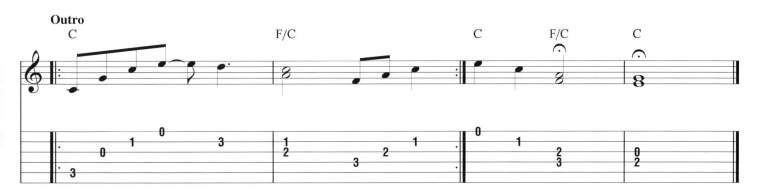

Additional Lyrics

2. Jesus freaks, out in the street, handing tickets out for God.
   Turning back, she just laughs. The boulevard is not that bad.
   Piano man, he makes his stand in the auditorium.
   Looking on, she sings the songs. The words she knows, the tune she hums.

The Tracks of My Tears

Words and Music by William "Smokey" Robinson, Warren Moore and Marvin Tarplin

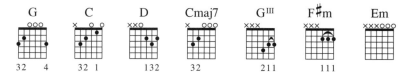

Strum Pattern: 6
Pick Pattern: 4

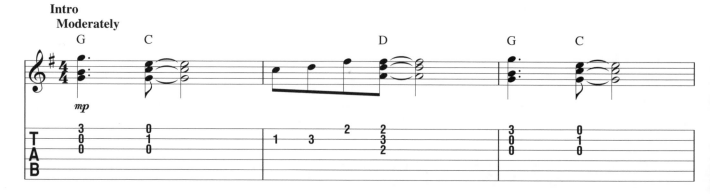

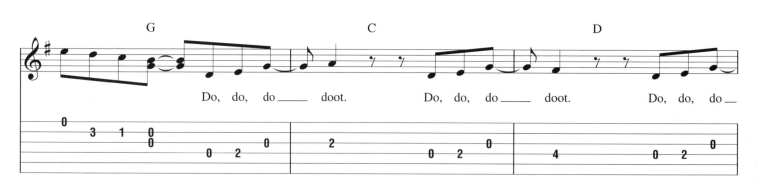

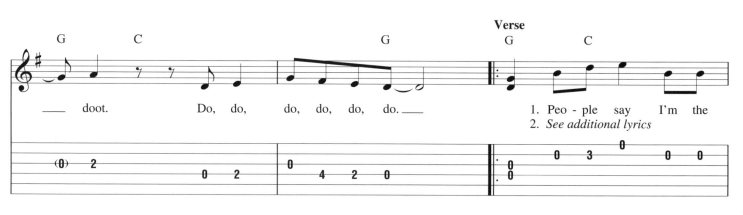

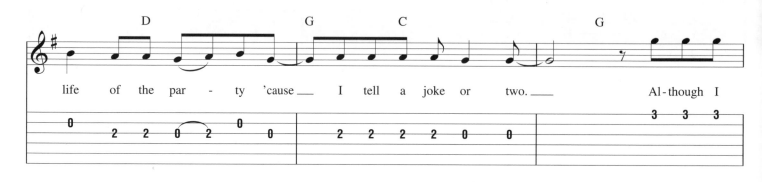

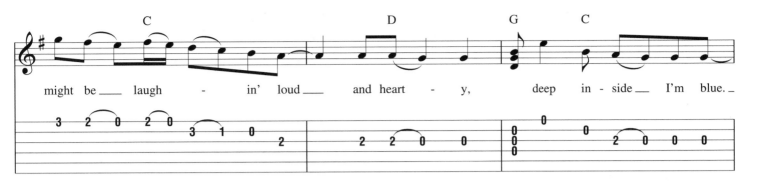

might be ___ laugh - in' loud ___ and heart - y, deep in - side ___ I'm blue. ___

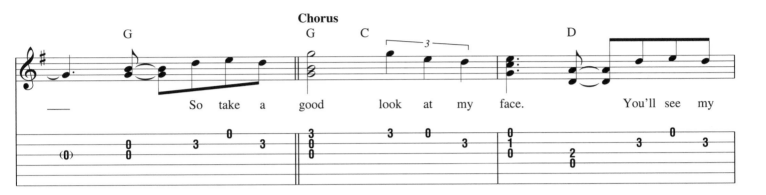

Chorus

So take a good look at my face. You'll see my

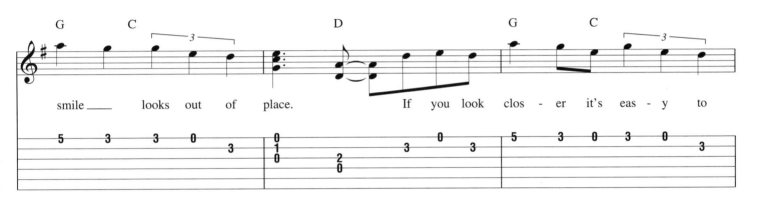

smile ___ looks out of place. If you look clos - er it's eas - y to

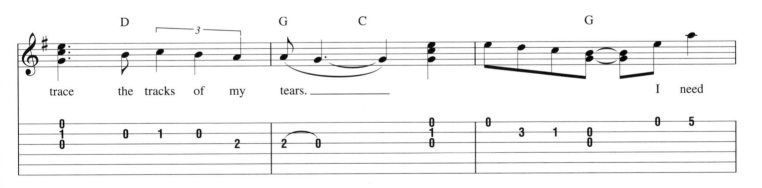

trace the tracks of my tears. ___ I need

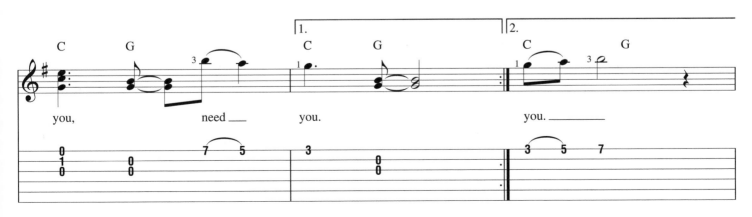

1.

you, need ___ you.

2.

you. ___

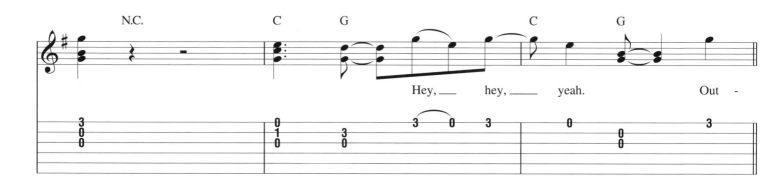

Hey, ___ hey, ___ yeah. Out-

Bridge

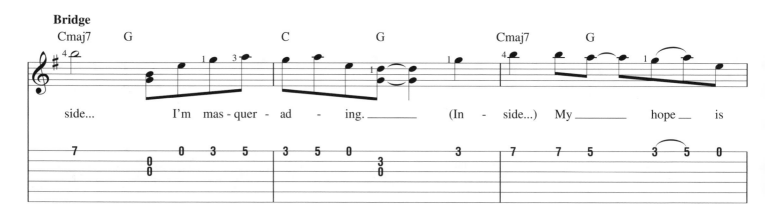

-side... I'm mas-quer-ad-ing. ___ (In - side...) My ___ hope ___ is

fad - ing. (Just a clown...) Ooh, yeah, ___ since you

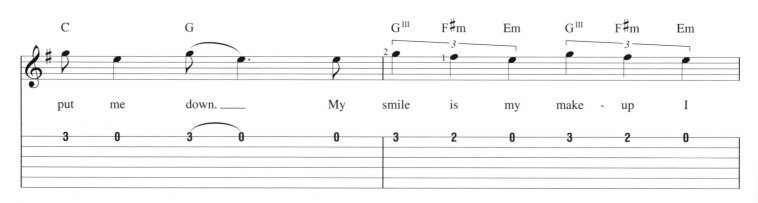

put me down. ___ My smile is my make-up I

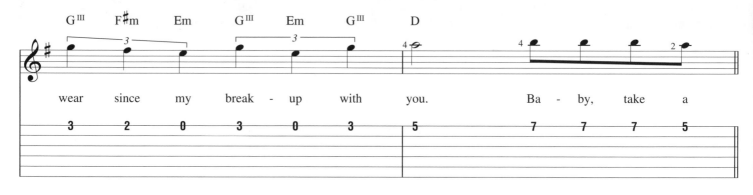

wear since my break-up with you. Ba-by, take a

Outro-Chorus

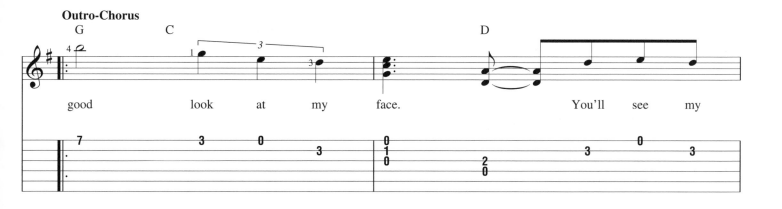

good   look   at   my   face.   You'll   see   my

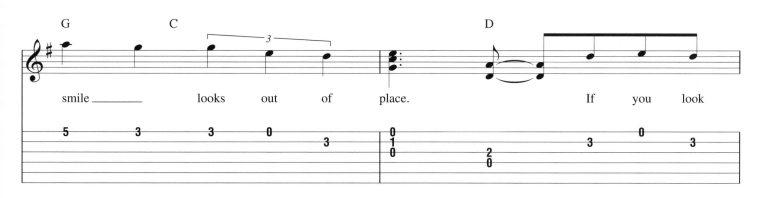

smile _____   looks   out   of   place.   If   you   look

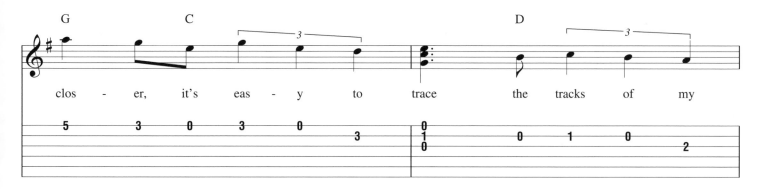

clos - er,   it's   eas - y   to   trace   the   tracks   of   my

Repeat and fade

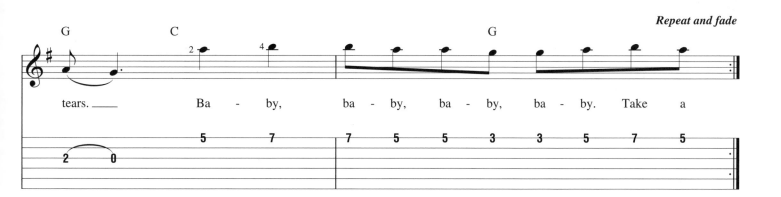

tears. _____   Ba - by,   ba - by,   ba - by,   ba - by.   Take   a

Additional Lyrics

2. Since you left me, if you see me with another girl,
   Seemin' like havin' fun,
   Although she may be cute, she's just a substitute
   Because you're the permanent one.

Vogue

Words and Music by Madonna Ciccone and Shep Pettibone

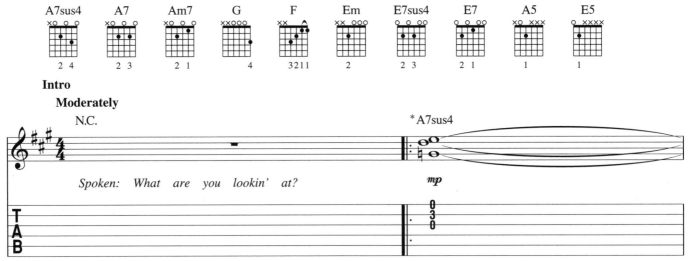

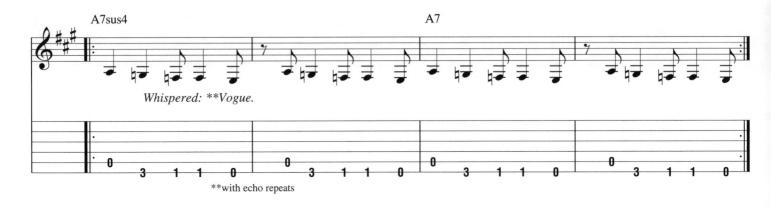

*Play chord once and let ring.

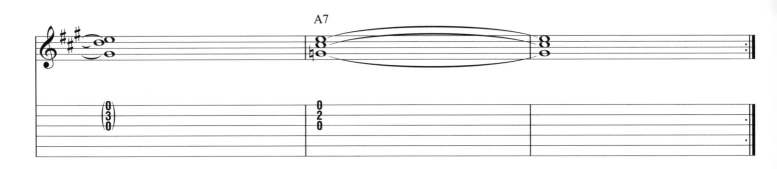

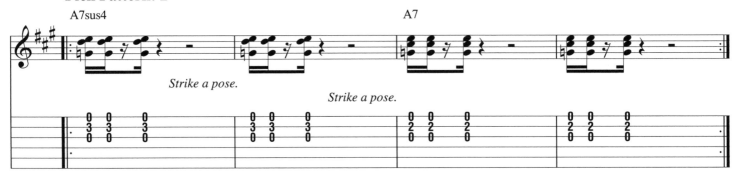

Strum Pattern: 1, 2
Pick Pattern: 2

Strike a pose.

Strike a pose.

Whispered: **Vogue.

**with echo repeats

Verse

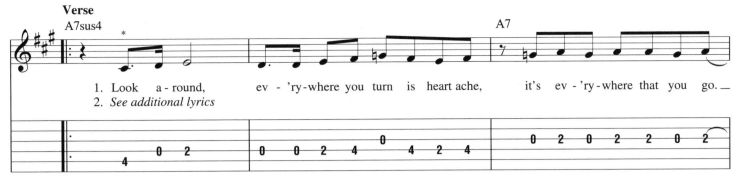

1. Look a - round, ev - 'ry-where you turn is heart ache, it's ev - 'ry-where that you go.

2. *See additional lyrics*

*Female vocal: sung one octave
higher than written.

You try ev - 'ry-thing you can to es - cape

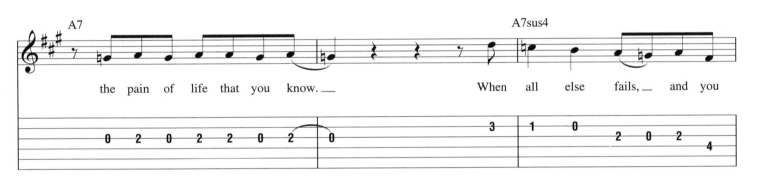

the pain of life that you know. When all else fails, and you

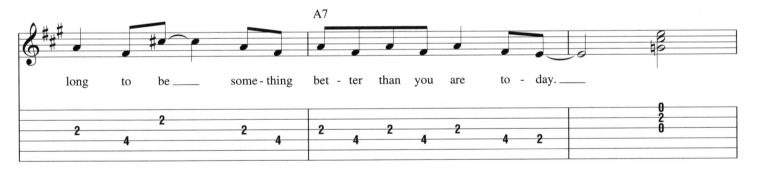

long to be some-thing bet - ter than you are to - day.

I know a place where you can get a - way, it's called a dance floor and here's what it's for, so

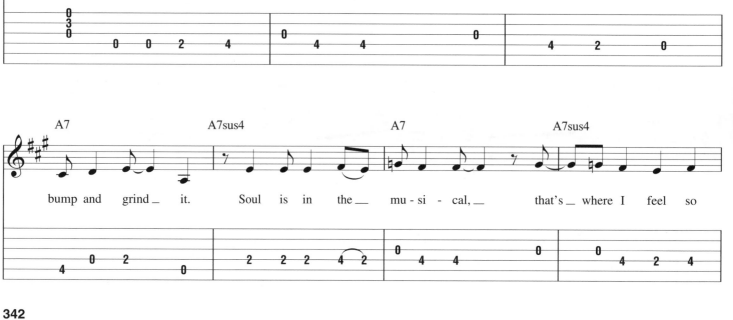

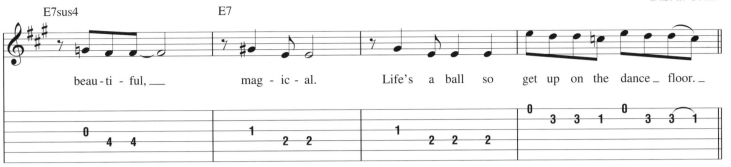

beau-ti-ful, ___   mag - ic - al.   Life's a ball so   get up on the dance _ floor. _

⊕ Coda

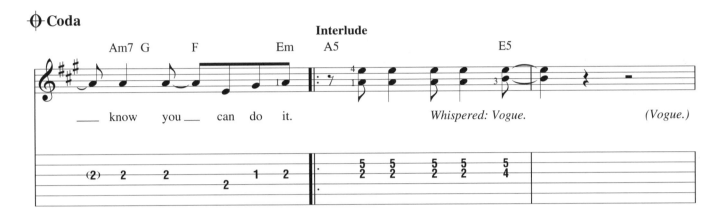

___ know you ___ can do it.   *Whispered: Vogue.*   *(Vogue.)*

Interlude

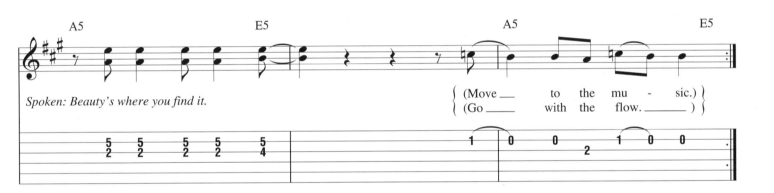

Spoken: Beauty's where you find it.   *(Move ___ to the mu - sic.)* *(Go ___ with the flow. ___)*

Spoken: Greta Garbo and Monroe,   *Dietrich and DiMaggio,*   *Marlon Brando, Jimmy Dean,*

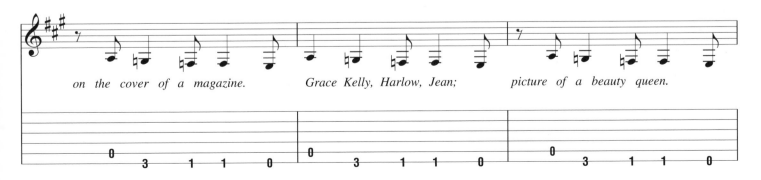

on the cover of a magazine.   *Grace Kelly, Harlow, Jean;*   *picture of a beauty queen.*

Outro

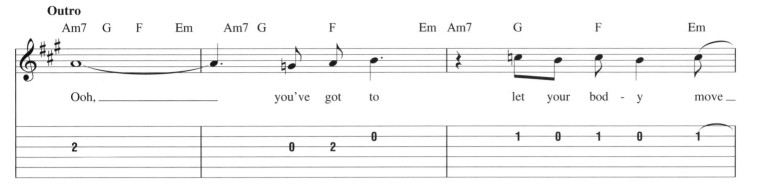

Ooh, _____ you've got to let your bod - y move _____

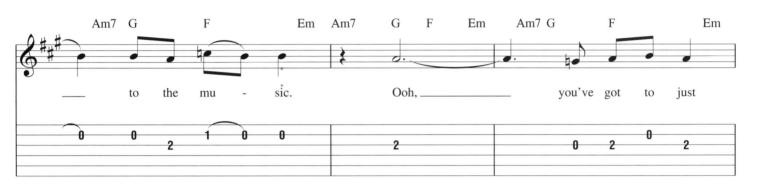

_____ to the mu - sic. Ooh, _____ you've got to just

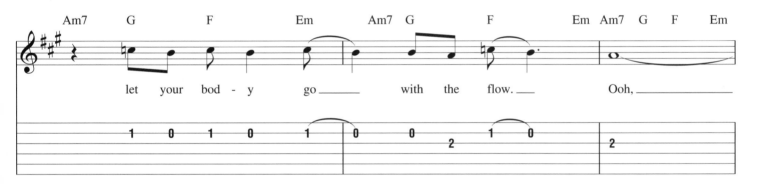

let your bod - y go _____ with the flow. _____ Ooh, _____

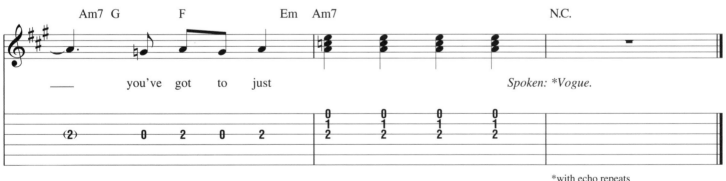

_____ you've got to just

*Spoken: *Vogue.*

*with echo repeats

Additional Lyrics

2. All you need is your own imagination,
So use it, that's what it's for.
Go inside, for your finest inspiration;
Your dreams will open the door.
It makes no diff'rence if you're black or white,
If you're a boy or a girl.
If the music's pumpin' it will give you new life.
You're a super star, yes, that's what you are , you know it.

Waterfalls

Words and Music by Marqueze Etheridge, Lisa Nicole Lopes, Rico R. Wade, Pat Brown and Ramon Murray

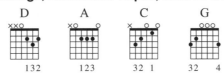

*Capo 1

Strum Pattern: 2
Pick Pattern: 4

Intro
Moderately slow

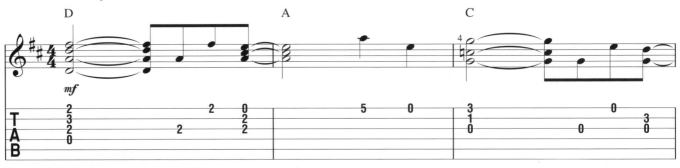

*Optional: To match recording, place capo at 1st fret.

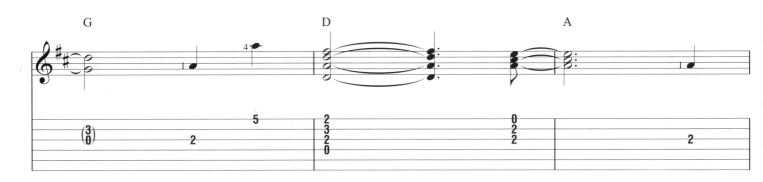

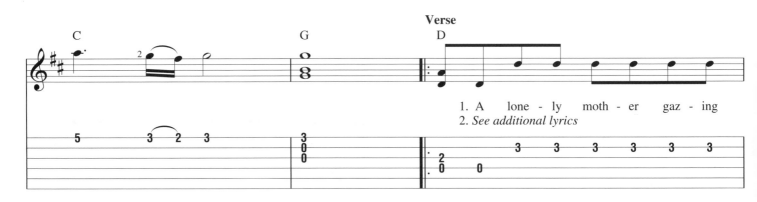

Verse

1. A lone-ly moth-er gaz-ing
2. *See additional lyrics*

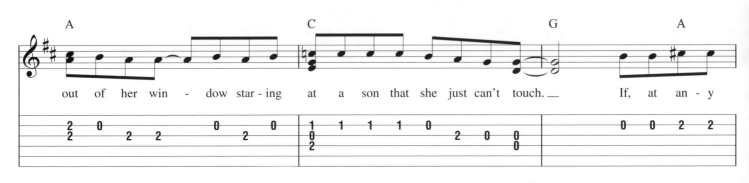

out of her win-dow star-ing at a son that she just can't touch. ___ If, at an-y

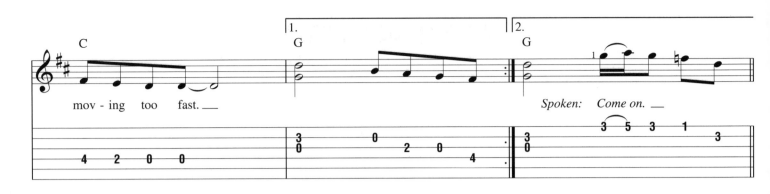

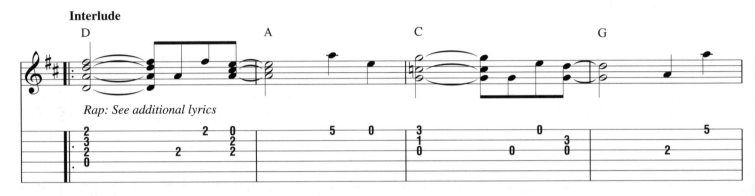

Interlude

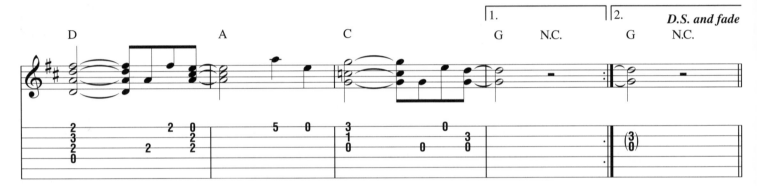

Additional Lyrics

2. Little precious has a nat'ral obsession for temptation,
   But he just can't see.
   She gives him loving that his body can't handle,
   But all he can say is, "Baby, it's good to me."
   One day he goes and takes a glimpse in the mirror,
   But he doesn't recognize his own face.
   His health is fading and he doesn't know why.
   Three letters took him to his final resting place.
   Y'all don't hear me.

Rap: *I seen a rainbow yesterday,*
   But too many storms have come and gone
   Leavin' a trace of not one God-given ray.
   Is it because my life is ten shades of gray?
   I pray all ten fade away,
   Seldom praise Him for the sunny days.
   And like His promise is true,
   Only my faith can undo
   The many chances I blew
   To bring my life to anew.
   Clear blue and unconditional skies
   Have dried the tears from my eyes.
   No more lonely cries.
   My only bleedin' hope
   Is for the folk who can't cope
   Wit such an endurin' pain
   That it keeps 'em in the pourin' rain.
   Who's to blame
   For tootin' caine in your own vein?
   What a shame,
   You shoot and aim for someone else's brain.
   You claim the insane
   And name this day in time
   For fallin' prey to crime.
   I say the system got you victim to your own mind.
   Dreams are hopeless aspirations
   In hopes of comin' true.
   Believe in yourself,
   The rest is up to me and you.

Wonderwall

Words and Music by Noel Gallagher

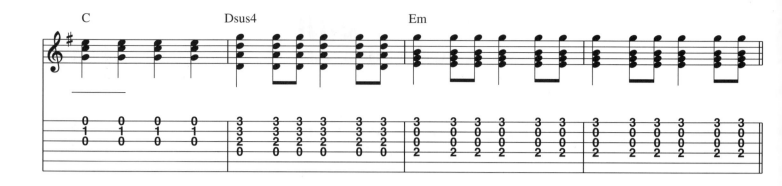

Verse

2. Back - beat the word was on the street that the fire ___ in your heart is out. ___
3. *See additional lyrics*

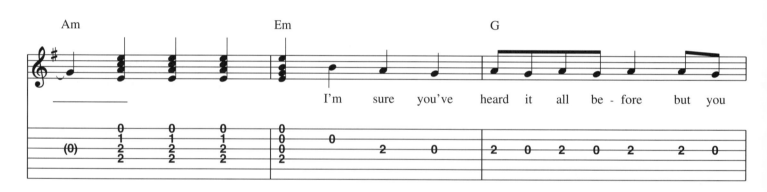

I'm sure you've heard it all be - fore but you

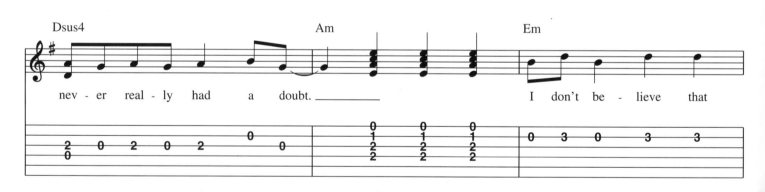

nev - er real - ly had a doubt. _____ I don't be - lieve that

an - y - bo - dy ___ feels the way I do ___ a - bout you now. ___

Pre-Chorus

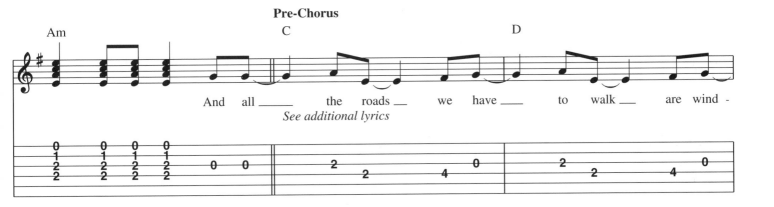

And all _____ the roads ___ we have ___ to walk ___ are wind -
See additional lyrics

- ing _____ and all ___ the lights ___ that lead ___ us there ___ are blind -

- ing. _____ There are man - y things ___ that I ___ would

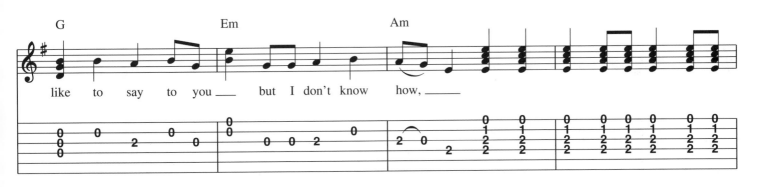

like to say to you ___ but I don't know how, _____

⊕ Coda

Additional Lyrics

3. Today was gonna be the day
   But they'll never throw it back to you.
   By now you should've somehow
   Realised what you're not to do.
   I don't believe that anybody
   Feels the way I do
   About you now.

Pre-Chorus And all the roads that lead you there were winding
   And all the lights that light the way are blinding.
   There are many things that I would like to say to you
   But I don't know how.

What's Going On

Words and Music by Marvin Gaye, Al Cleveland and Renaldo Benson

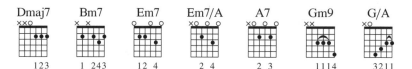

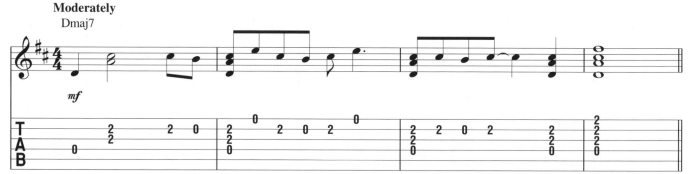

Strum Pattern: 2, 3
Pick Pattern: 4, 5

Intro
Moderately

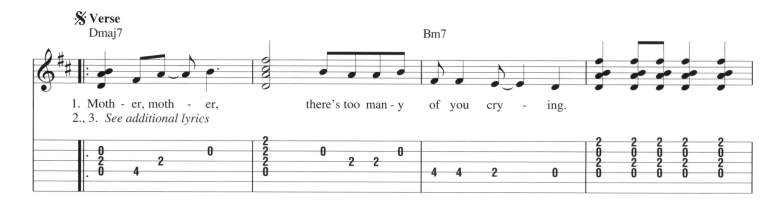

1. Moth - er, moth - er, there's too man - y of you cry - ing.
2., 3. *See additional lyrics*

Broth - er, broth - er, broth-er, there's far too man - y of you dy - ing. You know we've

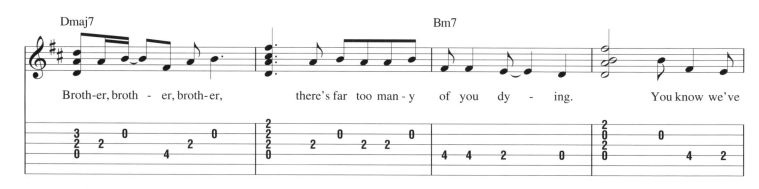

got to find a way ___ to bring some lov - in' here to - day, yeah. ___

Additional Lyrics

2. Father, father,
   We don't need to escalate.
   You see, war is not the answer,
   For only love can conquer hate.
   You know we've got to find a way
   To bring some lovin' here today, oh.

3. Mother, mother,
   Ev'rybody thinks we're wrong.
   Ah, but who are they to judge us
   Simply 'cause our hair is long?
   Ah, you know we've got to find a way
   To bring some understanding here today, oh.

Where Did Our Love Go

Words and Music by Brian Holland, Lamont Dozier and Edward Holland

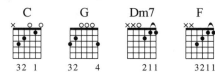

Strum Pattern: 3, 4
Pick Pattern: 3

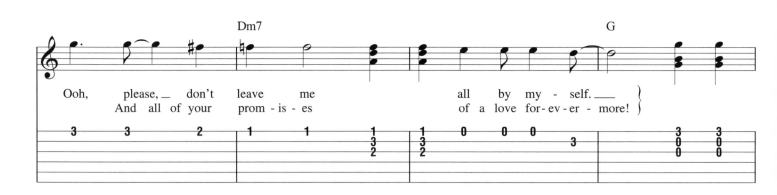

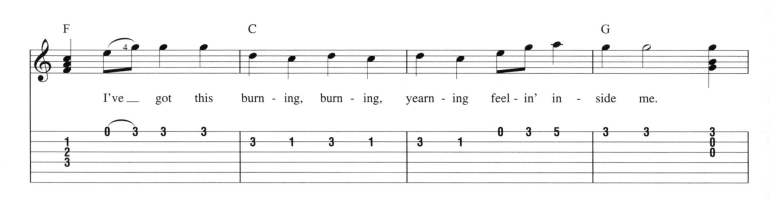

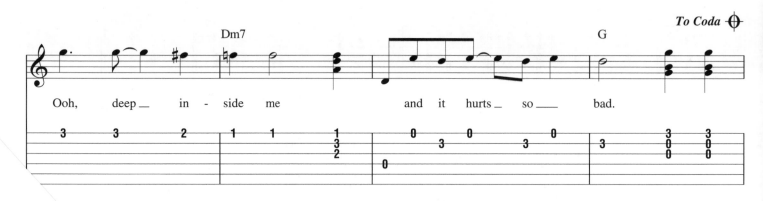

Chorus

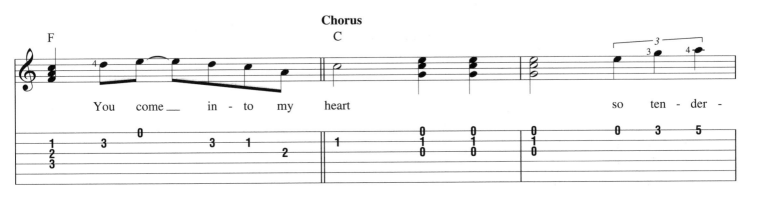

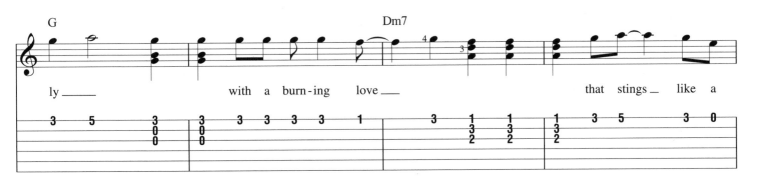

Verse

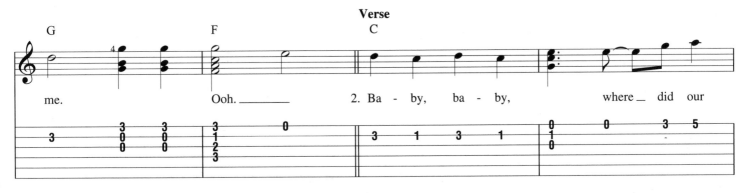

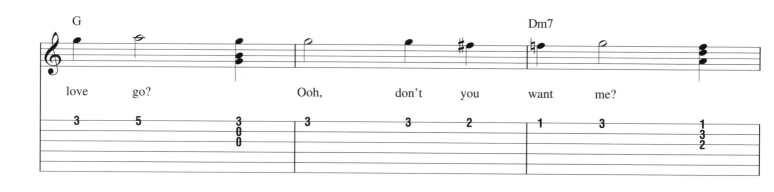

love go? Ooh, don't you want me?

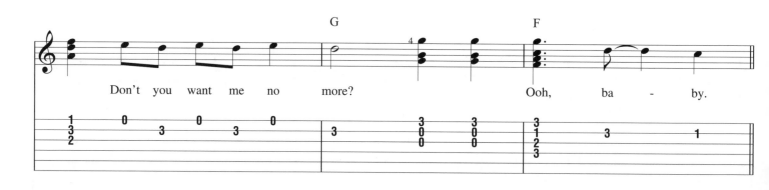

Don't you want me no more? Ooh, ba - by.

Sax solo

D.C. al Coda

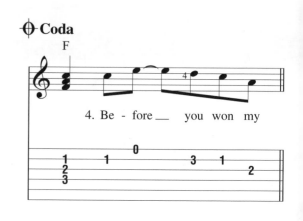

Coda

4. Be - fore __ you won my

Verse

C · · · · · · · G · · ·

heart, you were ___ a per - fect guy. ___

Dm7

But now ___ that you got me, you wan - na leave me be -

Outro-Verse

G N.C. C

hind. Ooh, ___ ba - by. Ba - by, ba - by, ba - by, don't

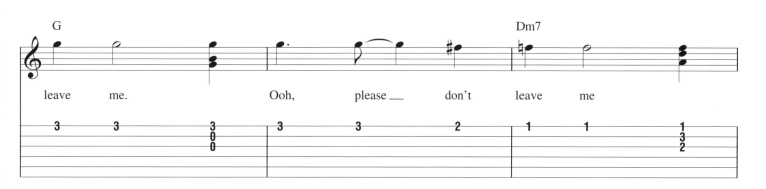

G Dm7

leave me. Ooh, please ___ don't leave me

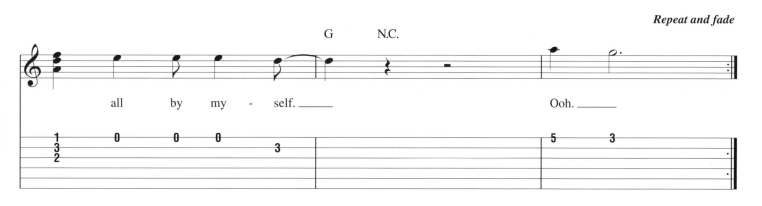

Repeat and fade

G N.C.

all by my - self. ___ Ooh. ___

Yesterday

Words and Music by John Lennon and Paul McCartney

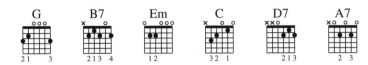

Strum Pattern: 2, 3
Pick Pattern: 2, 4

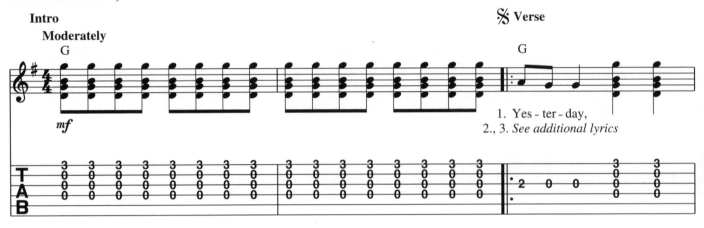

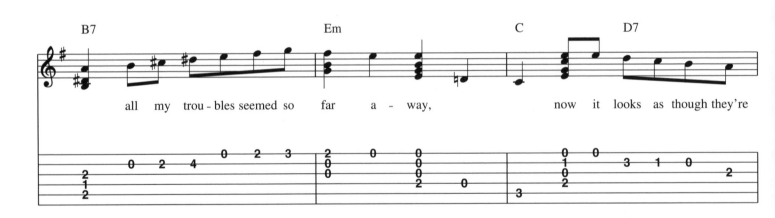

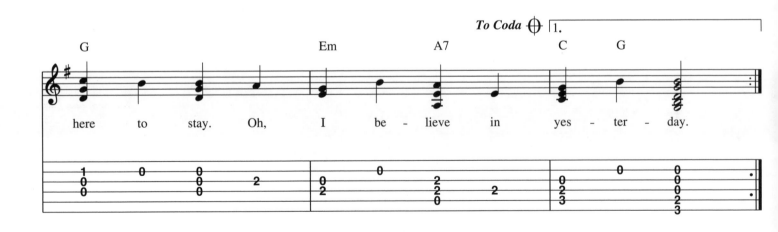

Additional Lyrics

2. Suddenly, I'm not half the man I used to be.
   There's a shadow hanging over me. Oh, yesterday came suddenly.

3. Yesterday, love was such an easy game to play.
   Now, I need a place to hide away. Oh, I believe in yesterday.

You Are the Sunshine of My Life

Words and Music by Stevie Wonder

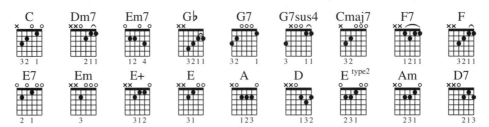

Strum Pattern: 5
Pick Pattern: 4

Chorus
Moderately

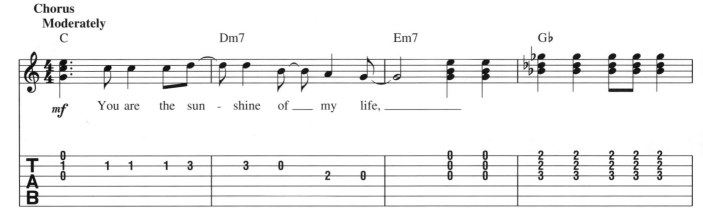

You are the sun - shine of ___ my life, ___

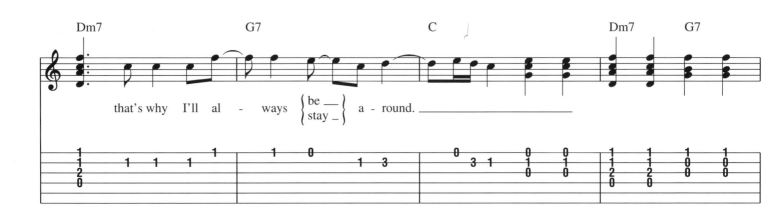

that's why I'll al - ways {be ___ / stay ___} a - round.

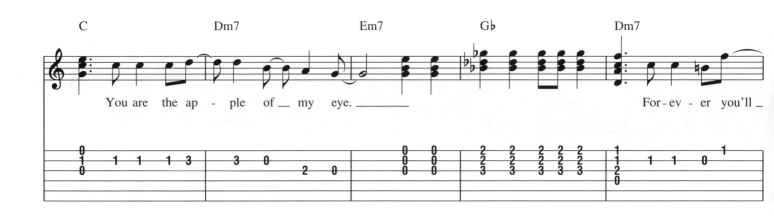

You are the ap - ple of ___ my eye. ___ For - ev - er you'll ___

Additional Lyrics

2. You must have known that I was lonely,
Because you came to my rescue.
And I know that this must be heaven;
How could so much love be inside of you?

You Oughta Know

Lyrics by Alanis Morissette
Music by Alanis Morissette and Glen Ballard

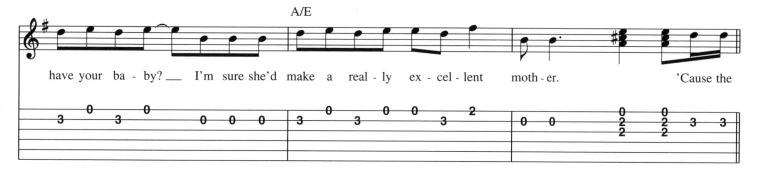

have your ba - by? ___ I'm sure she'd make a real - ly ex - cel - lent moth - er. 'Cause the

𝄌 Pre-Chorus

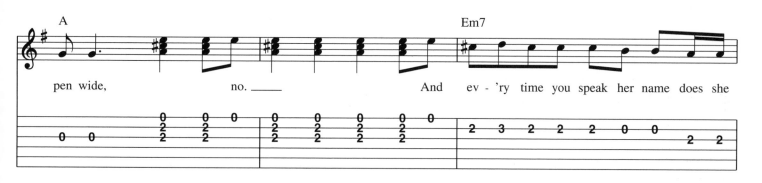

1., 2. love that you gave, that we made was - n't a - ble to make it e - nough for you to be o -
3. *See additional lyrics*

pen wide, no. ___ And ev - 'ry time you speak her name does she

know how you told me you'd hold me un - til you died, 'til you died? But

Chorus

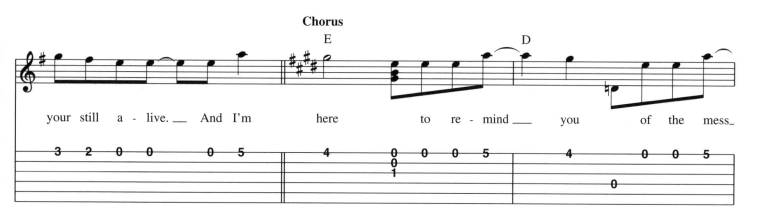

your still a - live. ___ And I'm here to re - mind ___ you of the mess ___

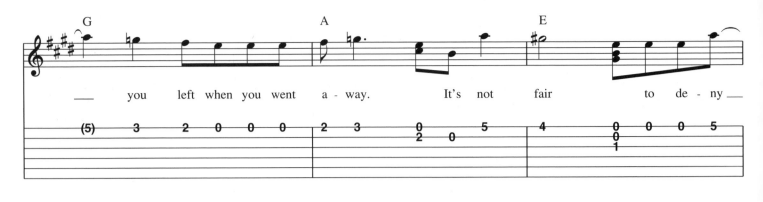

you left when you went a - way. It's not fair to de - ny

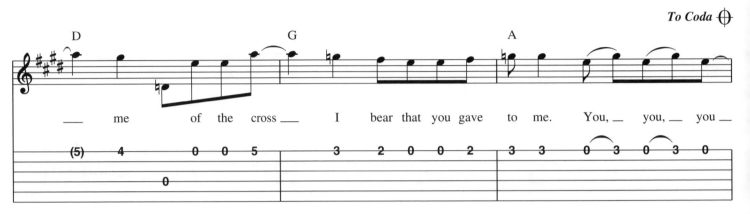

me of the cross I bear that you gave to me. You, you, you

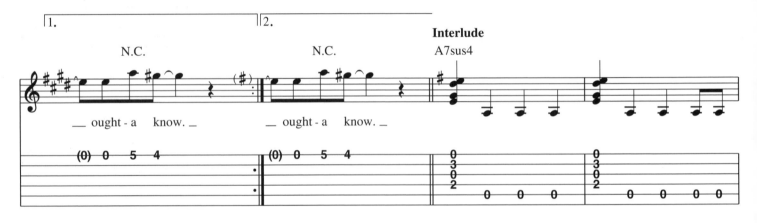

ought - a know. ought - a know.

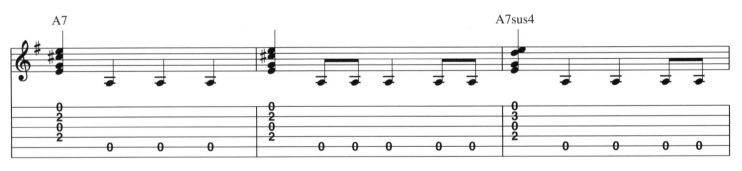

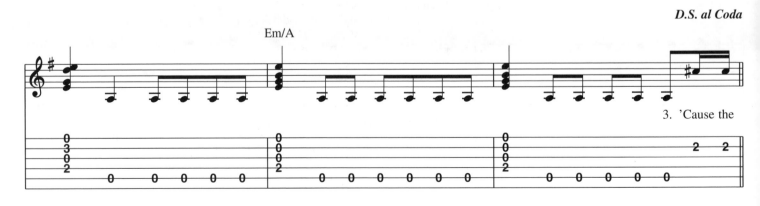

3. 'Cause the

Coda

Outro-Chorus

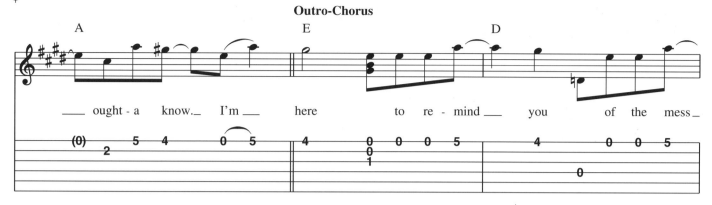

ought-a know._ I'm _ here to re-mind _ you of the mess_

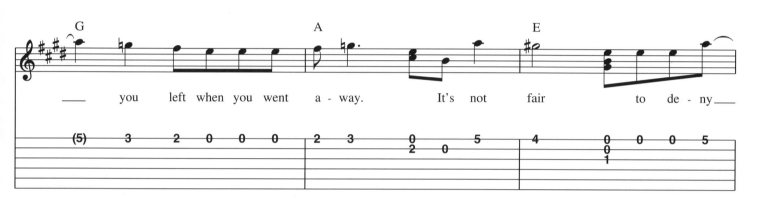

_ you left when you went a-way. It's not fair to de-ny_

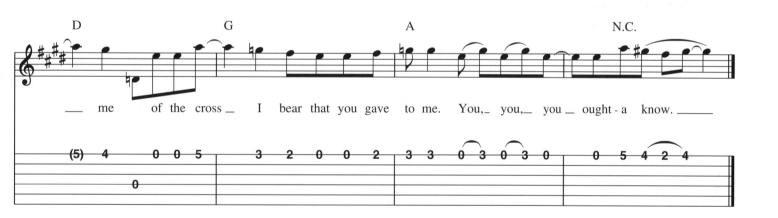

_ me of the cross _ I bear that you gave to me. You,_ you,_ you _ ought-a know. _____

Additional Lyrics

2. You seem very well, things look peaceful.
   I'm not quite as well, I thought you should know.
   Did you forget about me, Mister Duplicity?
   I hate to bug you in the middle of dinner.
   It was a slap in the face, how quickly I was replaced
   And are you thinking of me when you fuck her?

Pre-Chorus 3. 'Cause the joke that you laid in the bed was me
   And I'm not gonna fade as soon as you close your eyes,
   And you know it.
   And everytime I scratch my nails down someone else's back,
   I hope you feel it.
   Well, can you feel it?   Well I'm . . .

You Shook Me All Night Long

Words and Music by Angus Young, Malcolm Young and Brian Johnson

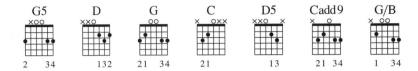

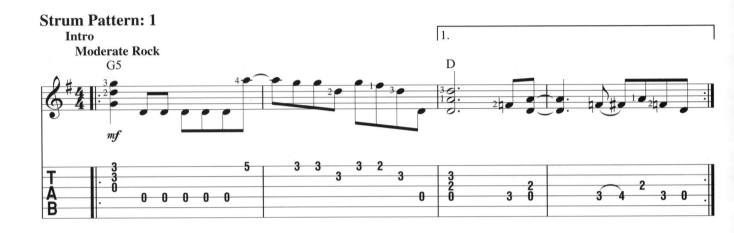

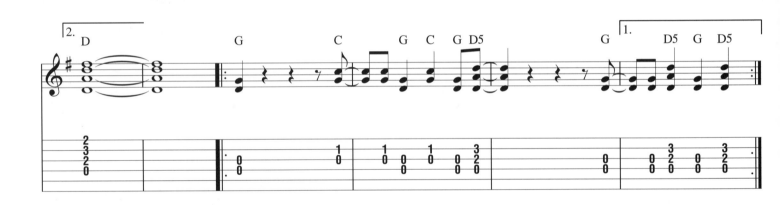

1. She was a fast ma-chine, she kept her mo-tor ___ clean, ___ she was the

2. *See additional lyrics*

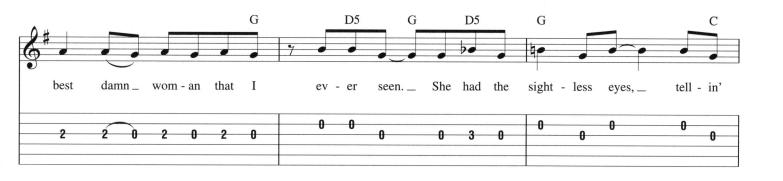

best damn_ wom-an that I ev-er seen._ She had the sight-less eyes,_ tell-in'

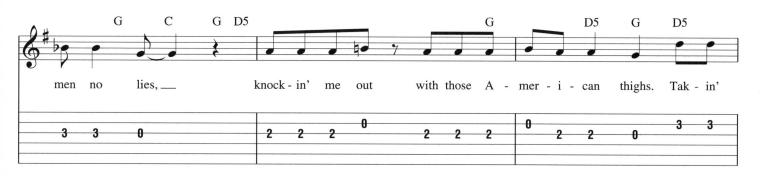

men no lies,___ knock-in' me out with those A-mer-i-can thighs. Tak-in'

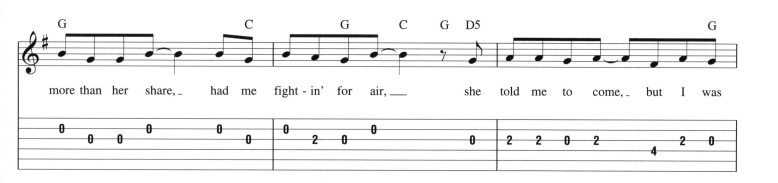

more than her share,_ had me fight-in' for air,___ she told me to come,_ but I was

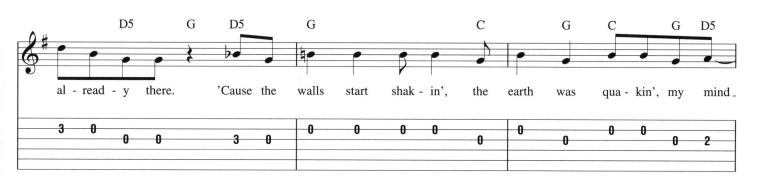

al-read-y there. 'Cause the walls start shak-in', the earth was qua-kin', my mind_

Chorus

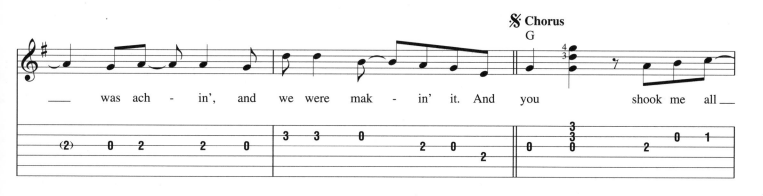

___ was ach-in', and we were mak-in' it. And you shook me all_

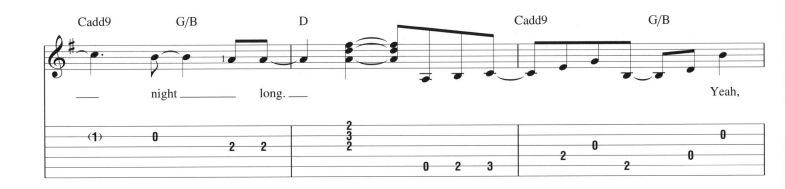

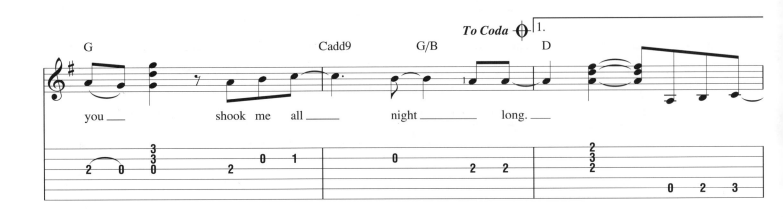

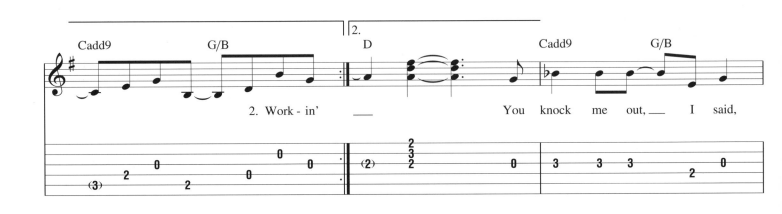

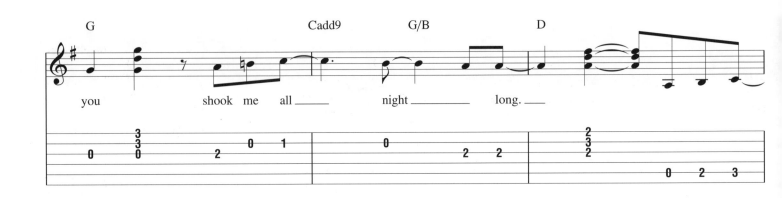

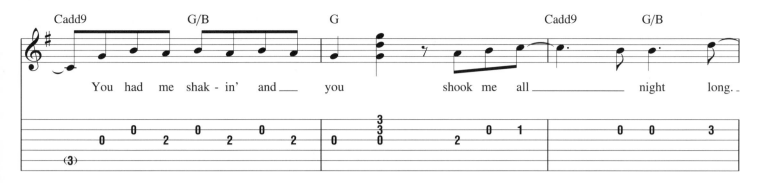

You had me shak-in' and ___ you shook me all _____ night long. _

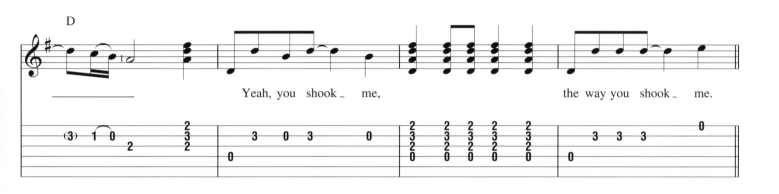

_____ Yeah, you shook ___ me, the way you shook ___ me.

Guitar Solo

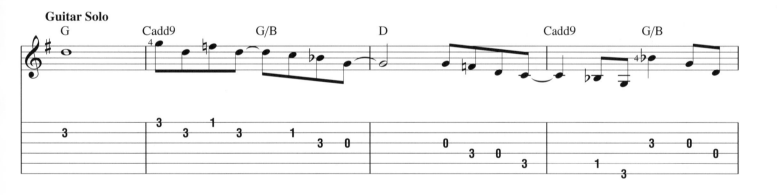

D.S. al Coda

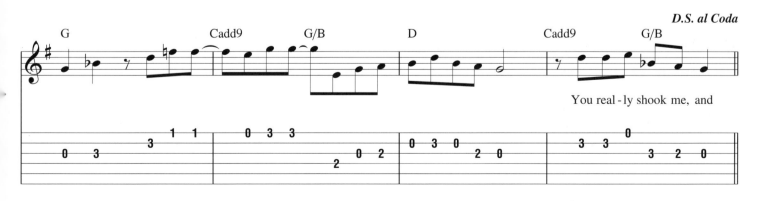

You real-ly shook me, and

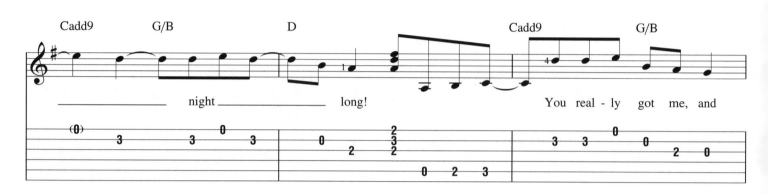

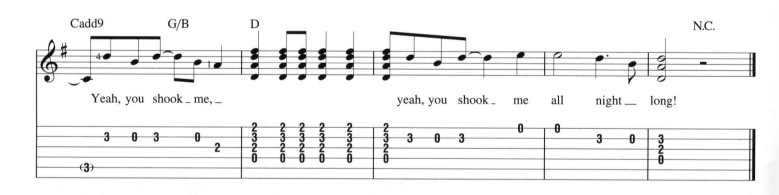

Additional Lyrics

2. Workin' double-time on the seduction line,
   She was one of a kind, she's just mine all mine.
   She wanted no applause, just another course,
   Made a meal out of me and came back for more.
   Had to cool me down to take another round,
   Now I'm back in the ring to take another swing,
   'Cause the walls were shakin', the earth was quakin',
   My mind was achin', and we were makin' it.

Your Song

Words and Music by Elton John and Bernie Taupin

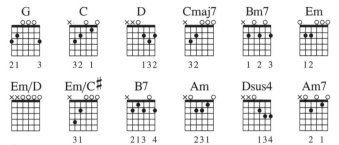

Strum Pattern: 2, 3
Pick Pattern: 3, 4

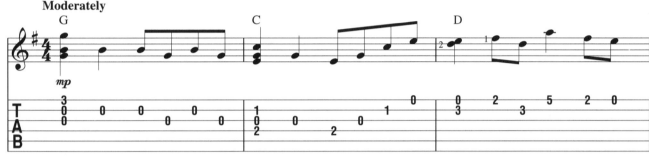

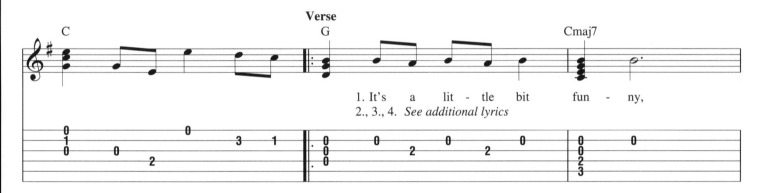

1. It's a lit - tle bit fun - ny,
2., 3., 4. *See additional lyrics*

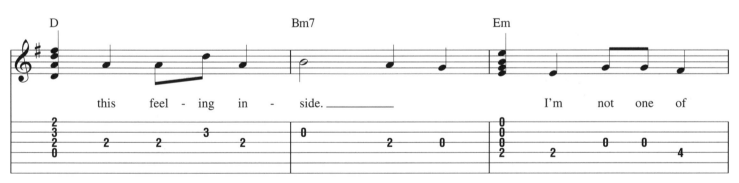

this feel - ing in - side. _____ I'm not one of

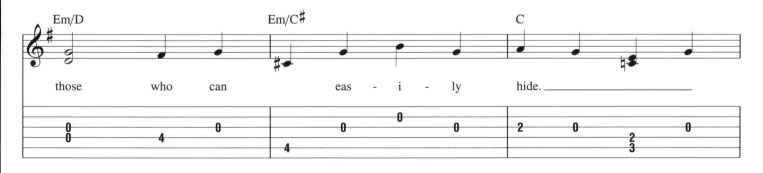

those who can eas - i - ly hide. _____

I don't have much mon - ey, but, ___ boy, if ___ I

did ___ I'd buy a big house where ___

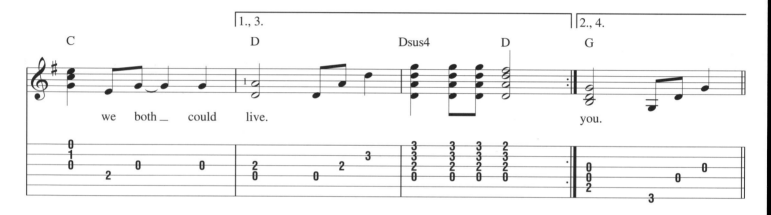

we both ___ could live. you.

Chorus

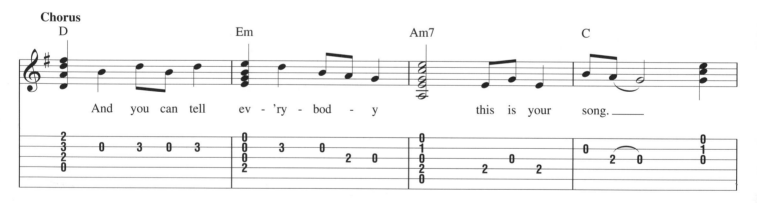

And you can tell ev - 'ry - bod - y this is your song. ___

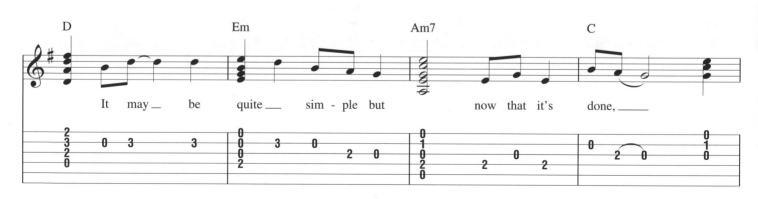

It may ___ be quite ___ sim - ple but now that it's done, ___

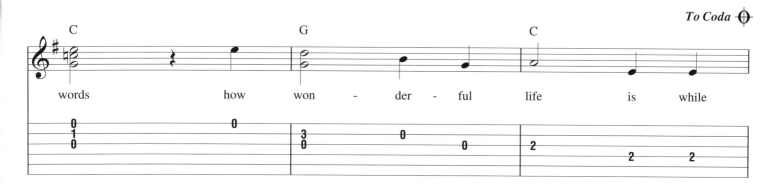

Additional Lyrics

2. If I was a sculptor, but then again no,
   Or a man who makes potions in a travelin' show.
   I know it's not much, but it's the best I can do.
   My gift is my song and this one's for you.

3. I sat on the roof and kicked off the moss.
   Well, a few of the verses, well, they've got me quite cross.
   But the sun's been quite kind while I wrote this song.
   It's for people like you that keep it turned on.

4. So excuse me forgetting, but these days I do.
   You see, I've forgotten if they're green or they're blue.
   Anyway, the thing is, what I really mean,
   Yours are the sweetest eyes I've ever seen.